Born To Be Wild
Attention Deficit Hyperactivity Disorder Alcoholism and Addiction

Born To Be Wild

Attention Deficit Hyperactivity Disorder Alcoholism and Addiction

Will Beyer, M.Ed., LPE
Robert D. Hunt, M.D.

Judy Wood Publishing Company & Consulting Services

Published by

Judy Wood Publishing Company & Consulting Services
12411 Southbridge Drive
Midlothian, Virginia 23113
Toll Free: 877-JUDY WOOD (583-9966)
Toll-Free Fax: 877-418-7860
Web: www.judywood.com

© 1999 Judy Wood Publishing Company & Consulting Services

No part of this book may be reproduced in any form or by any electronic or mechanical means including information storage and retrieval systems without explicit permission from the publisher, except by a reviewer who may quote brief passages. For further information, please address the publisher: Judy Wood Publishing Company & Consulting Services, 12411 Southbridge Drive, Midlothian, VA 23113.

ISBN 1-886021-12-0

Contents

Section 1   **Chapter 1**
Emergence of ADHD

Clinical Symptoms of ADHD/ADD	7
Responsibility & Blame	7
Clinical Symptoms of ADD	*7*
DSM-IV Diagnostic Criteria	*7*
Arousal and Stimulus Seeking	8
Adult ADHD	8
History and Etiology of ADHD/ADD	10
Historical Influences and Perspectives	10
Environmental Influences	12
Possible Nutritional Contributions	*12*
Brain Imaging	13
Genetic Studies	14
Interventions for ADD–Over the Lifetime	14
Nature Versus Nurture–The Functional Integration	15
Twin Studies: Separating Genetic and Environmental Influences	15
Comorbidity of ADHD and Addictive Behavior	17
Alcoholics Anonymous	17
Genetic Similarity	17
Family Genetic Relationships	18
Comorbid Problems Associated with ADD/ADHD	*18*
Stimulus Seeking	19
Failure to Inhibit	19
Emotional Causes of Addictive Behavior	20
The ADHD Scapegoat–Children of Alcoholics	20
Genetic Substrate for ADHD	21
ADHD and Scapegoats	22
Shared Characteristics	*22*
Nature Versus Nurture	22
Children of Alcoholics (COA)	
Behavioral Characteristics	23
Distinguishing ADHD from COA	24
Predisposing Factors in Alcoholism	24
Treatment Implications	25

Implications for Attributions and Treatment	25
Impact of Children's Behavior on Parents	26
Resilient Children	27
A Sense of Shame	27
Shaming of Children	*28*
Examples of "Parent to Child Shaming"	*28*
Examples of "Child to Parent Shaming"	*28*
In Defense of Mothers	*29*
Persistence of Disorganization	*30*
Repeated Relapses	*31*
Family Patterns of Repetition	*31*
Therapeutic Alternatives	31
The Genetic Connection	**32**
Overlapping Genetic and Symptomatic Characteristics	32
Comorbidity of ADHD & Addictions	33
Familial Genetics	33
Twin Studies for Alcoholism	*33*
Sons of Male Alcoholics (SOMAs)	*33*
Age of Onset	*33*
Predictors of Alcoholism	*33*
Comorbidity	*34*
Overlying Symptoms	*34*
Behavioral Symptoms of ADHD Versus ADD	*34*
Clinical Patterns of Comorbid Symptoms	34
ADHD and Alcoholism–Behavioral Similarities	*34*
Overlapping Symptoms	*34*
Types I and II Alcoholism	*35*
Platelet MAO in Type II Alcoholics	*35*
Evoked Potential in SOMAs	*35*
Behavioral and Cognitive Deficits in At-risk Alcoholics	*35*
Hyperactivity	*36*
Primary Versus Secondary Alcoholism	*36*
Juvenile Offenders	*36*
Adopted Sons of Alcoholics	*36*
Behavior of SOMAs	*37*
Psychiatric Problems	*37*
Follow-up Studies	*37*
Symptom Overlap	*37*
ADHD and Early Onset Alcoholism	*37*

ADHD and Substance Abuse 37
   Nicotine and ADHD 37
   Cocaine and ADHD 38
   Gamblers and Attention 38
Addictions, ADHD and Cognition 39
   Alcoholism and Vigilance 39
   Alcoholism and Problem-Solving 39
   SOMAs and Cognition 39
Attention and Learning in Alcoholism and ADHD 40
   Addictive Outcome of ADHD Children 40
   Gender Differences 40
   Neurochemical Components of Alcoholism
     and ADHD 40
   Genetic Aspects of Addictive Illness 40
   A Sociobiological View of Addictive Illness 41
   Alcohol Craving 42

Chapter 2
Questions and Answers About ADHD

What Are Some Characteristics Common to Individuals with ADHD? 47
What Are the Causes of ADHD? 47
   Genetic 47
   Environmental 49
Are Males More Likely to Have ADHD
   Than Females? 49
How Does ADHD Negatively Impact the Family? 49
   Frustration 49
   Anger 50
   Guilt 50
   Fear 50
   Confusion 50
   Exhaustion 50
   Denial 51
   Sadness 51
   Isolation 51
Grieving the Loss of Normalcy 51
How Many Individuals Have ADHD? 52
What Medications Are Used in Treating ADHD? 53
What Treatments Have Proven to Be Helpful? 53
At What Age Is ADHD Usually First Diagnosed? 54

Have There Been Longitudinal Studies of the
   Outcomes of ADHD Individuals in Adulthood
   and the Risk for Alcohol and Substance Abuse?
   How High Are the Risks? 54
What Is the Difference Between ADD and ADHD? 55
How Is ADHD Diagnosed? 56
Diagnostic Tests 58
Complex Diagnosis 58
Placebo or Appropriate Treatment? 61
An Increasing Diagnosis? 62
Quantitative Differences 63
Genetic Comorbidity Evaluation 63

Chapter 3
It Isn't Bad Parenting

It Isn't Bad Parenting 67
Grieve Your Loss of Normalcy 67
Change How You See Your Child 68
Confront Your Anger 68
Make Yourself Loveable
   "Treat Them Kind" 69
Change Your Environment 70
Look After Your Family's Mental and Physical
   Health 70
   *Distinguish Between Distractibility and
      Defiance* 73
   Join A Support Group 73
   Help Them to Get a Good Night's Rest 74
   Obtain a Tutor 74
   Provide Ample Time for Preparation 75
   *Help Your Child to See You As Someone
      Who Believes in Him* 75
   Recognize That You May Be ADHD 76
   Find the Right Teacher 76
   Know Your Rights to Special Education 77
   Play to Their Strengths 78
   Keep It in Perspective 78
   Share Responsibilities 78
   Watch Your Child Sleep 79

Chapter 4
Educational Services for ADHD Students

Educational Services for ADHD Students	83
Legal Advocacy	83
Forty Educational Interventions	84
Emphasize Quality over Quantity	*84*
Computer Instruction	*85*
Selective Seating	*85*
Cooperation Versus Competition	*86*
Multisensory Learning	*86*
Chunking	*87*
Teacher Prompts	*87*
Anticipate Ahead of the Child	*88*
Assist with Organization	*88*
Positive Incentive Programs with Continuous Reinforcement	*88*
Competency Development	*89*
Self-Monitoring	*90*
Textbooks on Tape	*91*
Reduction of Math Mistakes	*92*
Stimulus Reduction	*92*
Stimulus Enrichment	*92*
Physical Contact	*94*
Music	*94*
Sleep	*94*
Teach with Activity	*94*
Summer Tutoring	*95*
Tape Recorder/Video Camera	*95*
Secret Signal	*96*
Earplugs	*96*
Case Managers	*96*
Instruction about Word Processing	*97*
Instruction and Supervision of Socialization	*97*
Instruction of Core Subjects in the Morning	*98*
Exercise	*98*
Classroom Rules	*98*
Discipline	*98*
Encourage Free Inquiry	*99*
Use of Humor	*99*
Physical Coordination	*100*
Recognition of Individual Learning Styles	*100*

Values Training — *101*
Contracts and Reward Systems — *101*
Make Yourself Loveable — *102*
Career Guidance — *102*
If Your Child Comes Home with an F… — *103*

Chapter 5
Proposed Neurobiological Subtypes of ADHD-Spectrum Disorders

Proposed Neurobiological Subtypes of ADHD-Spectrum Disorders — 107

Validation of This Clinical Model for Neurobiological Subtypes Tests and Validation — 109
- *Measures of Brain Functioning* — *109*
- Subtype I—Cognitive Processing Deficit — 110
- Subtype II—Excessively Aroused ADHD — 112
- Subtype III—Impaired Behavioral Inhibition System — 113
- Subtype IV—Deficient Reward Systems — 115

Section 2

Chapter 6
Pharmacological Diversity— Medications Types and Effects

Pharmacological Diversity—Medication Types and Effects — 121
- *Major Medications for ADHD and Comorbidities* — *121*

Medication — 123
Risk/Benefit — 123
Treatment Effectiveness — 123
Clinical Variability and Subtypes — 123
Preparation for Medications:
    Before Medication Is Used, One Should Ask… — 124
Pharmacologic Treatments for Alcohol
    and Drug Abuse — 125

Chapter 7
Psychostimulants

Specific Medications for Treating ADHD — 131
Stimulants—Overview — 131
Psychostimulants — 131

    Mechanism of Action and Behavioral
        Effects of Psychostimulants   *131*
    Clinical Effects of Psychostimulants   *132*
    Behavioral Effects of Psychostimulants   *132*
    Cognitive Effects of Psychostimulants   *133*
Comparative Effects Of Psychostimulants   134
    Neurochemical Effects of Methylphenidate   *135*
    Mechanism of Action of Methylphenidate   *135*
    Studies on the Effect of Methylphenidate
        on Catecholamines in ADHD   *136*
    Methylphenidate Hydrochloride (Ritalin)   *137*
Is Ritalin an Addictive Drug?   138
Use of Stimulants in Substance Abusers   139
Methylphenidate for Substance Abusers   139
    Dextroamphetamine Sulfate (Dexedrine)   *140*
    Methamphetamine Hydrochloride (Desoxyn)   *140*
    Magnesium Pemoline (Cylert)   *141*
Adderall   142
    Adderall to Dexedrine   *142*
    Differences Between Adderall and Dexedrine   *142*
    The Clinical Significance of the Longer
        Duration of Action of Adderall   *143*
    Compared to Ritalin, Is There Any
        Advantage in Clinical Effects from Adderall?   *143*
    Patients' Preferences to Adderall   *144*
    Differences in Side Effects   *144*
    Clinical Experience: Comparison of
        Adderall to Ritalin   *146*
    Clinical Experience: Comparison of
        Adderall to Dexedrine   *147*
    Recommendations for Use   *147*
    Stimulants in Adolescents and Adults   *148*
    Adult ADD   *148*
    Long-Term Effects of Amphetamine   *149*
ADHD Spectrum/Pharmacological Diversity   149

Chapter 8
Antidepressants

Antidepressants   153
Tricyclic Antidepressants   154
Antidepressant Drug Therapy and ADHD   155

Imipramine Hydrochloride (Tofranil)	*156*
ADHD in the Classroom, Effects of Imipramine	*159*
Imipramine in Ritalin Non-Responders	*160*
Summary of Imipramine	*160*
Desipramine Hydrochloride (Norpramine)	*161*
Desipramine Compared to Placebo—	
Clinical and Neurochemical Response	*162*
Desipramine in ADHD Boys	*163*
Desipramine in ADHD with Associated TICS	*165*
Summary of Desipramine	*166*
Nortriptyline (Pamelor/Aventyl)	*166*
Clomipramine Hydrochloride (Anafranil)	*167*
Summary of Tricyclic Antidepressants	*167*
Monoamine Oxidase Inhibitors	*168*
Summary of Monoamine Oxidase Inhibitors	*169*
New Antidepressants	169
Bupropion (Wellbutrin)	*169*
Bupropion Study	*169*
Study of Bupropion on Preadolescent Males	*170*
Summary of Bupropion	*172*
Selective Serotonergic Reuptake Inhibitors	
Antidepressants (SSRIs)	172
Fluoxetine Hydrochloride (Prozac)	*174*
Comments on Use of Antidepressants	175

Chapter 9
Arousal Modulating Medications

Arousal Modulating Medications	179
Antihypertensives (Catapres/Tenex)	*179*
Clonidine in ADHD	179
Introduction	*179*
Clinical Indications	180
Therapeutic Efficacy	180
Clonidine Versus Placebo	*180*
Clonidine Versus Methylphenidate	*182*
Transdermal Clonidine	*183*
Differential Effects of Clonidine and	
Methylphenidate	185
Combined Clonidine and Methylphenidate	186
Clonidine + Ritalin	*187*
Neurobehavioral Mechanisms of Action	188

Neurochemical Mechanisms of Action	189
Pharmacokinetics	190
Oral Clonidine	*190*
Pharmacokinetics	*190*
Therapeutic Blood Levels	*190*
Clonicel	*190*
Clinical Guidelines for Using Clonidine in ADHD	**192**
Starting Clonidine	192
Side Effects of Clonidine	193
Monitoring Response to Clonidine	193
The Clonidine Skin Patch (Transdermal)	193
Proposed Relationship Between Symptoms, Neurochemistry, and Treatment	194
Mechanism of Action of Medication	195
Clinical Management of Clonidine in ADHD	196
Side Effects and Toxicity	*196*
Tenex	*199*

Chapter 10
Anticonvulsant Medications

Anticonvulsant Medications	**203**
Carbatrol (Tegretol)	203
Depakote (Valproic Acid)	204
Medications for Bipolar Disorder: Lithium	204

Chapter 11
Neuroleptics

Neuroleptics: Major Tranquilizers	**209**
Mellaril	*211*
Haloperidol (Haldol)	*211*

Chapter 12
Dietary Intervention

Dietary Intervention	**215**
Introduction	*215*
Amino Acid Supplementation	219
Introduction	*219*
Conclusion	220
Summary	222

Section 3

Chapter 13
Addictions, AA, ADHD Adults, and Answers

Stimulus Seeking	227
Positive Addictions	227
Treatment or Punishment	228
Alcoholics Anonymous	230
ADHD Adults	232
10 Keys to Managing ADHD in Adulthood	232
Acknowledge you have a disability	*232*
Acknowledge your strengths	*233*
Watch your appetite for thrill-seeking	*233*
Develop positive addictions	*233*
Become family and community oriented	*233*
Constantly work on organization, goal setting, and how to be more productive	*233*
Find a support group for ADHD adults or parents of ADHD children and attend	*234*
Learn to manage your moods	*234*
Manage your medication	*234*
Utilize counseling as needed	*234*
Summary	234

Chapter 14
Clinical Research and Developmental Diversity of ADHD

Research Into Clinical Typology	239
Clinical patterns of ADHD	*239*
Diagnostic Process	*243*
Developmental Aspects of ADHD	244

Chapter 15
Clinical Diversity of ADHD

Clinical Diversity of ADHD	249
Clinical Patterns of ADHD	250
Behavioral Dimensions of ADHD	251

Chapter 16
Neurobiological Systems for Cognition and Attention

Neurobiological Systems for Cognition and Attention	259
Neurobiological Systems in ADHD	*259*
Brain Regional Systems—Neuroanatomy of ADHD	*259*
Information Processing Systems	259

Chapter 17
Measures of Attention and Learning

Measures of Attention and Learning	267
Attention	*267*
Continuous Performance Task (CPT)	267
Matching Familiar Figures Test (MFFT)	268
Paired Associate Learning Task (PAL)	268
Inhibition Tasks	269

Chapter 18
Neurobiological Systems That Modulate Cognition and Attention

Neurobiological Systems That Modulate Cognition and Attention	273
The Arousal System	273
Behavioral Inhibition System	275
Affect Regulation System	279
Reward System	280
Neurochemistry of Brain Systems in ADHD	*280*
Brain Systems in Attention and ADHD	*281*

Chapter 19
Potential Role of Neurobiological Systems in ADHD/ADD

Potential Role of Neurobiological Systems in ADHD/ADD	285
Cognitive Failure in ADHD	285
Neurobiological Systems in ADHD/ADD	*285*
Overarousal in ADHD	286

Inhibition in ADHD 286
Arousal and Attention *287*
Reward Insensitivity in ADHD 287
Neurotransmitter Systems That Modulate Attention and Behavior 288
Neurotransmitters 288
Synaptic Regulation and Effects of Medications 289
Synaptic Regulation in the Brain *289*
Neurotransmitter Effects on Behavior *289*

Epilogue 293

References 297

Index 315

Section 1

Chapter 1

Emergence of ADHD

Chapter 1 **Born To Be Wild**

Emergence of ADHD

In 1904, Dr. George Still, a physician at the Royal College of Physicians, described 20 children whom he had seen in his clinical practice as having a "defect in moral control." He described this condition as a chronic behavior problem characterized by inattention, aggression, overactivity, a tendency to be "passionate" (emotional), "lawlessness," and a predilection to alcoholism, criminality, depression and suicide. Dr. Still suggested that many of these children came from families with adequate upbringing, and that there appeared to be a biological predisposition to these behaviors, likely to be hereditary (Still, 1902).

Dr. Still's description is still a valid one for children identified as manifesting Attention Deficit Hyperactivity Disorder. Over the past half century, there has been an enormous amount of research on this population of individuals. Our view has changed from one of a disorder of childhood to a disorder of the lifespan. We understand the enormous risk associated with the disorder when interventions are absent or lacking. During a counseling session, parents of these children often express their fears: "If something is not done soon, I fear the worst. I can see my child failing school, developing alcohol or drug problems, and eventually ending up in prison." Statements such as these are not simply unrealistic fears of parents who are overly stressed. They are, in fact, legitimate concerns by those who know this child best. Parents who make such statements have identified the sensation-seeking, insatiable, impulsive, "born to be wild" characteristics of their child. They have seen these characteristics often since infancy, and their observations certainly do have predictive value. They have seen their best interventions fail, even though they may have other children who have done exceedingly well. They may have begun their parenting experience as "environmentalists," assuming that they could and would shape their child's behavior to conform to their family's norms and values. However, they end up as "geneticists." They see their child as being like his grandfather who was the "black sheep" of the family, who always seemed to have a mind of his own, stubborn, strong-

> *"For him who has no concentration, there is no tranquility"*
> Bhagavad Gita

willed, and non-conforming, who may have been an alcoholic or have had other addictive qualities.

Clinical Symptoms of ADHD/ADD

Responsibility and Blame

As clinicians, these observations should not be minimized, nor should we be involved in "blaming parents" for their child's dysfunctional behavior patterns. These parents and children carry around enough guilt as it is. It is helpful to recognize these risks as legitimate and offer a support system to the parents who seek to minimize these risks. The research we have accumulated on alcoholism and addictive illness supports the genetic relationship of such behavior. Yet, socially, we continue to treat these difficulties as if they are predominantly environmentally caused, and often execute judgment against the victims of this disorder.

The cluster of ADD/ADHD symptoms often poses a risk for substance abuse. Both environmental and genetic factors contribute to the individual and social risks for these disorders. While the influence of environment on the behavior of children is profound, our culture has often ignored the hereditary factors and their influence. We have effectively identified the risk factors for alcohol and substance abuse in early childhood. These risk factors are predominantly genetic—hyperactivity, impulsivity, difficulty displaying gratification, attentional problems, motivational problems, low frustration tolerance, sensation seeking, and so on.

The risk for ADD/ADHD becoming a substrate for substance abuse increases with comorbidity. When ADD is linked to depression, oppositionality or conduct disorder, it poses a greater risk for subsequent substance abuse. ADHD patients at the highest risk for substance abuse (SA) are those stimulus-seeking patients with conduct disorder.

In spite of knowing the addictive risks of ADHD and ADD, our interventions for these children are far from adequate. Rather than treating them as a population at extreme risk for addiction, we have usually considered them to be simply defiant children in need of discipline. We

---

Clinical Symptoms of ADD

DSM-IV Diagnostic Criteria
Inattention—difficulties with
- *careless mistakes*
- *sustaining attention*
- *not listening*
- *not following through*
- *organizing tasks*
- *avoiding tasks*
- *losing things*
- *easily distracted*
- *often forgetful*

Attention Deficit Disorder
Hyperactivity
- *often fidgets, squirms*
- *leaves seat*
- *runs or climbs*
- *difficulty playing quietly*

Attention Deficit Disorder
Impulsivity
- *blurts out answers*
- *difficulty waiting in line*
- *onset before age seven*
- *symptoms in two settings*
- *significant distress or impairment in social, academic or occupational functioning*
- *not due to pervasive developmental, mood or anxiety disorder*

> **DSM-IV Diagnostic Criteria**
>
> *Conduct Disorder*
> **Repetitive and Persistent Pattern**
>
> **Violates Basic Rights of Others**
>
> **Violates Social Norms**
>
> **Lasts > 6 months; > 3 of the following**
>
> - often lies or breaks promises
> - stays out at night despite prohibitions
> - stolen items of significant value
> - deliberate fire setting
> - deliberate destruction of property
> - ran away from home overnight x 2
> - truant from school < 13 years
> - broken into house, building or car
> - often bullies, threatens or intimidates
> - initiates physical fights
> - uses weapons
> - stolen with confrontation of victim
> - physically cruel to people or animals
> - forced sexual activity
>
> *Conduct Disorder*
> - **Mild:** few problems, little harm
> - **Moderate:** several problems; some harm
> - **Severe:** many problems, considerable harm

increase the oppositional behaviors through our ineffective interventions, often acting in a manner which is the opposite of what is needed.

Arousal and Stimulus Seeking

Patients with the greatest risk for ADHD and SA tend to be highly stimulus-seeking. Their high level of energy and craving for novelty and excitement lead them to use drugs to intensify sensory experience. In other cases, some patients with ADHD use calming drugs such as marijuana to reduce sensory and emotional overload. Many patients with ADHD have described paradoxical reactions to substances of abuse, such as cocaine. They report actually feeling calmer and more focused on cocaine, in contrast to their friends who experience excitement and arousal.

Marvin Zuckerman (1990) developed a scale for measuring the preferred level of arousal that a person is seeking. His *Sensation Seeking Scale (SSS)* may be used to evaluate boredom, thrill and adventure seeking, disinhibition, and so on. Individuals with ADHD would tend to evidence an enormous amount of "sensation-seeking." It is this phenomenon that links this disorder to addictive illness. This characteristic does not necessarily diminish during adulthood.

Adult ADHD

There is a significant population of these individuals in adulthood who are still struggling with ADHD symptoms. Current research tells us that between 30 to 40% of male alcoholics manifest symptoms of residual ADHD. Yet, our treatment of these individuals often ignores the underlying contribution of ADHD to their alcoholism. We put them in hospitals for detoxification and training, from which they leave and relapse. We enter them in 12-step programs which they do not maintain. We deny them pharmacological management, suggesting that this would be "switching addictions." We blame their families for their unwillingness to offer assistance. (The family is often simply tired of trying; they have fought the war for years and have battle fatigue.) We use up their insurance benefits and leave them alone to try and survive.

Pathways to ADD
Clinical Subtypes

- Cognitive Dysfunction
  Inattention

- Arousal Modulation
  Hyperactivity

- Behavioral Inhibition
  Impulsivity

- Reward/Meaning
  Stimulus Seeking
  vs. Purpose

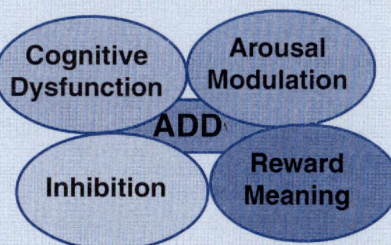

Brain Lesions

Clinical Patterns

This approach to treating the population with a strong genetic basis for addiction is poorly conceived and ineffective. It does not account for the root causes of this behavior in biogenetics. Our treatment orientation needs to change. To be effective, interventions must share the following characteristics:

- Treatment must begin early and it must often include lifelong pharmacological management.
- Clinicians must offer a strong support system to the family.
- Therapists must define the disorder correctly to the individual and must offer continuous assistance in the social, academic and work environments.

> *"People learn who they are and what they are by the way they are treated by the important people in their lives."*
> — William Purkey

History and Etiology of ADHD/ADD

Throughout this century, we have seen a multitude of labels identifying the population of patients now considered ADD. These titles reflected the similarity of ADD to brain damage or dysfunction, the importance of overactivity as a defining characteristic, and the centrality of inattention and impulsivity to the diagnosis. Listed below are just a few of these titles:

Minimal Brain Dysfunction—reflecting the similarity of ADD to head injury.
- Minimal Brain Dysfunction
- Postencephalitic Behavior Disorder

Hyperactive Child Syndrome—reflecting the overt symptoms of hyperactivity and fidgetiness.
- Hyperkinetic Impulse Disorder
- Organic Drivenness
- Restlessness Syndrome
- Hyperkinetic Reaction of Childhood Disorder

Attention Deficit Disorder with and without Hyperactivity—reflecting the importance of inattention to the diagnosis.
- Attention Deficit Hyperactivty Disorder
- ADHD - Predominantly Inattentive
- ADHD - Predominantly Hyper/Impulsive
- ADHD - Combined Type

Historical Influences and Perspectives

The various name changes have been reflective of our thinking about the disorder. For example, those who survived the *encephalitis* epidemic of 1917-1918 often had chronic symptoms of distractibility, difficulty regulating motor control, and impulsivity (Ebaugh, 1923). These are the core symptoms we see today in ADHD children. The reasoning then suggested that all individuals with these core symptoms must have some type of central nervous system injury (Blau, 1936). This thinking was further supported by studies of head injuries and by frontal lobe ablation in primates. These studies seemed to support the theory that the primary damage was within the frontal lobe of the brain (Blau, 1936; Levine, 1938). From the late 1930's through the 1940's, these individuals were often referred to as "brain injured children." It was from this label that eventually came the descriptors of "minimum brain damage" and later "minimal brain dysfunction." In the 1960's, the name changed again to "hyperactive child syndrome" (Laufer & Denhoff, 1957) and later as "hyperkinetic reaction of childhood disorder" with the focus on hyperactivity. We began to understand that hyperactivity could occur with no evidence of brain injury.

In the 1980's, the name became "attention deficit disorder," based primarily on the work of Virginia Douglas, a Canadian psychologist, whose research led her to believe that the primary deficit was "inattention." Douglas also described characteristics of "impulsivity," "inability to modulate arousal levels to meet situational demands," and "an unusually strong inclination to seek immediate reinforcement" (Douglas, 1983).

In the 1990's, we have begun to subtype ADD based on deficits resulting in hyperactivity, impulsivity, and distractibility. Currently, there is a great deal of research that suggests that the primary deficit may be a biologically-driven deficit in motivation. This may result in an "attention bias" (Zentall, 1986). Zentall researched how variables such as color and novelty affected ADHD individuals' performances as compared to controls'. Individuals with ADHD are attracted to situations which offer immediate, continuous, high magnitude reinforcement. It is this insatiable appetite for stimulation which puts in place the prerequisite components of addictive illness. The "cravings" for stimulation overpowers knowledge of the harmful effects of alcohol and/or drug abuse. Therefore it is a problem in doing the right thing, not in knowing the right thing to do, and may be described as a performance deficit rather than a skill or knowledge deficit.

Environmental Influences:
Possible Nutritional Contributions

In the search for answers, William Crook, M.D., (1978) wrote that adverse reactions to food might be implicated in hyperkinesis. During this same time period, Benjamin Feingold, M.D. suggested that hyperactivity and learning problems had their origin in *environmental agents* such as salicylates, dyes, preservatives, and so forth (Feingold, 1975). There is currently a growing body of research suggesting that some nutrients play a critical role in the production of opioid peptides, and may thus increase the production of neurotransmitters such as serotonin, dopamine and gamma-aminobutyric acid (GABA) (Blum & Payne, 1991). These *neurotransmitters* are strongly linked to "reward systems" in the brain. Such nutrients may possibly supplant medication management or may enhance medication effects. The bulk of this nutritional research currently lies in the treatment of addictive illnesses. In the past, these observations were more related to clinical observations and anecdotal reports of parents than to scientific knowledge. This controversy continues today.

At this point, there is no clear understanding of the etiological factors associated with these responses, yet theories abound. It appears that much of the early data was derived from clinical observation as opposed to double-blind studies. Some of the scientific community appears to have been unwilling to examine the data in an objective manner, but have acted in a rather "close-minded" way to the observations related to nutrition and ADD. Although the impact of diet has been difficult to quantify, controlled studies will be summarized later. Thus, strong divisions have developed within the therapeutic community. These dividing lines almost mimic religious division, with various camps of researchers clinging to what they believe to be the "truth" regarding the etiology and treatment of various behavior disorders.'

Brain Imaging

With the use of new brain imaging techniques such as PET Scans, SPECT Analysis, MRI's and others, we have ruled out brain injury as the most common etiological factor and have replaced these theories with biochemical explanations. These biochemical factors have a strong heritability and are viewed as primarily a dysfunction within the frontal-orbital-limbic systems of the brain. Recently, researchers using PET scans identified significant differences in the brains of ADHD individuals, as compared to the control group, in the metabolism of glucose within the striatal region of the brain (Lou, et al., 1989).

EEG's which measure electrical activity on the surface of the brain may be useful in ruling out a seizure disorder, but have not proven helpful in diagnosing ADHD. More advanced EEG's, referred to as QEEG's, can provide colorful tables and quantity data to provide a more detailed view of electrical activity, but likewise, are not able to diagnose ADHD.

Follow-up studies examining glucose metabolism with PET scans continue to suggest that the caudate nuclei and striatum are less active in individuals with ADHD. PET scans that involve the inhalation of a radioactive isotope in the form of xenon gas are not routinely administered. When methylphenidate (Ritalin) is administered, there is a redistribution of blood flow, and glucose metabolism in the brain increases in the caudate nuclei and right striatum.

Magnetic Resonance Imaging, which provides detailed volumetric data regarding specific areas of the brain, has revealed that children with ADHD have a smaller left caudate nucleus and caudate head with reversed asymmetry. Research also indicates a smaller volume within the right frontal region. Dr. Pauline Filipek, a lead researcher at the Department of Pediatrics, University of California Medical School, Irvine, conducting this research, recently stated, "The eye alone would not see any problem when looking at a clinical MRI of an ADHD child, so parents should not rush in and request an MRI. What this research means is that we are on the path to possibly finding specific, organic reasons for ADHD" (Filipek, et al., 1998).

Genetic Studies

These areas of the brain affect reasoning, moods and activity level of the individual. Therefore, we have come to view this disorder as primarily of biochemical and genetic origin, with ratios of male-to-female incidence at about 6:1. Studies of twins and adoptive children have likewise supported ADHD as primarily a disorder of genetic characteristics. Thus, we have conceptualized the disorder in numerous ways over the past century. No doubt, new conceptualizations will continue to occur based upon continual research. We currently see the ADHD individual not so much as a person with specific symptoms of neurological impairment, but rather as one who has a genetically determined neurochemical disability that predisposes him or her to difficulty with the regulation and control of drives for stimulation, activity level, mood, and decision-making. This predisposition may be suppressed through multimodal treatment or it may be enhanced through an absence of interventions, but it is not likely to be eliminated through the maturational process.

Interventions for ADD–Over the Lifetime

It also appears that, if interventions are to be effective in the long run, they certainly must begin early and often last a lifetime. When interventions are begun later, these individuals almost appear predisposed to be resistant to behavioral treatments. Hereditary influences may then supercede those of environmental upbringing. While in the past this disorder was viewed as one of childhood which was normally outgrown, it is now viewed as one primarily of the lifespan, with estimates ranging from 33 to 75% of those who were diagnosed in childhood still manifesting difficulty with core symptoms in adulthood (Shekim, et al., 1986).

Thus, ADD individuals often appear to be constantly seeking stimulation, and once they find something they like, they either can't seem to get enough of it or immediately begin to look for bigger and better stimulation.

Nature Versus Nurture–The Functional Integration

John Locke's view that the infant is born "tabula rasa" with a personality and character waiting to be completed, much like an empty chalkboard, has had little scientific support this century. However, we are still treating a multitude of disorders from a frame of reference which assumes this to be true. Included in this list are ADHD and alcohol and drug abuse.

The reason this occurs has more to do with theology and politics than with science. Awareness of a genetic contribution often evokes fear of "genetic determinism"– we are merely a manifestation of our DNA. Genetic influences on personality clearly exist–in shaping intelligence, attention, energy level and capacity for self-control. Collectively these characteristics comprise our *temperament*. We must distinguish between a predisposition to addictive illness and a predestination for addictions. There is a huge amount of research which suggests that many are predisposed to addictions, yet none which suggests predestination. The factors of nature and nurture combined, therefore, result in different levels of predisposition.

Twin Studies: Separating Genetic and Environmental Influences

During this past decade, research at the Minnesota Center for Twin and Adoption Research has discovered that many traits, previously considered to be primarily environmentally caused, are instead influenced significantly by genetics. These include such characteristics as extroversion, creativity, aggression, conformity, worry, cautiousness, optimism and paranoia, to name a few. This is certainly not news for parents who have adopted children. Many of them have come to realize, at least by their child's adolescence, that there are strong genetic factors which affect the adoptive child. We have done a disservice to these parents by refusing information regarding the biological parents'

This behavioral disability of ADD is characterized by

1) difficulty in *delaying gratification* (waiting for rewards; they are governed by the here and now)

2) a failure to *self-motivate* on tasks that are lacking immediate reward or consequence

3) chronic difficulty in *regulating mood and temperament* (prone to extremes in mood from depression to mania to anger)

4) behavioral *disinhibition or impulsive* decision-making (they fail to consider consequences before acting)

5) *stimulus-seeking* (individuals with ADHD are often described as risk-takers, suggesting that they are excitement-seeking, or they may also be described as experiencing rapid boredom and satiation of stimulus)

personalities. It is difficult enough to access information regarding such diseases as diabetes, cancer, schizophrenia, and others, yet it is very important that adoptive parents are made aware of characteristics of the biological parents such as temperament, hyperactivity, alcohol and drug abuse history, introvertedness or extrovertedness, and so forth.

Research supports a sociobiological theory of personality. We acknowledge an enormous hereditary influence on behavior of almost every insect and animal species in existence, except for humans, and then we only want to accept that it has to do with characteristics such as eye color, height, hair color, intelligence, and so on. Nature, in fact, demands that we accept the powerful influence of humankind's genes on personality and character. Thus, we can appropriately view others as truly autonomous individuals, who differ greatly in personal strengths and weaknesses of personality and character, as well as in physical and mental attributes. Therefore, we are ultimately more like snowflakes than paper dolls. Through this formulation we can become tolerant and merciful towards our fellow man.

Individuals with ADHD, as well as alcoholics, have historically been viewed as having a *moral deficit*. Due to their difficulty with delay of gratification, they frequently violated the normative limits imposed by society. Addicted individuals have been "shamed" by society through a homeostatic mechanism that says "conform to the rules of society or face the consequences." The use of aversive disciplinary approaches to the treatment of "moral deficits" has not proven effective, but may further alienate and embitter them from society. They have sought understanding and tolerance; they have been given blame and rejection. If we walked in the shoes of the alcoholic for but one day to try to understand the forces which operate upon the mind, we might experience the conflict of those who seek to do that which is right but repetitiously do that which is wrong!

Comorbidity of ADHD and Addictive Behavior

Alcoholics Anonymous

> "They are restless, irritable, and discontented unless they can again experience the sense of ease and comfort which comes at once by taking a few drinks...they cannot start drinking without developing the phenomenon of craving."
> — William Silkworth, M.D.

Researchers have identified a large number of comorbidities with ADHD. *Comorbidity* implies that when someone has one kind of disorder there is a good chance that he or she may also have another. There are numerous comorbidities associated with ADHD.

The interrelationship which exists among ADHD, alcoholism, Tourette's syndrome and other similar disorders suggests they share a common underlying psychophysiological etiology and may respond to similar pharmacological treatment.

Genetic Similarity

Recently the tryptophan 2, 3 dioxygenase (TDO2) gene has been implicated as a gene which may be semirecessive-semidominant and affect serotonin metabolism for ADHD (Comings, et al., 1993). These researchers have discovered that low platelet serotonin and blood tryptophan levels frequently occur in individuals diagnosed with ADHD, alcoholism or Tourette's syndrome.

Many of these disorders appear to overlap relative to the role of neurotransmitters such as dopamine, serotonin, and norepinephrine.

Research submitted in 1990 by Kenneth Blum and colleagues on the DRD2 gene (dopaminergic receptor gene) indicated they correctly classified 72% of the alcoholics and 77% of the non-alcoholics in the study by examining the DNA patterns in brain tissue. They had no other knowledge of the identity of the individuals studied. Replicated studies exploring other neuropsychiatric disorders found similar results in alcoholism, but also found a 40 to 50% presence of this allele in parents of children with attention deficit disorder.

Comorbid Problems Associated with ADD/ADHD

Addictive Behaviors
- *Alcoholism and Drug Abuse*
- *Pathological Gambling*
- *Sexual Addictions/ Paraphilias*

Disruptive Behaviors
- *Oppositional Defiant Disorder*
- *Intermittent Explosive Disorder*
- *Impulse Control Disorder*
  -Pyromania
  -Kleptomania
- *Conduct Disorder*
- *Antisocial Personality Disorder*
- *Borderline Personality Disorder*

Affective & Regulatory Disorders
- *Depressive Disorders*
- *Bipolar Disorder*
- *Sleep Disturbance*

Cognitive Disorders
- *Learning Disorders*

The neurophysiological mechanism of ADHD reflects the activity of the neurotransmitter dopamine in attention and reward processes within the brain. Dr. Blum hypothesizes in his book, *Alcohol and the Addictive Brain,* that his subsequent research found that individuals having the A1 allele had approximately 30% fewer D2 receptors than those having the A2 allele in an area of the brain called the caudate nucleus. The caudate nucleus is often referred to as the "reward center" of the brain due to its large concentration of dopamine-rich receptor cells. According to Dr. Blum, this reduction of receptors may create a type of disequilibrium among carriers of the A1 allele. Therefore, this may prompt pleasure-seeking behavior in the form of alcohol or substance abuse. Dr. Blum refers to this concept as the "stress-dopamine-genotype hypothesis of craving."

The presence of these areas of comorbidity may suggest a common genetic mechanism. Frequently, disorders associated with ADHD occur because of a failure to treat the core symptoms of ADHD. While the first disorder may be inherently genetic, the second disorder can often be prevented through adequate treatment of the first.

As can be seen in this list to the left, these are predominantly disorders of impulse control and mood. Many are expressed only in adulthood when there has also been a history of ADHD-type behaviors. Some of these disorders are no doubt related to a failure to acquire adequate socialization, rejection of the individual by significant others, or simply an absence of appropriate interventions.

Much has been written regarding other comorbid relationships. The comorbid relationship between ADHD and addictive illness has been relatively ignored.

Family Genetic Relationships

Literally, for centuries we have understood that alcoholism runs in families. Plutarch stated, "drunkards beget drunkards" (Burton, 1906). In recent years, we have come to understand the genetic component of alcoholism. As advances are made in the area of genetics, we are becoming more aware of the powerful predisposition towards alcoholism.

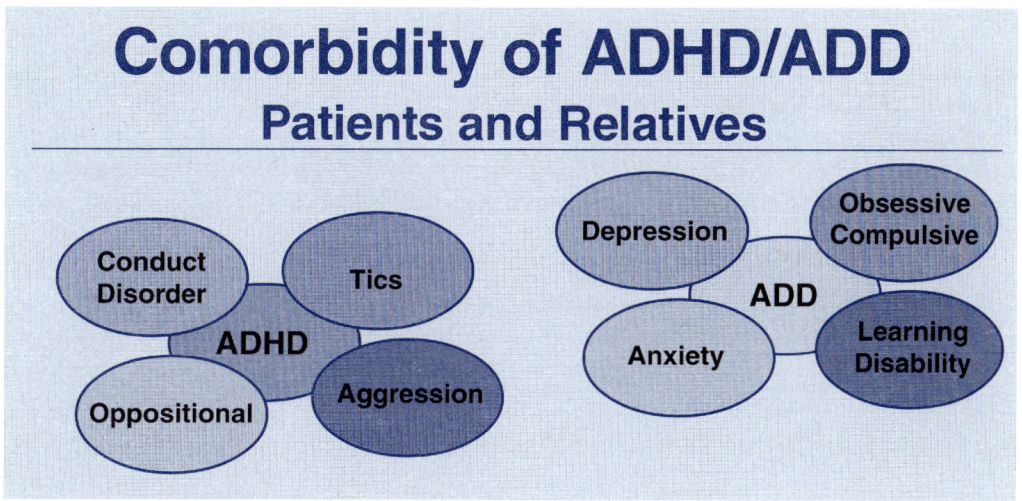

Stimulus Seeking

ADHD children, when placed in an environment which is lacking stimulation, will seek such in a variety of ways. Young children often climb into their parents' laps for affection, and older children may create a disturbance in order to increase the level of stimulation (even aversive). Adults may turn to alcohol or drugs to relieve this "boredom" which is almost intolerable to them. ADHD is often the precursor for a great many addictive illnesses, and mood and personality disorders. The failure to treat the underlying ADHD in the role of these related illnesses will result in a very inadequate plan of care.

Failure to Inhibit

Practitioners have witnessed this scenario many times: adolescents or adults who have been hospitalized for chemical dependency are placed on antidepressants and become model patients; then they are released from the hospital, and within days of removal of antidepressant medication, the individual relapses. What have we done? We have taken away from that individual the medication which maintained the levels of neurotransmitters, such as dopamine or serotonin, which helped him to control his impulsive-compulsive use of alcohol, cocaine, and so forth. These neurotransmitters help us to inhibit (reduce impulsive decision-making). Therefore they act much like the brakes on a car, helping us to slow down or stop prior to an accident. When we discontinue antidepressant therapy for individuals with difficulty inhibiting, going home from the hospital after therapy alone with no medication is like sending them to driving school to teach them to drive and then sending them home in a car with no brakes. They may know the right thing to do but are unable to carry out the plan. The alcohol and drug community often fears medication management for individuals with addictive illnesses, out of concern that these medications are addictive or simply bandages. Yet, these are the very medications that help the programs to work. THESE MEDICATIONS ARE NOT ADDICTIVE! The individual is not switching addictions. In fact, these medications often reduce the craving and emptiness that fuels addiction in ADHD patients. They provide the "brakes" to impulsive behavior.

Emotional Causes of Addictive Behavior

Developing a chemical dependency may have been enormously destructive to the individual, but his life was already in complete disarray long before he ever began to abuse alcohol or drugs. Why? Because he was failing school, he had poor social relationships, he violated rules at home and school, he became frustrated easily, he was hyperactive, he was restless, he was highly impulsive, he was disorganized, he was defiant, he was oppositional, he was rapidly bored, and ONCE HE FOUND SOMETHING HE LIKED, HE COULDN'T GET ENOUGH OF IT (SEX, DRUGS, GAMBLING, AND SO ON).

The ADHD Scapegoat–Children of Alcoholics

His core symptoms were ADHD. His parents and teachers didn't understand it. This child was not necessarily the product of poor parenting. It was highly likely, though, that either Mom or Dad also had the same problems in childhood and still does. So the alcohol and drug community has given a name to this child. In literature on children of alcoholics, he is referred to as the "scapegoat." He is described as defiant, argumentative, hyperactive, aggressive, impulsive, and socially immature. He will probably have low self-esteem, fail school, and begin to use chemicals early in life. We would suggest to you that the scapegoat is often the ADHD child who likely has a chemically abusing parent, who is also likely ADHD, and for whom primary intervention for ADHD has been nonexistent or of a single modality. The ADHD child and the child of the alcoholic manifest these behavior patterns because of a common genetic anomaly rather than by environmental shaping. Other players within the alcoholic family, who may also be ADHD children, are those labeled the "mascot" or "distracter." They are described as lacking seriousness, often clowning, easily distracted, poorly motivated, highly impulsive, hyperactive, disorganized, and so on.

These may be ADHD children who have rationalized "it's better to laugh than to cry." They often have failure in school and are described as emotionally immature. With little or no objective research, the alcohol and drug abuse treatment community has seen the behaviors and so labeled them. Having done this, they then had to try to explain the behaviors, which was easily done by taking notice of the alcoholic in the home. Yet there was no objective data to suggest that the BEHAVIORS BEING EXHIBITED WERE CAUSED BY NURTURANCE.

Genetic Substrate for ADHD

There is, however, enormous data that suggest that these behaviors are related to genetics. In fact, the presence of the "hero" child in the home supports this. The "hero" child is the child of an alcoholic who often assumes responsibility for the household. This child is often performing very well in school and also caring for others in the household. While there is little doubt that this role is frequently visible within the home of an alcoholic, there is also a considerable amount of evidence that this child's early behavior patterns were considerably different from those of the "scapegoat." These behavior patterns are more indicative of biogenetics than they are of nurturing.

What is even more unfortunate is that we suggest to parents of these children that they caused this child to take on the role of the scapegoat because of the parents' alcoholism. The perpetuation of this cycle is much more indicative of genetics than of environment. Junior is likely exhibiting the same behavior patterns that the addictive parent exhibited when he or she was a child and continues to exhibit as an adult.

ADHD and Scapegoats

Consider the following shared characteristics of ADHD children and the "scapegoated" children of alcoholics.

Shared Characteristics
Hyperactivity
Restlessness
Impulsivity
Distractibility
Motivational Failure
Insatiability
Compulsivity
Low Frustration Tolerance
Sleep Disturbance
Irritability
Moodiness

Nature Versus Nurture

Clinically and personally, we must begin to differentiate between genetic/biological markers for addictive illness and environmental stress responses to family pathology. Failure to do this results in playing the "blame game" and encouraging the growth of guilt within the parents as if they caused this child to have these behavioral difficulties. It is interesting that as parents often describe their children, they view these behavioral difficulties as present even from the womb, long before the forces of nurturance come into play.

ADHD Genetic-Biological	COA Environmental-Social
early onset of hyperactivity	later onset of hyperactivity
relatively chronic and cross-situational	temporary and situational
high scatter* on IQ scores	little scatter* on IQ scores
motor coordination problems	coordination appropriate
chronic impulsivity/behavioral disinhibition	knowledge and skill deficits
low anxiety	high anxiety
difficulty with temperament in infancy	difficulty with temperament in later childhood
absence of somatic complaints	frequent somatic complaints (headaches, stomachaches, diarrhea)
early onset of insatiable addictive behavior to foods, sex, video games	late onset of addictive behaviors
chronic sleep disturbance	short-term sleep disturbance
nighttime enuresis	night and daytime enuresis/encopresis
rapid, sloppy handwriting	average to good handwriting
chronic difficulty with sequential tasks	periodic difficulty with sequential tasks

Scatter refers to the variability and range in subtest performance on measures of intelligence.

Children of Alcoholics (COA): Behavioral Characteristics

Are there behavioral characteristics common to children from alcoholic families? Certainly. However, we must better distinguish them from ADHD characteristics. We have to be able to identify whether the child's patterns of behavior are likely to be genetically linked or environmentally linked. This is not as difficult as it may sound. The rationale for the DSM-IV using an early age of onset for these behaviors when diagnosing ADHD suggests that they are more likely caused by genetics or pre/perinatal factors than by nurturance. If we cannot adequately distinguish etiological factors, then our treatment plan is likely to be ineffective.

Distinguishing ADHD from COA

Consider the following list of characteristics which may be used to distinguish these two groups.

Both groups are likely to develop addictive illnesses. However, those with genetic markers are likely to have an earlier onset, need a different approach to prevention, and need a very different approach to treatment. Our failure in prevention and treatment has been due to not recognizing these subgroups and using a "shotgun" approach.

Predisposing Factors in Alcoholism

Zucker and Gomberg (1986) proposed that etiology for alcoholism was related to several factors, among them biological, psychological, and social. These authors suggest that childhood factors such as achievement deficits, increased activity levels, antisocial behavior patterns, marital conflict, and deficient child-rearing practices all influence the development of alcoholism in the individual.

One could easily identify these characteristics within the homes of children identified with ADHD. Parents of ADHD children frequently appear to have "deficient child-rearing practices," but one must realize that these patterns emerge only after enormous frustration and often present themselves with the ADHD child alone. For other children of the household, these patterns are not present. ADHD children, therefore, appear to elicit these negative responses from their parents.

Treatment Implications

As we examine treatment implications, we must move away from suggesting that parents "cause" these behavior patterns in ADHD children. Our treatment for children of alcoholics with a genotype for alcoholism manifested as childhood ADHD must follow a very different approach than the one we would utilize for children of alcoholics without the genetic markers.

ADHD COA	NON-ADHD COA
high risk for relapse and treatment failure	lower risk for relapse and treatment failure
high risk to substitute addictions	lower risk to substitute addictions
higher risk for academic failure	lower risk for academic failure
higher risk for conduct disorder and anti-social behavior disorders	lower risk for conduct disorder and anti-social behavior disorders
long-term medication management possibly needed	short-term medication management needed
therapy should be oriented towards a disability and self-management	therapy should be oriented towards trauma and coping

Implications for Attributions and Treatment

When we view the individual or COA who manifests a genetic/biological etiology for addictive illness, we:
1. *Recognize the importance of multimodal treatment,* including possible long-term pharmacological treatment.
2. Redirect therapy to *self-management/self-monitoring.* We recognize the need to develop educational and home behavior management plans. We offer knowledge to the parents and the child.

3. *Remove an enormous burden of guilt from the parents.* They have been told that the COA's behavior is caused by the family dysfunction. Those therapists who believe the child's behavior is related to poor parenting should have the child live with them for about six months. The therapist may emerge out of that six-month experience an alcoholic herself. What she will likely find is that even with the best of parenting skills, these are difficult children to raise. It is easy for the "experts" to sit in their offices and give the answers to solving the mysteries of parenting these children. For years, we have examined the role of parenting styles on children. When are we going to look at the effects of children on parents? Several researchers studied how children who exhibit difficult behaviors affect the parents' level of alcohol consumption and found that, indeed, when distress is increased due to the child's externalizing behaviors, the fathers drank more alcohol (Lang, et al., 1989).

Impact of Children's Behavior on Parents

Are there children who by virtue of their resistance to parenting strategies affect their parents' smoking, drinking, or self-medicating levels? Certainly! Can these difficult children encourage their mothers to become clinically depressed? Certainly! Are there children who by virtue of their behaviors lead parents to become abusive? Certainly! These are not popular notions, but they are real.

When practitioners see children "acting out," they may immediately draw conclusions that there are environmental forces causing these behaviors. Just because A and B occur together does not mean that A causes B, and, yet, that is exactly what some practitioners are suggesting. They may see the child in the alcoholic family who is "acting-out" and immediately—with little or no assessment—suggest that the family dynamics have led to the child's behavior patterns. This is then followed by a plan of treatment that is usually ineffective. There is a wealth of data that suggests just the opposite—that these chronic behaviors cannot be created by poor parenting or family dysfunction. Rather, they are inherited.

When the parent says, "I have two other children, neither of whom are having these problems," therapists may have responded with, "You see, she is the hero child or the peacekeeper, or adjuster." No matter how the parents respond, they are made to feel as if they have damaged this child. Even the child who is doing exceptionally well is described as damaged because of the parent's alcoholism. Let's get real! Are we really going to say to the parent that your child is making straight A's, and this is because of something wrong that you have been doing? It is bad enough to blame parents for a child's bad behavior patterns, but must we blame them for a child's good behavior patterns, too? We need to stop blaming parents for the child's genetically linked behavior, and begin to educate the parents regarding the cause, course and treatment of a genetically based developmental disorder and its genetic relationship to addiction.

Resilient Children

Emmy Werner (1986), over an 18-year span, followed 49 children of alcoholics. Some appeared resilient to the influences of the alcoholic in the home, while others developed severe psychological problems. Those who were resilient were usually girls. These children manifested little or none of the characteristics common to ADHD. There is no evidence that this "resilient" behavior was taught in these families. Rather, it appears to be more indicative of genetic factors.

A Sense of Shame

When we view these individuals' behavior as having little or nothing to do with genetics:
We will find the individual constantly searching for his *dysfunction*. He will be told it was related to being raised in an alcoholic home; that his grandparents were alcoholic (intergenerational COAs); that his parents were codependent; that they were shamed, and so on. There is absolutely no scientific support for these conclusions!

Shaming of Children

There is little doubt that "*shaming*" occurs in these homes. However, the shaming goes both directions.

Examples of "Parent to Child Shaming"
- "Why won't you act your age? Grow up!"
- "I can't stand to be around you."
- "Why are you so stubborn and lazy?"
- "You're not even trying!"

Examples of "Child to Parent Shaming"
- "I hate you."
- "I wish you would die."
- "You're a jerk."
- "Why aren't you like other parents?"

This process of shaming is often present in families with ADHD children. It is a symptom of how the disorder influences the family, rather than being a cause for dysfunction. It is a response which is born of frustration. A closer look will often reveal that it is a process which begins with the child rather than the parent. Shaming statements, made by family members, are not indicative of true feelings but rather are often an impulsive response to anger or frustration.

As an example, one day in an office between appointments, an ADHD child was playing a video game while his mother sat in a chair beside him reading the paper. The child suddenly threw the game down and turned to his mother and said, "You idiot, you made me mess up!" The mother looked at the therapist and sighed. Later, in speaking with the mother about what happened, she confided, "This kind of thing happens all of the time. Any time he gets angry or frustrated, he takes it out on me."

Mothers are often the victims of such verbal aggression. There is little doubt that, at times, these mothers reach a point of frustration themselves and as a result may lash out at their child. To an outside observer, it would be rational and logical to assume that this was a mother who had not taught her child to respect her, due to a lack of discipline. Such was not the case. In fact, typically these are children who are disciplined much more frequently and harshly than other children.

The rational assumption is that, if appropriate discipline is enacted, the child would not behave in that manner. This is the big myth. These are children who typically respond to discipline with increased defiance and resentment. The good old advice by well-meaning experts that this child may need "more trips to the woodshed" is wrong. This child has probably already made more trips to the woodshed than there are trees in the forest, yet his behavior is relatively unchanged. It is for this reason that we must change our view of this child and see him as having a behavioral disability, rather than just being mean.

In Defense of Mothers

In a research project directed by Russell Barkley, Ph.D., he commented that when one watched the children and mothers interact, one almost viewed the mothers as "neurotic." However, when the child was *medicated*, the mother's behavior became much more normal. What this says is that the use of appropriate medication management for the child may help prevent a cycle of verbal and physical abuse from occurring within these families.

ADHD children are exceptional at eliciting negative responses from those they are around the most. This may be explained by "familiarity." The more novel the environment, the better behaved the child becomes. However, when placed in a very familiar environment, they can be at their worst. Thus parents sometimes hear from others: "I don't understand why you have so much difficulty. He never is a problem when he is with me." Mothers are the ones most likely to hear this type of comment and are often viewed as "creating" this defiant child by weak parenting. Far from it! To suggest that this is a parenting problem is likely the greatest insult you could give to this mother. She has gone far beyond her "call to duty" in caring for this child and in seeking to preserve his well-being. She should be praised for her perseverance in parenting a child who others just don't seem to understand.

It is the mother first and foremost who has the clearest picture of what the future holds for this child. She will know him best. She will be the "realist." As clinicians, we should listen carefully to the mothers of these children. Mothers desperately need the support of other family members, and especially of the grandparents. The child will often encourage her feelings of ineptness; she certainly doesn't need negative criticism from others.

Persistence of Disorganization

We will find that **even when traditional treatment for chemical dependency is utilized, the individual's life may continue in disarray.** The core symptoms of ADHD will not go away just by following the 12-step treatment program. We must remember that ADHD is a disorder of the *lifespan*.

- He may still have *financial* problems due to impulsive spending.
- He may have *relationship* problems. (In the same way it is hard to parent an ADHD child, it is also hard to be married to an ADHD adult.)
- He may have *other addictions* (tobacco, caffeine, sex, work, religion) and periodic relapses to his drug of choice.
- He will likely still be a *risk-taker* (driving too fast, gambling, excitement-seeking, often having affairs).
- He will still act *immaturely*.
- There is a long history of *sexual impropriety* associated with alcoholics.
- They will often have *children* who will act much as they did as children and they will grow frustrated and feel like a failure as parents and go to therapists who will blame the child's behavior on the parents' addiction!

This pattern of social immaturity has contributed to this scenario: When a person begins using alcohol or drugs, social maturity is halted at that point. Thus, alcoholics are frequently described as 30-year-olds acting like 16-year-olds. Where is the research that supports this conclusion? Yet, due to the impulsive nature of ADHD and excellent research, we can often describe them in this manner: As ADHD adults, they are still immature-acting, risk-takers, have difficulty delaying gratification (waiting for rewards), and are stimulus-seeking, restless and/or hyperactive, inattentive, and so forth.

This book's view of the *primary alcoholic*, then, is one who has been predisposed to a variety of addictive behaviors as a result of neurological deficits in inhibitory systems, whose etiology is likely of genetic origin and is expressed through a dysfunction of biochemistry of the brain.

The Genetic Connection

There has been considerable controversy regarding the etiology and treatment of ADHD and of alcoholism. Since ADHD has, in the past, been viewed as primarily a disorder of childhood, and alcoholism as a disorder of adulthood, the most obvious connection has been overlooked. The genetic connection suggests that they are closely related disorders! The characteristics which manifest in childhood of the genetic form of alcoholism is ADHD by description and by definition. We might say that **the behavior patterns of ADHD lead to alcoholism or other addictive illnesses**. Our clinical experience suggests that follow-up and fallback studies of the early development of alcoholics who are prone to relapse from sobriety will demonstrate a high incidence of ADHD. We predict that research studies will demonstrate ADHD with very early onset in life.

Overlapping Genetic and Symptomatic Characteristics

The body of evidence connecting the two disorders is growing. Studies of twins, residual studies, brain imaging studies and longitudinal studies are all contributing to our understanding of these two disorders. Treatment modalities overlap tremendously, with the use of antidepressants playing a major role in the treatment of both disorders. What do the antidepressants do? They help the person to inhibit—to stop and think before he acts, to overcome a sense of restlessness and craving for stimulation, and to improve frustration tolerance.

Whether the individual is age 10 or age 40, these are the core symptoms of both disorders. When we view ADHD as alcoholism and alcoholism as ADHD, we gain insight into the treatment modalities for prevention and intervention. We may use 12-step-like programs for ADHD adolescents to accept responsibility for their behavior and promote a social consciousness. We may use medication management more effectively for the alcoholic in maintaining sobriety.

Comorbidity of ADHD and Addictions

Considerable research has addressed the comorbidity between these two disorders from the perspectives of family genetics, gender differences, overlapping symptoms of clinical patterns, and neurobiology and microbiology of genetics. Key findings from this research further illustrate the interrelationship between specific patterns of ADHD and addictions.

Familial Genetics

1. ***Twin Studies for Alcoholism:*** Studies of twins have consistently shown that there is a greater risk for alcoholism among *identical twins* than among fraternal. There is a 74% concordance between identical twins and alcoholism, while there is only a 32% concordance among fraternal twins (Kaij, 1960).

2. ***Sons of Male Alcoholics (SOMAs):*** They are three or four times more likely to be alcoholic than sons of non-alcoholics (Goodwin, 1979; Tarter, 1981; Cloninger, 1991).

3. ***Age of Onset:*** Familial alcoholics show the first signs of dependency at *a younger age* than do non-familial alcoholics. Children of familial alcoholics are most commonly described as hyperactive, impulsive, and oppositional (Goodwin, 1983).

4. ***Predictors of Alcoholism:*** The strongest predictor of future alcoholism is *biconditional*: the parent is alcoholic, and the child has a history of hyperactive and impulsive behavior (Goodwin, 1985).

5. ***Comorbidity:*** 30 to 40% percent of alcoholics qualify for DSM III-R diagnosis of *residual ADHD* (Horton, 1985; Wood, Wender & Reimherr, 1983).

6. ***Overlying Symptoms:*** Children of alcoholics are frequently described as manifesting behavior patterns associated with attention deficit hyperactivity disorder (Fine, 1976). They have difficulty regulating excitement and mood (Lund, Landesman & Dwyer, 1979).

7. ***Behavioral Symptoms of ADHD versus ADD:*** When Russell Barkley, Ph.D., and colleagues studied 48 children with ADD plus hyperactivity and 42 ADD children without hyperactivity, it was found that the ADD plus H children had more externalizing and internalizing symptoms. They were off task more, and had more family substance abuse and aggression (Barkley, et al., 1990).

Clinical Patterns of Comorbid Symptoms

ADHD and Alcoholism—Behavioral Similarities

1. ***Overlapping Symptoms:*** SOMAs often demonstrate symptoms of ADHD:
   - They appear impaired in their ability to *concentrate*, to pay attention and to control their motor behavior sufficiently when required to do so.
   - They often break rules, act out and have *conflict* with those in authority and their peers. They are more often described as hyperactive or conduct-disordered.
   - They also show differences in their *sensitivity* to alcohol's reinforcing effects and differences in patterns of psychophysiological response.
   - In addition, they evidence a variety of verbal and abstract *cognitive* deficits (Peterson & Finn, 1990).

2. ***Types I & II Alcoholism:*** Researchers identified two subtypes of alcoholics.
   - *Type I* alcoholism is primarily one of social learning. It typically progresses at a slower pace, often at a later age and responds more favorably to 12-step programs.
   - *Type II* (or "male-limited") has a high genetic penetrance from father to son and minor environmental association, which also onsets prior to age 25 and is accompanied by persistent consumption of alcohol with aggression (Cloninger, 1987). Type II alcoholics are described as exhibiting behaviors consistent with antisocial personality, with high degrees of impulsivity and excitability (high novelty-seeking), brash and uninhibited behavior (low harm avoidance), and distant social relations (low reward dependence).

3. **Platelet Monoamine Oxidase in Type II Alcoholics:** Researchers found significant differences in type II (male-limited) alcoholics as compared to type I alcoholics. The type II alcoholics had significantly lower platelet monoamine oxidase levels than controls or type I alcoholics (Von Knorring, et al., 1985).

4. **Evoked Potential in Sons of Male Alcoholics:** Begleiter and colleagues (1984) found that the P300 wave of sons of alcoholics evidenced reduced amplitude compared to sons of non-alcoholics. The P300 wave normally appears during the performance of cognitive tasks involving visual memory and attention. Therefore, the reduced presence of the P300 wave suggests an increased risk factor for alcoholism.

5. **Behavioral and Cognitive Deficits in At-risk Alcoholics:** Neurological deficits in the frontal-midbrain were associated with temperament traits which placed individuals at high risk for developing alcoholism. These traits provide the link

between genetics and environment. The traits included: 1) a high activity level, 2) diminished attention span, 3) slow ability to calm following stress, 4) high sociability, and 5) labile emotional expressivity (Tarter, Alterman & Edwards, 1985).

6. **Hyperactivity:** An excessively high activity level in childhood has been shown to be a risk factor for alcoholism (Morrison & Stewart, 1973; Cantwell, 1972).

7. **Primary Versus Secondary Alcoholism:** 17 of 22 (77%) of *primary* alcoholics were classified as high in childhood hyperactivity and minimal brain dysfunction, as compared to only 9 of 33 (27%) of *secondary* alcoholics (De Obaldia, et al., 1983).

8. **Juvenile Offenders:** A study conducted at the University of Ottawa on the prevalence of substance abuse and coexisting Diagnostic Statistical Manual-Version III psychiatric disorders in 111 juvenile offenders found overlapping behaviors. "Significantly higher rates of attention deficit disorder and aggressive subtype of conduct disorder were present in those offenders who abused drugs and alcohol (54%) versus 14% of non-substance abusers demonstrating comorbid psychiatric diagnosis" (Milin, et al., 1991).

9. **Adopted Sons of Alcoholics:** A study of 5483 men in Denmark who were adopted in early childhood assessed the genetic influence for alcoholism. Researchers found that the sons of alcoholics adopted by nonalcoholic families were more than three times as likely to become alcoholics than were the adopted sons of nonalcoholics. The onset of alcoholism also occurred at an earlier age (Goodwin, et al., 1973).

10. **Behavior of Sons of Male Alcoholics:** A study following 134 sons of male alcoholics for 20 years compared them with sons of nonalcoholic in Denmark. The results indicated that sons of male alcoholics were more restless, impulsive, repeated more grades, had more reading difficulties and unhappier childhoods (Knop, et al., 1985).

11. **Psychiatric Problems:** Sixty percent of all patients admitted to chemical dependency programs are children of alcoholics (Liepman, White & Nirenberg, 1986).

12. **Follow-up Studies:** Longitudinal studies (prospective and retrospective) have continually shown that ADHD boys are at increased risk for alcohol abuse as both adolescents and later as adults (Bloun, Bornstein & Trites, 1978).

13. **Symptom Overlap:** A study on "inherited behavior traits that predispose to substance abuse" evidenced significant positive correlation among activity level, emotionality, sociability, and substance abuse among adolescents (Tarter, 1989).

14. **ADHD and Early Onset Alcoholism:** Hesselbrock, et al. (1985) found that attention deficit hyperactivity disorder and conduct disorders before the age of 12 predicted the onset of alcohol abuse.

ADHD and Substance Abuse

1. **Nicotine and ADHD:** Nicotine is a dopamine antagonist that was found to improve performance on attention tasks and increased arousal in smokers and non-smokers when given through a patch for a week. (Connors, et al., 1996).

   Milberger and Colleagues (1997) found that ADHD is a significant risk factor for early initiation of cigarette smoking in children and adolescents. This risk occurred independent of socioeconomic status, IQ and psychiatric comorbidity.

In follow-up studies of comparisons of siblings with ADHD and non-ADHD probands, Milberger, Biederman and Colleagues (1997) confirmed higher rates and earlier onset of cigarette smoking among siblings with ADHD.

There will no doubt be further research regarding the connection between tobacco products and ADHD individuals. One only has to attend an A.A. meeting to observe the connection between stimulants: nicotine and caffeine and alcoholics. Without stimulants these same persons become very restless, inattentive, and impulsive—the triad of symptoms of ADHD.

2. ***Cocaine and ADHD:*** In a study of 298 treatment-seeking cocaine abusers, 104 or 34.9% had a previous history of childhood attention deficit disorder (Rounsaville, et al., 1991). This is in contrast to a normal population, which exhibits a rate of ADHD of 3 to 5%.

   Carroll and Rounsaville (1993) found that "cocaine abusers with childhood ADHD were younger at presentation from treatment and reported more severe substance use, earlier onset of cocaine abuse, more frequent and intense cocaine use, higher rates of alcoholism and more previous treatment."

3. ***Gamblers and Attention:*** A 1993 study entitled "Neuropsychological assessment of attention problems in pathological gamblers" compared 33 non-substance abusing pathological gamblers with 33 nonaddicted controls on nine attention measures and childhood behavior questionnaires. The results indicated that "gamblers performed significantly worse than controls on higher order attention measures and reported more childhood behaviors consistent with attention deficits." This was suggestive that "attention deficits may be a risk factor for addictive disorders" (Rugle, 1993).

Addictions, ADHD and Cognition

1. ***Alcoholism and Vigilance:*** Research conducted at Four Winds Hospital in New York utilizing the continuous performance test led to the conclusion that impairments in attention may be associated with early onset alcohol abuse and that previous conceptions of the role of attentional impairments in risk prediction for alcohol abuse are supported. This research also delineated worse performance by alcohol abusers than by other substance abusers (Pogge, Stokes & Harvey, 1992).

2. ***Alcoholism and Problem-Solving:*** In a study entitled, "Persistence and problem-solving skills in young male alcoholics," (Cynn, 1992), it was found that "alcoholics persisted for significantly shorter periods of time on both measures of unsolvable anagram and diagram problems than their matched controls." ADHD has often been described as a "failure to persist" or "motivational deficit."

3. ***Sons of Male Alcoholics and Cognition:*** In a study of 16 sons of alcoholic fathers, with 25 sons of nonalcoholic fathers, the results indicated that teenage sons of alcoholics performed worse on tests measuring attention, memory, perceptual-motor coordination, motor speed, spatial sequencing, and language capacity. The study further described the lower scores were likely linked to not only family dysfunction but also to neuropsychological capacity. This suggests that there is a hereditary neurobiological vulnerability to alcoholism often identified by these factors in combination with environmental conditions (Hegedus, Alterman & Tarter, 1984).

Attention and Learning in Alcoholism and ADHD

Addictive Outcome of ADHD Children

In a 1993 study "Adult outcome of hyperactive boys," involving a longitudinal study from 13 to 19 years, the conclusion was that "childhood ADHD predicts specific adult psychiatric disorders, namely antisocial and drug abuse disorders" (Mannuza & colleagues, 1993).

Gender Differences

ADHD is six times more prevalent in boys than girls. Studies on genetics and ADHD conducted by the Institute of Child Health in London, England, indicated that at least half of the variance for hyperactivity is best explained by genetics (Goodman, 1989).

Girls of substance-abusing parents generally were more likely to have attention deficit, hyperactive, aggressive and conduct disorder problems than girls of non-substance-abusing parents (Gabel & Shindledecker, 1992).

Neurochemical Components of Alcoholism and ADHD

Alcohol consumption increases if the synthesis of brain serotonin is prevented. When serotonin brain receptors are blocked, alcohol consumption increases. Alcohol consumption decreases when brain serotonin receptors are stimulated.

Alcohol consumption also increases when dopamine receptors are blocked. Alcohol consumption decreases when dopamine receptors are stimulated. Alcohol consumption decreases when the synthesis of norepinephrine is blocked. (Blum & Payne, 1991; Kenneth Blum and James Payne have contributed enormously to our knowledge of alcoholism and genetics.)

The neurotransmitters dopamine, serotonin, and norepinephrine are implicated in both ADHD and alcoholism.

Genetic Aspects of Addictive Illness

Research on the prevalence of the A1 allele of the Taq 1 polymorphism of the dopamine receptor gene (DRD2) that among all known controls (n = 314), the A1 allele was significantly increased for ADHD (46.2% N = 104) **and for alcoholism** (42.3% N = 104) requiring P< .0009 for significance. The authors concluded: "The similar prevalence of the A1 allele in Tourette's syndrome, ADHD, autism, alcoholism and drug abuse is consistent with our proposal that these are a part of a spectrum of disorders that share common pathophysiologic genetic mechanisms. One feature these disorders have in common is a substrate of impulsive-compulsive addictive behaviors" (Comings, et al., 1990).

Later, in examining the role of serotonin on these disorders, these researchers found a strong connection to defective serotonin metabolism.

Drinking in Rats: Research indicates that there are significant neurochemical differences found in the brains of alcohol-preferring (P) rats versus the brains of non-alcohol-preferring (NP) rats. There was a consistent major difference in the amount of the neurotransmitters serotonin and dopamine (Murphy, et al., 1982, 1987). (These are the two primary suspect neuro-chemicals implicated in the etiology of ADHD children.) These researchers found that administration of fluoxetine (Prozac) raised serotonin levels at the point of synapse and prevented its reuptake by neurons. This resulted in reduced alcohol consumption by alcohol-preferring rats!

Dopamine Receptors: Blockage of dopamine receptor interferes with oral self-administration of alcohol in rats (Pfeffer & Samson, 1986).

Dopamine Levels: Dopamine levels are higher and serotonin levels are lower in alcohol-preferring rats in

A Sociobiological View of Addictive Illness

Genetic	Environmental
Difficult temperament	Pre/Perinatal influences
Behavioral disinhibition	CNS insult/injury
Distractibility	Parenting failure
Sensation-seeking (difficulty with delay of gratification)	Academic failure (educational intervention)
Overarousal (hyperactivity)	Community failure (antisocial)
Intellect (cognitive deficits)	Socioeconomic failure (poverty)

comparison to non-alcohol-preferring rats (Wong, et al., 1988).

Treatment Effects: Gorelick (1986) in a double-blind placebo study, "Effect of fluoxetine on alcohol consumption," in which one group received a placebo and one group received fluoxetine and where both groups had free access to alcohol, found that the fluoxetine group consumed significantly less alcohol than the control group.

Alcohol Craving

Dr. Kenneth Blum and James Payne (1991) in their book, *Alcohol and the Addictive Brain,* describe a "motivational model of alcohol craving." They describe three phases: (1) setup, (2) substitution, and (3) destruction. In the setup phase, Dr. Blum describes an individual who has a reduced supply of enkephalins or a "reduced natural release of these neurotransmitters in the hypothalamus." The result is a lower amount of serotonin, an increase in the amount of opioid receptors, and a reduced number of dopamine D2 receptor binding sites. The result, according to Dr. Blum, is that "the person under normal resting conditions cannot achieve feelings of well-being because not enough dopamine is being released, and not enough can bind to the dopamine D2 receptors in the reward part of the brain." With this setup in place, the person seeks to substitute. Alcohol may be the substance which causes a release of dopamine, offsetting temporarily the genetic dopamine deficiency. As the person continues to abuse alcohol, "destruction" of dopamine receptors occurs along with a decrease in enkephalins and serotonin in the hypothalamus, thus leading to damage of the reward centers and thereby intensifying the need for agents to release dopamine.

This, then, may explain the ADHD individual's constant seeking of sensation. This may also explain the association with high stimulus carbohydrate use described by mothers of ADHD children. The risk-taking, stimulus-seeking behavior may lead to addictions to sex, gambling, food, aggression, video games, and so forth. The ADHD individual has been described as "having a tank which cannot be filled." This places him in a state of "drive" in trying to fulfill this need. This explains why he disdains "boring" environments and why he continues to engage in behaviors which he knows are destructive to him.

William D. Silkworth, M.D., the author of "The Doctor's Opinion," in the book *Alcoholics Anonymous*, stated back in the 1940's: "We believe, and so suggested a few years ago, that the action of alcohol on these chronic alcoholics is a manifestation of an allergy; that the phenomenon of craving is limited to this class and never occurs in the average temperate drinker. These allergy types can never safely use alcohol in any form at all…. They are restless, irritable, and discontented unless they can again experience the sense of ease and comfort which comes at once by taking a few drinks…they cannot start drinking without developing the phenomenon of craving. It has never been by any treatment with which we are familiar, permanently eradicated. The only relief we have to suggest is entire abstinence."

Dr. Silkworth could not adequately explain the etiology of the chronic alcoholic. However, he knew from his experiences in treating literally thousands of alcoholics that they were not all alike. He saw many about whom he could only postulate that allergy was responsible for their response to alcohol. He could see no other explanation. He saw that, once they began to drink, they could not limit their intake or gain satiation. No such allergy has been found. Rather, we are now beginning to understand that it is within the functioning of the neurochemistry of the brain that the answer must lie. We are exceptionally close to real answers. We are beginning to understand the role of dopaminergic centers such as the nucleus accumbens and the basal ganglia as they play a role in pain prevention, reward and pleasure. We are beginning to understand the neurochemistry associated with the use of alcohol, heroin and cocaine on general and specific areas of the brain. It is with this information that the role of pharmacology may ultimately assist us in either blocking the effects, reducing the craving, or controlling the mood. What is inordinately clear, however, is that there are populations which we can identify who are at "extreme risk." It is upon these populations that we must begin to place our emphasis. The "shotgun" approach which we have previously used in prevention has proven itself too large, too costly and largely ineffective.

The studies presented here are only the "tip of the iceberg." What this research says is that, for years, we have understood the relationship among genetics, ADHD characteristics and addictive illness. Since we are in the middle of fighting the drug war (I include alcohol as a drug of abuse), why have we not utilized this information in prevention and treatment? ADHD has become the "disorder of the 90's," and yet, we have, for the most part, ignored the role it plays in contributing to addictions. Are we assessing for ADHD in families which we are treating for addictive illnesses, and if we are, how are we using this information? The authors are angered that we have individuals completing multiple treatment programs for addictions and spending thousands of dollars, who have ADHD diagnosed in the psychological evaluation which is then ignored in treatment as if the core symptoms of ADHD have had nothing to do with their present condition. It has had everything to do with their current condition! It is what is wrong! It is why they are failing treatment! We must stop blaming their addictions on environmental causes and look at an addictive personality empathetically. We understand how to treat and manage this hereditary illness effectively. It is past time for us to begin to do so! We can do a much better job in assessing these genetic markers and developing treatment plans which are more appropriate for these individuals. This research suggests that these are people whose social, academic and personal survival depends heavily upon a multimodal treatment program which likely involves consistent pharmacological management of specific symptoms along with therapy.

No one questions the impact of environmental influences on addictive behavior patterns, but to intervene successfully we must recognize the hereditary factors involved.

We must not, for instance, assume that irresponsible behavior is a learning or social skills deficit. In fact, frequently these individuals know the right way to behave, but they act the opposite. To try to teach the appropriate behavior for the occasion is probably a waste of time and money. There is little or no evidence that these people transfer this learning to their natural environment. Rather, we must seek to increase the individual's ability to self-monitor and manage his or her behavior patterns from a view of disability.

Chapter 2

Questions and Answers About ADHD

What Are Some Characteristics Common to Individuals with ADHD?

> *"Fifty years from now it will not matter what kind of car you drive, what kind of house you live in, how much you had in your bank account, or what your clothes looked like. But the world may be a little better because you were important in the life of a child."*
> —Hiam Ginott

Motivational deficits
Insatiability/rapidly form addictions
Hyperactivity/restlessness
Rapid boredom
Inconsistent pattern of productivity
Difficulty complying with rules and authority
Rapid mood changes
Excitability
Organizational difficulties
Distractibility/attention deficits
Difficulty delaying gratification
Aggression
Short sleep cycles
Low frustration tolerance
Impulsivity

These are the same core symptoms we would see in 30 to 40% of alcoholics even before the disease progresses to an addiction.

What Are the Causes of ADHD?

An enormous amount of research exists regarding the etiology of ADHD. We have identified many etiological factors. These may include both genetic and environmental causes.

Genetic

We are still unsure about the mechanism. However, the heritability of ADHD is without question. Based on laws of genetics, we understand that, if a parent manifests the disorder through a dominant defective transmitting allele then: 1) The trait is transmitted by a parent to about half of his or her children (assuming a heterozygous relationship exists). Thus, if a family has three or four children, the trait is usually expressed in every generation. 2) If a parent does not express the trait, then he does not transmit it to his children. In the case of a recessive allele, then we would expect to see the trait in a sibling, but not in the parents. On the average, one-fourth of the siblings of parents, both of whom are known to be carriers of the recessive allele, would be affected. These same genetic relationships will generally hold true for alcoholism, depending, of course, on the person's decision of whether or not to drink.

Currently, the belief exists that there is a gene which interferes with dopaminergic and/or serotonergic transmission either directly or as a modifier. Dopamine plays a major role in processes of attention, motivation, activity control, memory, or what may be described as "executive functioning." Stimulant medications such as methylphenidate and dextroamphetamine sulfate (which are dopaminergic agonists) increase central nervous system arousal which results in improved cortical inhibition. They may also increase the availability of norepinephrine at the synaptic cleft. Likewise, cerebral blood flow is increased, and glucose metabolism may be increased. Serotonin plays a major role in behavioral inhibition, mediating depression, aggression, and other aspects of mood. Medications, such as tricyclic antidepressants of which imipramine and desipramine are two examples, appear to inhibit the reuptake of dopamine, while newer antidepressants such as Prozac, Paxil, Zoloft, and Effexor appear to inhibit reuptake of serotonin. Other theories of genetic origin are based upon the genetic influence on glucose metabolism in the brain, resistance to thyroid hormone or even morphological differences in periventricular structures within the brain, such as the right striatum of the caudate nucleus. Hemispheric dominance and function also continue to be studied. It is likely with the astounding amount of information being obtained through genetic research and through the introduction of improved brain scanning single-photon emission computed tomography (SPECT), positron emission tomography (PET), magnetic resonance imaging (MRI), mental activity network scanner (MANSCAN), and magnetoencephalography (MEG) that we will have a much clearer picture of the etiology within the next decade. There are many genetic disorders, such as fragile X and Tourette's syndrome, that may mimic symptoms associated with ADHD.

Environmental

Certainly pre/perinatal injury such as intraventricular hemorrhages, ischemia, toxemia, and so on may create symptoms associated with ADHD. Environmental agents such as lead, alcohol, cocaine, marijuana, pesticides, and others have also been examined and likely make up some of the etiology of ADHD. However, it may be possible to differentiate many of these causes by other symptoms inconsistent with ADHD.

While psychological trauma may create symptoms similar to ADHD, the lack of chronicity and pervasiveness of symptoms should lead practitioners to rule these out through their differential diagnoses.

Are Males More Likely to Have ADHD Than Females?

The ratio of males to females receiving a diagnosis has varied between 4:1 and 6:1. This may be due to a combination of factors. The male of any species is, generally speaking, more susceptible to genetic disorders. Homo sapiens males are also by nature more aggressive, and this may lead to more referrals and eventual diagnoses.

How Does ADHD Negatively Impact the Family?

Listed below are feelings by parents (especially mothers) of ADHD children:

Frustration

This results from the resistance that these individuals

have to change. Parents often say, "No matter what we do, nothing seems to change." The children are described as stubborn, strong-willed, having a mind of their own, oppositional, defiant, and so on.

Anger

Parents often become angry because "life is not how we expected it to be." Why does my child have this problem? Why does he continue to make the same mistakes over and over? Why doesn't he act his age? Why is she so stubborn? Why doesn't he follow rules? Why must he constantly argue? Why is he so moody? Why doesn't she do her work? Why is he always demanding things? Why is he never satisfied? Why does he constantly lie? Why don't others understand?

Guilt

Often, out of frustration, parents displace their anger and focus it on their children, punishing them verbally and physically. Coercive discipline may bring about immediate results but in the long run will likely worsen matters, leading to increased aggression and lowered self-esteem of the child.

Fear

Parents are often afraid for this child's future. Will he finish school? Will he be injured? (ADHD children have three times the accident rate of other children.) Will he violate laws? Will he become sexually active early? Will he develop alcohol or drug problems? Will he be able to find a career he can stick with? All parents have fears similar to these, yet statistically these are very real possibilities for this population.

Confusion

Which professionals should be involved? Psychologist? Psychiatrist? Physician? Neurologist? What "really" helps?

Exhaustion

When do we get to rest? When will this improve? Dealing with ADHD is day in and day out. Parents end up "being parents" much longer than they would like. When the child is age 40, he is still acting irresponsibly and immaturely.

Denial

They look normal. Why won't they act age-appropriately? ADHD is a "hidden disability." There are no physical features that identify the disorder.

Sadness

Many tears are shed over this individual. Many prayers are proffered. Upon diagnosis, a "grief period" often occurs related to acceptance of the disorder and understanding of its implications.

Isolation

Parents stop visiting with their child in others' homes. They stop going out for meals. They stop taking family vacations. They stop going to public places like church, malls, or ballgames. They fear embarrassment from being unable to adequately control their child.

Grieving the Loss of Normalcy

In the 1960's, author Elizabeth Kubler Ross wrote of five stages of grief common with the terminally ill. They are denial, anger, bargaining, sadness, and acceptance. These same five stages are often seen in parents of ADHD children. Initially, they may deny that their child has anything wrong with him. They often suggest that he is just "going through a stage" such as the "terrible twos." When teachers or child care workers begin to describe developmental differences in the pattern of behavior expressed by the child in quantitative terms, the parents often deny the child's differences. Eventually, the parents' denial is overwhelmed by the behavioral difficulties. When this happens, they begin to search for answers, and, if a diagnosis is made, there is often a sense of relief with the question becoming "What can we do to overcome this?" When working with those practitioners who suggest that this disorder is "managed" rather than "cured," the parents may hover again around denial. When a cure is not immediately discovered, the parents may begin to migrate towards interventions outside the traditional scope of psychology and medicine. This then begins the bargaining stage. During this stage parents may seek novel "cures" involving various unproven interventions such as biofeedback, dietary management, orthomolecular (megavitamins), or chiropractic. Many parents stay "locked" into this mode with little or no change occurring, except that which is likely placebo-related. As frustration over a lack of progress grows, parents often begin to feel anger which they frequently project onto others. Thus, the parent may become angry at his or her spouse, teachers, doctors, counselors, and especially at the child himself for not improving his behavior. This anger, often created by a "loss of normalcy" in the life of the parent, can be terribly destructive to these relationships and impede the child's progress. There is also a deep feeling of sadness associated with this loss. As many as 20% of mothers of ADHD children become clinically depressed. Since ADHD is a chronic illness, the pervasiveness of parenting a child with severe behavioral problems often simply "wears down" the resistance to stress, leading to depression. It is essential that the parents of ADHD children manage this stress and monitor their physical and mental health frequently. Eventually most parents begin to accept the ADHD as "real," change their view of the child and become an advocate for him or her.

How Many Individuals Have ADHD?

Estimates vary, but likely 3 to 5% of our population may be diagnosed with ADHD. There is little doubt that in many settings, ADHD is overdiagnosed. Simply meeting the diagnostic criteria for ADHD is not sufficient for diagnosis since there are many conditions which may mimic ADHD. Likewise, ADHD is oftentimes underdiagnosed. This seems to occur when the child's behavior is simply described as a failure of parenting. This is terribly unfair to those parents who are already experiencing a great deal of guilt over the child's behavioral difficulties.

What Medications Are Used in Treating ADHD?

Chapter Six will focus specifically on medications. At this stage, suffice it to say that stimulant medications, antidepressants, antiseizure medications, hypertensive medications and some major tranquilizers may play a role in treatment.

What Treatments Have Proven to Be Helpful?

Medication Management—Single-modality treatment of medication alone has not proven to help in the long run.

Parental Education—This is a vital intervention. Parents do not create ADHD by poor parenting. However, they must learn how to become "better than average" parents to reduce the risk associated with their child.

Individual Therapy—This is associated with self-management and understanding of ADHD. At times, specific skills must be built. However, this has been misunderstood by many practitioners. Most ADHD individuals have knowledge of how to behave; they just don't do it. That is very different from a skill deficit.

Educational Interventions—School creates a foundation for one's belief about self. School success can lead to a healthy self-concept and high self-esteem, while school failure can create the opposite. It is essential that interventions begin early and continue throughout the formal educational years. Unfortunately, many teachers and administrators lack understanding of how ADHD impacts the child. In recent years, federal laws have been reinterpreted to include ADHD as a disability under the "other health impaired" category of the Individuals with Disabilities Education Act. This allows ADHD children to receive special education services when the ADHD adversely affects their learning. ADHD children may also receive modifications in their educational program through Section 504 of PL 93:112. This is a civil rights law which prevents discrimination based upon a handicapping condition. ADHD may be viewed as such, depending upon severity.

At What Age Is ADHD Usually First Diagnosed?

This can certainly vary depending upon the parents' and careproviders' awareness and knowledge of ADHD. However, usually during the first one or two years of school, ADHD children show quantitative differences in their behavior. That is to say that the kind of behaviors they exhibit are not that different from those of other children their chronological age, but the frequency of their occurrence can be dramatically different. If the child is a firstborn child, then the age of diagnosis is often further delayed, due to a lack of comparison for first-time parents. If the child is a girl, then likewise the diagnosis is often delayed as teachers are sometimes more tolerant of a female child's behavior problems than those of a male. It is not unusual for parents to have the child's hearing checked due to concerns about the child not following through on instructions, or repeated questions of "What did you say?" This behavior is characteristic of distractibility. The parent will often say, "He can listen when he wants to."

Have There Been Longitudinal Studies of the Outcomes of ADHD Individuals in Adulthood and the Risk for Alcohol and Substance Abuse? How High Are the Risks?

Only in the last decade have we studied outcomes in adulthood. In 1993, Salvatore Mannuzza and colleagues released research conducted on 91 white males representing 88% of a cohort systematically diagnosed as hyperactive in childhood and 95 (95%) comparison cases of similar race, gender and age, whose teachers had voiced no complaints about their school behavior in childhood. The study involved intervals ranging from 13-19 years. The results indicated significantly higher rates of antisocial personality disorders (18 versus 2%) and DRUG ABUSE DISORDERS (16 versus 4%). They also found that, among the subjects, educational and occupational achievements were significantly compromised.

Prior to Mannuzza and colleagues, Weiss, Milroy, and Perlman did a 15-year follow-up of 63 hyperactive children with an average age of 25 years. The results showed antisocial personality disorder was significantly more prevalent than among controls (23 versus 2%, P<.01) as was alcohol abuse (68 versus 33%, P=.01). Deficits were also found in academic achievement.

What Is the Difference Between ADD and ADHD?

ADD is an entirely different disorder from ADHD. The name ADD refers to the absence of hyperactivity, but there are a great many other differences. Research has shown us that individuals with ADD are more likely to come from families where there are more anxiety disorders and learning disabilities. The root symptom is slow neural processing. These individuals are often described as lethargic. They do not have the oppositional/behavior problems common with ADHD. Instead, they often go unnoticed except for academic underachievement. They have difficulty with selective attention and thus have more of a true attention deficit. Children with ADHD are more likely to come from families where there is a history of alcoholism or antisocial behavior. They have more difficulty with motivation, impulsivity, and hyperactivity. Since it would probably be better to rename ADHD to more accurately describe its characteristics, some have suggested "hyperactive-impulsive disorder." Children with ADHD can attend adequately when motivational factors are high.

Both disorders respond positively to stimulant medication. Children with ADD usually require much lower dosages. Etiologically, they are entirely different disorders caused by different brain mechanisms. Researchers at the

Department of Neurology, University of Texas-Southwestern Medical Center in Dallas have suggested that ADD may be better described as a "primary disorder of vigilance," suggesting that the core characteristics are inattentiveness, daydreaming, boredom, restlessness and sleepiness (Weinberg & Brumback, 1990).

A comparison of the two disorders reveals significant differences between them

ADHD	ADD
Etiology Prefrontal-limbic-striatal **Deficits** Inhibiting, Sustained Attention, Motivation **Characterized by** Hyperactivity, insomnia, aggression	**Etiology** Posterior associative cortical-subcortical, or possible hippocampus dysfunction **Deficits** Processing speed, Short-term memory, distractibility **Characterized by** Lethargy, somnambulence, apathy

How Is ADHD Diagnosed?

There is no single medical, psychological, or educational test that can diagnose ADHD. As earlier noted, great advances have been made in brain imaging techniques which include CAT scans, MRI, PET scans, or SPECT analysis. However, none of these can conclusively identify ADHD. Psychological tests, such as intellectual evaluations, determine intellectual strengths and weaknesses and, to a small degree, measure distractibility; however, they do not offer sufficient data to diagnose ADHD. An adequate differential diagnosis must include a clinical interview of developmental history, rating scales from teachers and parents, a clinical interview with the child, observation of the child in a natural environment (or accurate observations by others), and a medical evaluation to rule out a medically remediable cause for the behavior. Additional testing may be needed if comorbidities, such as learning disabilities, are suspected. Thus, a number of different professionals like teachers, psychologists, and physicians are often used in gathering data.

While there are those who question that validity of the diagnosis of ADHD, we recognize the following:
1. There are definable symptoms that constitute a valid cluster for identification.
2. There is a predictable course to the disorder with identifiable patterns of outcome.
3. There exists a brain dysfunction that is identifiable.
4. There is a genetic pattern to the disorder evident in familial studies and now in molecular genetic studies.
5. Treatment can be defined that has predictable effects.

These criteria are clearly met by ADHD in childhood and continuing into adulthood (Spencer, et al., 1998).

> *"Some people see a closed door and turn away. Others see a closed door, try the knob, and if it doesn't open they turn away. Still others see a closed door, try the knob, and if it doesn't open, they find a key, and if the key doesn't fit, they turn away. A rare few see a closed door, try the knob, and if it doesn't open they find a key, and if the key doesn't fit...they make one."*
> KEYMAKERS
> (Author Unknown)

Assesment-ADD/ADHD
Essential Components

Comprehensive
- **History:**
  Patient, Development, Medical, Family
- **Behavioral:**
  School, Home, Play
- **Cognitive:**
  Measure Attention, Learning, LD
- **Physical:**
  Dysmorphia; Coordination; Fine & Gross Motor
- **Psychiatric/Emotional**

Cost and Time Effective
- **Standard Clinical Pathway**

Diagnostic Tests

As was previously mentioned, there is no single medical, psychological, or educational test that can currently diagnose ADHD. Therefore, it cannot be diagnosed by EEG's, MRI's, CT scans, bloodwork, and so on. Nor can it be diagnosed by the continuous performance test or freedom from distractibility formulas on the Wechsler Intelligence Scale for Children—Version III, and so on. Nor can it be diagnosed by teachers' observational data through checklists or measures of achievement. ADHD cannot be diagnosed in a brief period of time in the pediatrician's or psychologist's office. What then are the appropriate tests and measures which diagnose ADHD? The answer is that no single piece of data can confirm a diagnosis, but rather that ADHD should be diagnosed based upon a detailed review of developmental history, including family genetic relationships, and direct observational data as supplied by parents, teachers, and practitioners. Other information such as intellect, neural processing, achievement, medical history, and other factors may lend supporting information that may assist in confirming diagnosis or in ruling out diagnosis.

Complex Diagnosis

While a diagnosis of ADHD seems very simple, it is not. It is increasingly complex. There are probably 20 or more other kinds of problems which, at least on a short-term basis, may look much like ADHD. These may include traumatic brain injury, tumor, learning disabilities, allergies, trauma or abuse, poor parenting, substance abuse, epilepsy, fragile X syndrome, Asperger's disorder, mental retardation, neurocutaneous disorders and hyperthyroidism to name a few. We know of no better source of interview forms than those which have been developed by Russell Barkley and colleagues. In his book *Attention Deficit Hyperactivity Disorder: A Clinical Source Book,* Dr. Barkley offers, in these authors' opinions, the best diagnostic materials available today. Dr. Barkley is well known for his expertise regarding ADHD. In his clinical interview forms, Dr. Barkley includes questions about pre/perinatal history, school achievement, similar neuropsychiatric disorders and criteria, medical history, genetic relationships, and family stability. In addition, there are excellent rating scales available for parents and teachers which examine specific criteria related to diagnosing.

The information gathered by the psychologist can often be easily composed into a report to share with the child's physician when discussing rationale for diagnosis. The psychologist should make every effort to observe the child in a school-type setting prior to diagnosis. Many ADHD individuals do quite well in the clinician's office where novelty is high. It is because of this that many mothers have left the pediatrician's office with a prescription for herself, such as Valium or Xanax, to assist her with anxiety because she is the one who appears to have the "problem," rather than her child. When children are stripped to their underwear and placed on a table, remembering that in times past they received a shot in the buttocks under similar circumstances, they have the ability to listen attentively to the physician and behave wonderfully, much to the mother's frustration.

Physicians should avoid diagnosing until data regarding the child's performance in the school setting can be determined. Psychologists should refrain from diagnosing until medical data from the physician is obtained. Therefore, while either *may* diagnose, neither *should* diagnose until they have collaborated with the other. For the school psychologist, it is vital that he or she likewise collaborate with the physician and the parent. It is entirely inappropriate to try and diagnose a child with ADHD based upon test data and teacher observations alone. To do so is to leave out major amounts of information that may influence the diagnosis.

When psychologists are evaluating, they must recognize that the novelty of taking an individualized intelligence test often results in a sample of observable behavior that is incongruent with the child's behavior in his naturalistic environment. That is to say, he may be very different when placed in a class setting with 20 other children. One should also keep in mind that a factor analysis of the subtests that yield a freedom from distractibility formula suggests that actually only a small portion of that child's score is measuring distractibility. Certainly we must recognize that the child's arithmetic subtest score is measuring first and foremost numerical reasoning. We must recognize that digit span is measuring short-term auditory memory and that coding is measuring hand-eye coordination and speed of processing. It is altogether inappropriate for the psychologist to suggest that the child's weak performance on freedom from distractibility is indicative of a child with attention-deficit hyperactivity disorder. This information only becomes meaningful when combined with other data. Therefore, a diagnosis of attention-deficit hyperactivity disorder should be based on data collected by the physician and psychologist. Once this information is shared, the diagnosis may be made by either party.

Of great concern is that practitioners often seem to practice on the "fringes." That is to say, there are those who insist that a battery of testing must be completed prior to diagnosis. With this battery of tests comes a very expensive price tag. This practice applies to both psychologist and physician. The result is that the child's health care benefits may be virtually exhausted by the assessment process prior to treatment ever occurring. This is unethical, in our opinion. On the other end of this spectrum of services are those who claim to be able to diagnose ADHD by a very brief clinical interview. A 20-minute interview with either the physician or psychologist is insufficient to make such a diagnosis. These are individuals who appear to know the "symptoms" of the disorder with scant other knowledge about its treatment, course, or outcomes. Families would be advised to avoid practitioners whose training falls outside the scope of behavioral medicine, pediatrics, family practice, neurology, clinical psychology or psychiatry. As with any type of difficulty, it can be especially helpful to seek services from someone who has had first-hand experience in parenting or has a sibling or close relative with ADHD. The education this provides cannot be obtained through text or training. If this is not practical or possible, certainly it is important to find someone who has stayed up-to-date on the research about ADHD. We have likely learned more about ADHD in the past 10 years than in the previous 100 years. A practitioner who has not kept abreast of this information may seek to use interventions that have a very weak research base.

Placebo or Appropriate Treatment?

Families should likewise avoid falling victim to those who claim to be able to "cure" ADHD. Miracle cures always seem to appear when dollars are available. Currently, families are very vulnerable to fraudulent practices. There is little or no data, for example, that supports the use of dietary management, megavitamin/mineral treatment, chiropractic, or biofeedback in the treatment of this disorder. Likewise, the use of single-modality treatments such as therapy or medication, while appropriate in a multimodal treatment program, may be very ineffective when used in isolation from other interventions. Individuals should not minimize the influence of the "placebo" effect when beginning new treatments. The benefits of unproven treatment programs are usually short-lived. Thus, in searching for a food or environmental agent associated with the child's behavior, one may see initial benefits only to see a return to baseline behaviors in weeks to come. The result is an eternal search for the cause of the child's behavior.

However, it should also be stated that, if something works, then common sense suggests using the intervention as long as there are no risks associated with its use. For example, if a parent finds that indeed "chocolate" worsens behavior, then a substitute item may be given. The more likely explanation is that sweet foods increase excitement level and behavioral difficulties follow. This is not created by the food but rather by a "pleasure principle" which causes a similar response when the child is given a toy.

Involvement in the assessment process for children and adults with ADHD over the years has shown that one could usually find either a very high genetic relationship to ADHD or similar comorbid conditions in the relatives of these individuals. If genetic relationships were absent, then one could usually find evidence of pre/perinatal birth trauma, the presence of alcohol or drug abuse in utero, or traumatic brain injury.

An Increasing Diagnosis?

The question has recently been asked, "Why are there so many more children with ADHD now than in the past?" The answer involves many factors, one of which is that many of the children who are being diagnosed with ADHD are children who have had central nervous system injury due to their mother's use of alcohol or other drugs. While a lot of attention has been given to fetal alcohol syndrome, many practitioners have overlooked "fetal alcohol affected" children. These children often have low average IQ's, ADHD symptoms of hyperactivity, impulsivity, and difficult temperament, in addition to learning problems (expressive or receptive language impairments, speech impairments, dysgraphia, visual-motor impairments, slow neural processing, and so on.) In the past, these children often fell through the cracks. They would not qualify as learning disabled in many states due to discrepancy formulas in which there was no significant discrepancy between IQ and achievement. When laws were reinterpreted to include ADHD children under the "other health impaired" category, many of these children could finally receive special educational services by qualifying as ADHD. Treatment modalities do not differ significantly for fetal alcohol affected children, with the exception that they may need more time-intensive interventions and greater assistance with learning. Early interventions are very important for these children. The same can be said for "crack babies." These children, again, manifest symptoms common to ADHD children and, in fact, may be defined as ADHD. ADHD is commonly viewed as a collection of symptoms or diagnostic criteria, as opposed to a specific genetic disorder. While etiology for ADHD is often described as unknown, in fact it usually can be established as either genetic or environmental, based upon developmental history. We may also see more children diagnosed as ADHD due to the fact that we have more birth mothers who are younger and who are in poor health. Technology and advances in medicine have enabled children who are born prematurely to survive. However, with their survival comes a wide range of neurological problems and birth defects. With teen pregnancy at all-time highs, along with health issues like smoking, alcohol use, crack use, and others, we are going to continue to see more children who are born with these kinds of difficulties.

We may also consider that changes from an agrarian society to an industrial/technological society may be making ADHD children more recognizable. While the rapid pace of society is not causing ADHD, it is likely leading to more children being diagnosed in nations which require increasing amounts of classroom education. Society does not tolerate very well those who do not fit neatly into our educational, occupational, and social domains. "Diagnostic criteria" for ADHD in one sense simply suggests that these are individuals who do not conform to societies' expectations for behavior control.

Quantitative Differences

When compared to his or her same-age peers, the ADHD individual is quantitatively different. For example, all children from time to time have difficulty with sustaining attention, interrupting conversations, and difficulty staying seated. ADHD children seem to have these kinds of difficulties more often than their same-age peers. These differences are highly situational. They do not occur in all settings. In fact, they typically occur only in those settings which require a considerable amount of rigidity relative to following rules (i.e., school, home, church, work). As has been previously suggested, these differences in performance likely have more to do with genetics than with environment.

Genetic Comorbidity Evaluation

We may determine the genetic risk factors for ADHD and comorbidities through examining the genetic relationships by developing a detailed genogram with the biological parents.

The value of this is that, for young children who are displaying several of the characteristics below, we can assess the probable risk associated with their development. Thus we may be able to determine the seriousness of these characteristics. While all of these characteristics are shaped by forces of nature and nurture, the outcome of close relatives may tell us there is a need to modify the nurturance process in order to minimize these risks. For children whose families reflect high risk relative to comorbid disorders, specific educational materials should be gathered from which the child may benefit to reduce the potential risk. The child whose family has evidenced significant problems with endogenous depression should, at an early age, be taught the core symptoms of depression. The child whose family has had special difficulty with alcoholism should be taught that they may lose control due to alcohol intake more quickly than others. The parents of children where ADHD symptoms have persisted may need assistance in managing their own lives. The following characteristics may be reviewed regarding genetic propensity:

> Childhood hyperactivity
> Inattention or distractibility
> Impulsivity or disorders of impulse control
> Learning disabilities or special difficulty in reading, math, spelling or language
> Alcohol or drug abuse
> Anxiety disorders
> Depression, including bipolar disorder
> Schizophrenia
> Antisocial behavior/criminality
> Temper difficulties
> Mental retardation
> Tourette's syndrome or tic disorders
> Other genetically driven disorders such as fragile X, neurofibromatosis, autism, etc.

The research on genetics should certainly reinforce the need to be looking long and hard at the other family members and the age of onset of particular problems.

Chapter 3

It Isn't Bad Parenting

It Isn't Bad Parenting

It is important to remind the reader that ADHD is not caused by weak parenting. Many of the parents of these children have other children who are doing very well. These parenting interventions are developed to encourage parents to see their child as manifesting a behavioral disability, rather than just disobedience. No one will be more important and influential in the life of the child than the parents. Kahlil Gibran wrote, "You are the bows from which your children as living arrows are sent forth…you may give them your love but not your thoughts, for they have their own thoughts. You may house their bodies but not their souls."

Grieve Your Loss of Normalcy

While most parents have rest periods between their child's behavior problems, such is not the case with parents of ADHD children. The pervasiveness of this disorder suggests that there are typically problems in the morning before school, possible problems at school, problems after school, problems when eating out, problems when company comes over, problems in going to church, problems when going on vacation, and so on. The result is a parent who often feels completely "whipped" by the child.

When a diagnosis is initially made, there is often a sense of relief and also one of grief. Parents have been looking for an explanation, but they haven't found a cure. It is important for the parent to grieve this loss of normalcy much the way the parent would if a child were diagnosed with juvenile diabetes. With the grief comes an acceptance that this is "real" and that it must be dealt with. This grief process occurs more easily with mothers than with fathers. Fathers tend to stay in denial of the legitimacy of the disorder, or to blame the mother for the child's behavioral problems. This grief must be tempered, however. An old Japanese proverb says, "When birds of sorrow fly over your head, don't let them build a nest in your hair." This is especially true for the mothers of these children. Some 20% of the mothers of ADHD children become clinically depressed. This is understandable but is also preventable.

> "They came to tell your faults to me, they named them one by one;
>
> I laughed aloud when they were done,
>
> I knew them all so well before;
>
> Oh, they were blind, too blind to see.
>
> Your faults had made me love you more."
>
> Sara Teasdale, "Faults," *Collected Poems of Sara Teasdale*

Change How You See Your Child

It is easy to see your child as lazy, defiant, stubborn, and so forth. For those who do not fully accept the diagnosis, this is exactly how they will view this child. It is essential for parents to see their child's strengths as well as his weaknesses. We may describe a child as poorly motivated, terrible at math, rude, belligerent, and impatient, or we may describe the same child as highly creative, determined, intelligent, loves to work outdoors, interested in animals and computers, and courageous. It is all a matter of where we put our focus. There is nothing inherently wrong about wanting to do things quickly, enjoying having fun, or liking action. Rather, we sometimes are trying to make these individuals act the way we think they should act according to our own pattern of behavior. It is sometimes helpful, as noted before, to view these children as being 20% developmentally younger. In fact, they often have friends slightly older or slightly younger than themselves, yet have difficulty making and keeping friends their own age. Older kids are often more tolerant of their immature behaviors or like their risk-taking attitudes, while younger children are socially more on their developmental level.

Confront Your Anger

It is easy to become angry at your child for not following rules. Get used to it, and get over it! Do not think that you will ever likely bring his behavior up to his chronological age. To try to do so will result in your continually being frustrated. These are children who are easy to abuse. Be careful of how you respond to them when you are angry. Place some limits on your responses. Have a plan to de-escalate arguments and conflicts. Think conflict management, rather than conflict resolution. Avoid power struggles. They aren't worth winning. You may resolve few conflicts, but you can learn to manage them. Also, there will be many who will not understand the cause of your child's behavior and will blame you for it. They are uneducated and ignorant regarding ADHD, as you and I both were once. Teach them! If they do not have such a child in their household, they will never understand it as well as you. Sometimes clinicians have worked with these children for 20 years, and they still have no understanding of what is going on. Only by living with someone who has this disorder can you fully appreciate how difficult this can be. Turn your anger into advocacy.

> ## Make Yourself Lovable
> Consider the words in the poem below.
>
> ### Treat Them Kind
> *by Kim Israel*
>
> *The child spoke not a word as he saw her face was a frown*
> *He knew that he had done something wrong; he heard not a sound.*
> *He quietly went upstairs to his room knowing she was mad*
> *He hoped that tomorrow he could tell of the day he'd had.*
>
> *He woke the next morning excited to start again*
> *Hoping that his mom would now be his friend*
> *He could always see the disappointment in her eyes*
> *When she looked at him and gave those awful sighs.*
>
> *He walked into the kitchen to a blank and somber face*
> *Seeing she still remembered yesterday's disgrace.*
> *"Why do you always..." she started out, and*
> *"You should do that and this..."*
> *He just wanted to make her happy; a single day of bliss.*
>
> *Parents seldom realize the impact that they can claim*
> *On these little lives-these children-so much from us they gain.*
> *So no matter if they are right or wrong or their choices bad or good*
> *Love your children and treat them kind, the way a parent should.*

ADHD children are great at eliciting negative responses from those around them. It is so important to balance the negative with positive. Never pass by a chance to compliment and encourage. Choose your fights carefully! Ask yourself if what you are correcting is a skill they will need to have in adulthood. Frequently we as parents and teachers are seeking to control the behavior of these children within our own comfort level of noise and activity.

Change Your Environment

Parents of ADHD children understand that their children have enormous risks of injury. Research on accident proneness indicates that 46% of parents of ADHD children describe them as such, with 15% of ADHD children having had at least four or more serious accidents (Hartsough & Lambert, 1985; Mitchell, et al., 1987). Thus, it is imperative that parents examine closely the environment of these children to determine the risk. For young children this may mean locking up guns, fire-starting materials, poisons, and so on. A good way to begin this process is to walk into a room or setting and ask yourself, "If I were he, what might I get into?" As this child matures, special care must be exercised in his riding a bike on the street, and later, driving a car. Many of these children end up in the emergency room due to the combination of hyperactivity and impulse control difficulties. I have seen signs in yards "Warning: slow, deaf child lives here" and have thought that implication of inability to determine danger almost applies to the ADHD child. They will likely not stop and look before running into the street.

Adolescents with ADHD must be taught the value of abstinence, both in alcohol and drugs and in sexual relationships. If they drink, they will soon drink to excess. If they have sex, they are not likely to stop and consider the risks. Open discussion of these topics is essential between the parent, counselor, and child. Parents of these children are encouraged not to drink alcohol at all. While they may be able to limit their own intake, they send a dangerous message to this child that, as an adult, they too will be able to use alcohol responsibly. Such is not the case.

Look After Your Family's Mental and Physical Health

In order to be of help to your child, you need to examine your own lifestyle. Do you work too long, drink too much, smoke too much, exercise too little? A wellness approach should be implemented. Seek a support group to share your frustrations. **Vacation away from your ADHD**

child! Do not feel as though you must have the traditional family summer vacations. A long drive with a hyperactive child will certainly not leave you feeling rested, relaxed and recovered. Rather, it may leave you feeling exhausted, tense, and as if you need a vacation! Mini-vacations are important for the parents.

Finding a suitable babysitter can be extremely important. It is not unusual for parents of ADHD children to go through many babysitters before finding one who will stick it out. Pay well, and seek someone with lots of patience who enjoys activity with children. Provide the babysitter with literature about ADHD and seek to answer questions. Discuss thoroughly how discipline problems should be managed.

Be aware that, as a parent of an ADHD child, you are a likely candidate for depression due to stress. Be aware that your child's relationship within your family can affect your relationship with your spouse and with your other children.

Protect your other children from mental or physical abuse by the ADHD child. It is not unusual to find that a younger sibling is frequently emotionally upset due to witnessing conflicts between the ADHD sibling and the parents. The child may also be a victim of constant manipulation or physical aggression by the ADHD child. Separate rooms may help reduce some of this. The non-ADHD child needs education about his sibling's behavior patterns. It is not unusual to find that in the intervention process, the sibling of the ADHD child is often excluded.

Provide more powerful rewards and consequences. Expect that you will punish your child more than other parents do theirs, but also expect that you will need to reward your child more than other parents. It is when this ratio of punishment to rewards gets out of proportion that we are beginning to destroy self-esteem. The result of too much punishment and too little reward is a good formula for creating an angry, oppositional child. Remember, these children are great at eliciting a negative response from you. As parents and teachers interact with these children, they would benefit from prompts and cues to remind them to offer a positive interaction with the child. Without the prompts and cues, most parents typically punish more than they reward.

ADHD children are governed by the moment. Delaying rewards will frustrate them and will be highly ineffective in bringing about a significant change in behavior. Reinforcement must be of high magnitude and immediate. Extrinsic motivators of a material nature will likely be more effective than motivators such as praise. While partial reinforcement is a powerful phenomenon for most children, it is typically ineffective for ADHD children. Continuous reinforcement usually works much better. When developing a menu of rewards, it is important to discuss with the child what will be motivating to him or her. Frequently, parents are surprised at the kind of things that will motivate. One good way to determine potential motivators is to notice what causes the child to appear happy, contented, or satisfied and to make a list of these things. By doing this, we find that routine things like soft drinks, television time, phone time, and video games are potential motivators.

Contracting may be used to agree upon a plan of how the reward may be obtained. Whenever a token system is utilized, it is essential that the child experience success in obtaining the reward, at least initially. Otherwise the response will be something akin to, "This is stupid! I'm not going to do this. I hate this dumb contract." Common mistakes in reward systems are to put too many items on the list, to have weak reinforcers, or to include too many items which the child is not currently doing. Frequently, verbal contracts should be made to prompt and govern the child's behavior at a particular time. An example would be: "Billy, as we go into this restaurant I want to go over the rules with you.

1. I will tell you what you may select from on the menu.
2. Do not eat with your fingers.
3. Do not talk loudly or whine.

If you follow these rules, you may have a dessert. If you do not, you will not get dessert. In addition, when you break a rule, I will record that in my notebook, and you must sit for five minutes in time-out when we are at home for each rule you broke. Do you understand? Please tell me the three rules."

It is essential that, when such contracts are laid out, the parent sticks to the contract. To fail to do this and to allow flouting of its provisions will result in a continuation of the undesired behavior. Dr. Thomas Phelan, (1987) a well-known author on behavior management with ADHD children, advocates that parents must see themselves more as "animal trainers" than as parents. Avoid talking too much. Dr. Phelan says, "Act, don't yak!" This is very good advice.

Distinguish Between Distractibility and Defiance

When a child is given an instruction and he responds that he will follow the instruction, but then does not complete the task, this is likely to be distractibility. That is to say that the child's intentions were to complete the task, but he got sidetracked by something that was probably more interesting. Redirection is needed. Therefore, it is very important to pay attention to the amount of distracters that are in the environment. When giving instructions, turn off the TV or radio. If the child, when given an instruction, looks at you and says, "Leave me alone, or do it yourself," this is defiance and may need discipline.

Join a Support Group

ADHD parents often feel that they are the only ones in the world with a child like theirs. It can be extremely helpful to meet with other parents of ADHD children to gain some empathy and understanding. Also, support groups enable parents to access local resources and to learn from each other. Parents have often learned many interventions which are not yet in the textbooks. When my own son was quite young and we were sitting in church one morning, he became quite restless. Even with medication, this was almost an intolerable environment for him. It offered little or no reward, and from his perspective, was terribly boring. I discovered, however, that I could control his restlessness by simply rubbing his back, arms, hands, hair, and so on. It was as if he had this terrible need for stimulation, and there was none around. When I began to scratch his back he leaned over and was content. I shared this in our support group, and had many positive responses from parents that indeed, this type of intervention was very helpful when they noticed their child's frustration level climbing. I took this same concept into the classroom where we found that, by giving ADHD children something to hold onto, they were able to stay more focused on their work rather than becoming distracted by it.

Help Them to Get a Good Night's Rest

It is very important when a differential diagnosis is made that a sleep disorder is ruled out as a cause for the child's behavior or learning problems. Only in the past five years or so have we come to understand and appreciate the number of individuals who have difficulty with sleep. Studies of ADHD children suggest that as many as 26% have restless sleep. We must consider what we are doing when we have a child who is only getting three or four hours of quality sleep a night, who then wakes up grumpy, and is given a stimulant. For many ADHD children, a medication like clonidine, which may create some drowsiness and help them to get a good night's rest, may significantly improve daytime behavior and attention. There are many suggested behavioral manipulations to assist with sleep difficulties. Among these are establishing a routine, or the use of music or "white noise" to filter out background sounds. Many parents of colicky infants put them in their car seat, roll down the windows and go for a drive. The humming noises often help the child to drift off to sleep. There are many economical devices which may be purchased that simulate soothing sounds like the wind, ocean, or rain. These can be very helpful in getting the child to sleep.

Obtain a Tutor

One of the most common causes of friction in the home is trying to complete homework or to prevent academic failure. If you have to make a choice between dollars spent for therapy versus a tutor, you may get more for your money with the tutor. Tutoring may not be needed due to learning problems as much as for motivational problems. To have someone who will work with the child at a designated time, to prepare him for tests, to help him stay organized, and to work problems with him one-on-one is invaluable.

Provide Ample Time for Preparation

ADHD individuals frequently need twice as much time to get ready as other individuals. Trying to rush them is like pouring gasoline on a fire. Lists which help to organize can be very helpful, especially in the mornings when preparing for school or work. How often are parents called to bring something to school that has been forgotten? I have made tapes of songs which the children would listen to in the mornings on their personal stereos, interspersed with a D.J. who gives instructions such as, "Hey, Billy, it's getting time to be finishing your breakfast. Remember to put your dishes in the sink, and then go brush those pearly whites."

Help Your Child to See You As Someone Who Believes in Him

There will be plenty of people who will not understand ADHD and will have little or no tolerance for those diagnosed with it. It is therefore essential that your child see you as being supportive and encouraging. Put a list up of 100 ways to encourage your child and practice them. William Glasser, the author of *Reality Therapy*, wrote, "If there is but one significant person in the lives of individuals, they can overcome enormous negative social forces." Glasser is absolutely right. This significant person needs to be the parent. You may feel you need the patience of Job, but you can get it done. A story is told of a family who went to a store in which an adjacent sidewalk has been recently cemented and was still wet. The ADHD child immediately bolted out of the car and ran to the wet cement where he began to write his name and then wipe his hands on his new clothes. The father was almost livid. The mother reminded the father of his great love for his child, to which the father responded, "I do love him in the abstract, but not in the concrete." As parents of ADHD children, we have to remind ourselves to love them even in the concrete. Hopefully, there will be a day when we can look back and smile. It is at times like this that I must remember my own mother's reaction when, as an 8-year-old, I came running to the house crying after trying to catch a skunk by the tail. Sometimes it is indeed better to laugh than to cry!

Recognize That You May Be ADHD

As has been stated, it is certainly not uncommon for at least one of the parents to state that the child is just like he or she was. Often, the parent, in grieving for the child, is in fact grieving his or her own unhappy childhood. It is tough enough to have a child with ADHD, but to have a child and a parent with ADHD can be extremely difficult. The other spouse often acts like a referee to maintain some kind of order. If this is the case, the person with ADHD Residual may need to be seeking assistance for his or her own disorder.

Many parents tend to isolate their child from their peers due to ridiculing and teasing by other children. While it is natural to want to protect your child from hurt, this is not the best way. Peer interaction is essential to the socialization process of maturity. Parents rather need to supervise settings such as taking their child and a friend to a ballgame, out for pizza, a movie, a sleepover, and so on. By supervising their time together, you can encourage a positive relationship to be built. Therapy can also be very helpful in assisting the ADHD child in understanding how to build relationships. Due to their egocentric natures, they can come across as very rude, selfish, and mean children. It is likewise important for the therapist to assist the ADHD child in responding to rejection. They are often hurt very badly. While on the outside they can appear very callous, on the inside they are very vulnerable to hurt.

When they appear hurt, try to restate and reflect their feelings and ask open-ended questions to encourage them to talk about how they feel. Avoid denying the feeling by saying, "You don't need to feel that way."

Find the Right Teacher

The time to do this is during the summer. It is often possible to meet with the principal or guidance counselor during this time and discuss your child's needs. Ask for someone who makes learning fun, enjoys teaching, is creative, is patient, accepts ADHD as legitimate, communicates well with parents, and overall is a strong teacher. The most important criteria are his or her attitude about ADHD and simply being an outstanding teacher. Although the administrator will rarely guarantee a particular teacher, by knowing your wishes and learning about your child, he or she will be better able to place your child in classes with some of the better teachers. Do not, however, expect the teacher to be able to do for your child what you cannot do yourself. That is to say, the teacher will not cure the ADHD. Like yourself, he or she will seek to manage, monitor and communicate with team members to offer the best possible instruction and services for your child, but he or she cannot do the impossible. Keep in mind that the teacher may have several other children in the classroom with ADHD or other needs, and it is not possible to provide time-consuming interventions without assistance. The process of "inclusion" is addressing the problem of providing assistance with the regular classroom teacher for special-needs students.

Know Your Rights to Special Education

School systems have the responsibility of providing you with a copy of the rights of children with disabilities. This is available through the "local education agency" (LEA). All children have the right to a free, appropriate public education (FAPE). Children with ADHD may be eligible for special education services under the Individuals with Disabilities Education Act (IDEA), or may be eligible for modifications within the regular education environment under Section 504 of the Rehabilitation Act of 1973 as amended by 29 U.S.C. 794. IDEA governs the treatment of students with disabilities or students with suspected disabilities in public education. IDEA requires schools to "search and find" students with disabilities starting at three years of age. Thus, when an educator or parent suspects that a student has a disability, a referral should be made for the student to have an evaluation. No more than 40 days should pass between the time of the referral to the placement of the student. The school should appoint a staff member to serve as the IEP team chairperson for this student within ten days of the referral. During the time the referral has been made, the student should be treated as if he or she were already in special education in regards to disciplinary matters. Section 504 prevents discrimination based upon disability. It applies to any program or activity receiving federal financial assistance.

Play to Their Strengths

It is so very important to build on their talents. Find something they can succeed in, and reinforce this. Look for participation in sports such as track and field, swimming, karate, and many others. These children often do not do well in sports like baseball or basketball. Their problems with distractibility often result in making mistakes which influence the team and thus bring feelings of resentment. Individual sports are better than team sports. Likewise, organizations like scouting and 4-H can encourage interest and build skills, such as working in groups, along with teaching values.

Keep It in Perspective

While your child's disorder is very real and can be quite handicapping, do not make it worse than it is. With appropriate interventions, your child can be very successful and live a relatively normal life. This cannot be said for many disabilities. Reflect frequently upon your child's strengths of intellect, creativity, humor, or athleticism in order to focus upon a positive outcome. There are many adults with ADHD who have done very well. Career guidance is vitally important for offering direction for the adolescent to adult transition. Remember, the disability appears most prominently in settings which impose rigid standards. There are many occupations that allow great flexibility in work hours and work settings and reward those who have many ADHD characteristics.

Share Responsibilities

We truly feel sorry for single parents with these children. Both the child and the parent may feel abused. It is important to be able to say to someone else, "I'm at my limit! Please care for this child for a while; I need a break." Unfortunately, in working with families it's usually the case that mothers have most of the responsibility for childcare.

Fathers need desperately to become involved in helping with homework, assisting in the socialization process, trips to the doctor, and so forth. Both mothers and fathers need to build a relationship with the child. This often means that each parent needs to find something special that he or she and the child can enjoy doing together. It is often these bonds which help families make it through the difficult days intact. It is also important that the grandparents become educated about ADHD and are consistent in carrying out the discipline plan in the home of the ADHD child. They can often undo a lot of effort by the parents with the child.

Watch Your Child Sleep

Why watch your child sleep? Because it helps you to reaffirm in your own mind the value of the child. When he or she is asleep, he or she is finally still and quiet. You realize that he or she really can be quiet! In sleep, the innocence and beauty of the child is reflected. Few parents can watch their child sleeping and not offer a kiss on the cheek. While the child is sleeping, forgive the child for any offenses of the day and relive once again the hopes and dreams you have for your child.

Parenting the ADHD child is a special challenge. Few will understand the challenges it imposes. Few will know the prayers which are offered. Few will know the love that grows. Few will know…unless they have one of their own!

Chapter 4

Educational Services for ADHD Students

Educational Services for ADHD Students

Legal Advocacy

> *"No use to shout at them to pay attention.... If the situations, the materials, the problems before a child do not interest him, his attention will slip off to what does interest him, and no amount of exhortation or threats will bring it back."*
> John Holt,
> *How Children Fail*

For many years, ADHD children were not eligible for special educational services without a diagnosis of a specific learning disability, emotional disturbance, or other handicapping condition. Due to heavy lobbying and a massive educational campaign by parents, this has changed. As noted earlier, ADHD children may now be served under the Individuals with Disabilities Education Act within the "other health impaired" category, when the child evidences chronic or acute impairments that result in limited alertness, which adversely affects educational performance. The child may also be eligible for modifications within the regular educational environment under P.L. 93:112 Section 504 of the Office of Civil Rights category of the Rehabilitation Act of 1973. This legislation prevents discrimination against any person with a disability. Included in this is the responsibility of schools to identify, evaluate, and if deemed eligible, to afford access to appropriate educational services. This legislation then offers services to anyone who "has a mental or physical impairment which substantially limits one or more major life activities (caring for oneself, performing manual tasks, walking, seeing, hearing, speaking, breathing, learning, and working), has a record of such impairment, or is regarded as having such an impairment." ADHD students may meet the criteria for emotionally disturbed (ED), but this does not mean that this is the most appropriate placement for them. The criteria for emotionally disturbed are written in a manner which is very broad and open to a considerable amount of interpretation. They do not correspond to any particular mental disorder of DSM-IV. Rather, they describe in general terms children who have been unable to acquire appropriate socialization and are underachieving due to this failure. In addition, ADHD students may qualify as learning disabled (LD). While a significant population of ADHD children do, in fact, have neurological processing deficits often inherent in learning disabled children, many do not. Their admittance to this category of special education in many states is based rather on a significant discrepancy which exists between their intellect and their achievement. Frequently, these discrepancies expand through improper teaching methods rather than because of an inability to learn due to neurological processing deficits.

Individuals outside of the educational system frequently need training regarding special education and the special provisions that surround such services. For example, many physicians believe that a child may need special educational services but have no idea of how to bring this about. They often feel that they can simply write a prescription for a child to receive resource help. That's comparable to the school psychologist who would like to write a prescription for Ritalin but obviously doesn't have the authority or training. It is a failure of collaboration between these two parties that often results in a delay of services. There is a need for the physicians and school psychologists to establish a policy for defining how services will be obtained. Physicians need to understand what psychologists mean by "discrepancy formulas" and other such jargon associated with psychological evaluations. Psychologists need to understand information associated with, for example, EEG's or medication. Parents should, when meeting with either party, sign a release form so that the physician, school psychologist, principal, and teacher can freely communicate about the child.

Forty Educational Interventions

Emphasize Quality over Quantity

It is especially important to remember the rationale for homework. Homework is for practice, not for instruction. For the ADHD/LD student, rapid boredom is his number one enemy; therefore, remember that tasks which are repetitious and boring with little or no rewards or consequences are not likely to be completed. It is this intolerance for the rote and repetitious task that causes ADHD children not to complete their assignments or in some cases to not even begin their assignments. It is essential that the teacher be willing to modify the length of the assignment. It is an invalid assumption that all students in the class work at the same rate and should thus do the same amount of homework or seatwork. Teachers have rationalized for years that they should treat all of their students "alike," thus giving them the same amount of work. This is nonsense. None of us wants to be treated *alike*. We want to be treated *fairly*. "Fair" represents a volume of work required to obtain competency. ADHD children can typically do grade level work; however, they may not be able to do grade volume work. Russell Barkley, Ph.D., suggests a good rule of thumb is to think of them as 20% developmentally behind their chronological age in terms of their behavior and the amount of work they can do.

Computer Instruction

ADHD/LD children frequently perform exceptionally well through the use of computer instruction. With computer instruction comes color, novelty, one-to-one learning, and fun. Typically, it is the child who finishes his work first who gets to use the computer, rather than the ADHD child, but it is the ADHD child who needs the computer instruction. The other child will learn without it. For the ADHD child, however, it can make the critical difference between staying on grade level and falling behind. The obvious solution is to buy more computers. Unfortunately, this will not happen for a while. We can no doubt dream of the day when every child will have a computer and an individual educational program. When this happens, we will not need to "label" so many children under special education.

Selective Seating

The ADHD child should be surrounded by students who typically stay on task well. A learning partner may even further assist in helping the student to stay organized and on task. The student should also be seated near the front of the classroom. The student should not be seated beside the teacher's desk or in a position which would be an embarrassment to him. We should also realize that near the teacher's desk is likely the most distracting spot in the entire classroom. While the child is seated, he should be allowed some freedom of movement. This may involve changing positions in his desk or, in some cases, standing for a short period of time beside his desk. Teachers sometimes become "neurotic" about requiring students to have both feet on the floor at all times.

Cooperation Versus Competition

For much too long, we have stressed competition in the classroom, rather than cooperation. In athletics we understand the value of cooperation by the members of the team. Yet, in the classroom, children learn from an early age that you do not help others (that's cheating). Research on learning tells us that if we teach someone else, then we have a better chance of putting that information into long-term memory. How often do we allow students to teach each other? We need to allow students to instruct each other throughout the educational process. We have many educated individuals in our country who cannot work with others because they have no "instructional skills." For the ADHD student, this process of teaching others causes the learning curve to remain much more constant across time, rather than the student having a rapid decay or loss of information.

Multisensory Learning

Hear it, see it, say it, write it, then you will know it. Much of the learning which occurs in classrooms today is "silent." Have you ever been introduced to someone, and then a couple of minutes later you cannot remember his name? That person's voice is unfamiliar to your brain, yet had you said, "Fred Jones, nice to meet you, Fred," then your brain would have recognized your voice and you would have recalled his name. How often in class do students get to speak? We can learn complicated musical pieces by hearing and repeating. This process of repetition has gone by the wayside in modern education, yet it is just as important as ever, especially for ADHD/LD students. Other students may learn without this process, yet for these students it makes a critical difference.

Chunking

The human brain has an almost infinite capacity for learning. However, the information must be entered in small "chunks." "Miller's theory" (Coons,1995) tells us that humans can remember seven bits of information, give or take two. What this says is that for all students, we need to reduce the information we are imparting to chunks of probably three or four. Again, for the ADHD/LD student this is essential. Other students may acquire the information with persistence when not instructed in this manner. ADHD/LD children, however, grow rapidly frustrated and quit. When we ignore our method of instruction and give long lists of information, we are exhibiting a "teaching deficit" and creating failure. Likewise, instructional time should be delivered in chunks. Most middle- and high-school-age children will retain more information using a distributed practice schedule of 25 minutes instruction, 5 minutes break, and 25 minutes instruction, than they will with 55 minutes of instruction. Current attempts at "block scheduling" of 90-minute classes for high-school-age children without these breaks is a very ineffective use of time for the students. Research tells us that going beyond 50 minutes of instructional time is to create "retroactive interference" in which recently learned information is decaying before new information can be acquired. For ADHD children, even 50-minute periods go beyond their ability to sustain attention.

Teacher Prompts

As teachers, we often need to remind ourselves of the need to "create success" with a child. There are many ways to do this, such as by placing ten coins in your left-hand pocket, and each time you "set the child up for success" by asking a question that she can answer, you move one coin from your left-hand pocket to your right-hand pocket. At the end of the day you know how many times you helped the child to succeed. This may also be done by placing a symbol representing that child in a noticeable place, such as near a clock, where it will remind you throughout the day of your goal.

Anticipate Ahead of the Child

This involves "being the child's frontal lobe." Doing this means stopping and thinking for the child. We ask the question, "What will happen if…?" By doing this, we can often prevent difficulties. For example, "What will happen if Johnny and Billy sit beside each other on the bus during the field trip?" or, "Billy, before you go into the assembly, tell me the rules for how we should act."

Assist with Organization

Teachers sometimes say in meetings, "When are we going to stop babying him? He has to learn to do it on his own. Maybe if he fails he will learn to start doing these things," and so on. These type of statements reflect either a disbelief or lack of understanding of the core nature of this disability. It is the same message that so many of these students have heard throughout their lives, and that is, "You've got to try harder." Why can't we accept that maybe they are trying as hard as they can now, and we need to try and meet them on middle ground? Certainly, we need to teach organizational skills; however, when we stop assisting with organization the result is failure, and this failure does not lead to a change in behavior due to its consequences. Rather, it leads to a downward spiral of self-esteem. These are individuals who, in adulthood, will need a good secretary or a spouse to help them stay organized. This is not separate from their disability. The inability to sequence, plan or organize is part of the disability and should be seen as such. When you see these children's desks, you begin to understand the disorganization that exists. It has been said in a joking manner that you could almost diagnose this disorder just by looking at a desk and its disorganization. There is some degree of truth in that statement. Organization may be improved by weekly homework assignment sheets, daily schedules, color coding books, spiral notebooks with dividers, day planners, and so forth.

Positive Incentive Programs with Continuous Reinforcement

While partial reinforcement has proven to be beneficial with most individuals, research with ADHD children suggests that continuous reinforcement is needed to change behaviors. Rewards need to be immediate. These are people who are truly motivated "moment by moment." Teachers need to accept that and initiate behavior contracts with these students. This is comparable to grandma's rule of "first you eat your vegetables, then you get your dessert." In psychology this is referred to as the Premack principle, which states: If you pair a behavior with a low probability of occurence with a behavior with a high probability of occurence, then the low probability behavior will increase. "First you do your homework, then you get to watch TV." While we should be hopeful that new behaviors will habituate and that we can gradually reduce the amount of extrinsic motivators, don't count on it. Rather, we are likely to have to change motivators or manipulate the value of the motivator to continue the behavior.

Competency Development

For years, ADHD children have gone into therapy with the intent of improving self-esteem. Self-esteem is built by success. If children have success in an area, then they will feel good about themselves as the success relates to identity. For example, if a child is a good baseball player, then he will feel competent while playing that sport. Self-esteem will be high as it relates to that sport. The same is true of the classroom. If a child has success with reading or math, then she will feel academically competent and will demonstrate high self-esteem in the classroom setting. The problem is that acquiring these competencies is a difficult process for most ADHD children. It doesn't always occur naturally.

Over the years I have seen children with extremely low self-esteem who were in foster care and who had been abused for years. We provided therapy, we provided medication when appropriate, we provided loving foster parents, and we provided structure. But, in my opinion, what led to a change in their self-concept and their self-esteem was that we found a way to build competency. This may have been through piano lessons, scouting, sports, art, singing, or academics. As they began to feel competent, their personalities changed from one of anger or sadness to one of loving life.

In my clinic, I have sought to refer children to "mentors"

who assist in the development of these competencies. This is a low-cost service which appears to make a tremendous difference. There are certainly other factors in self-esteem, such as providing a safe environment and establishing significant relationships, but the need for building competence cannot be overemphasized. If you follow these children around throughout their day, you will see chronic failure. They have chronic failure in relationships with parents, siblings, teachers, and peers, academic failure, sports failure, and many others. They often begin to ask the question, "Why am I like I am?" or "Why don't people like me?" or "Why can't I do things right?" If we simply toss them to the sea and say, "sink or swim," most of these kids are going to sink. We must provide, as Robert Brooks, Ph.D., has most eloquently stated, an "island of competence," where this child can succeed. The feeling of success in getting a base hit, performing at a recital, competing in a karate tournament, or medaling at a track meet cannot be duplicated in the therapist's office, no matter the skills or talents of the therapist. What is the result of not acquiring this feeling of competence? The result far too often is a movement towards more antisocial behavior, such as gang participation, alcohol and drug use, sexual promiscuity, and so forth. We all need success like the air that we breathe.

Self-Monitoring

This refers to procedures that require the individual to keep track of whether he or she engages in particular behaviors. The procedure involves a tone which is heard periodically. The student responds "yes" or "no" to the question, "Was I paying attention?" Research has shown that, in many instances, there is an increase in "on task" behavior even over that accomplished by stimulant medications. Another advantage of this approach is that there is no stimulus generalization by the rest of the class to the teacher's instruction for "Johnny" to return to his work. The steps are: 1) determine the base and ceiling attention span of the student while on task; 2) model the desired behaviors to the student; 3) model the undesired behaviors to the student; 4) have the student model the desired and undesired behaviors; and 5) explain the function of the device. For example:

"Johnny, you know how paying attention to your work is sometimes difficult for you. You've heard teachers tell you 'Pay attention, get to work' and things like that. Well, today we're going to start something that will help you help yourself to pay attention better." (Teacher models desired behavior.) "This is what I mean by paying attention." (Teacher models inattentive behaviors such as glancing around and playing with objects.) "Now you tell me if I am paying attention." (Teacher models attentive and inattentive behaviors and requires the student to categorize them.) "Okay, now let me show you what we're going to do. While you're working you will hear a little sound like this." (Teacher plays the tone.) "When you hear that sound, quietly ask yourself, 'Was I paying attention?'

If you answer 'yes,' then put a check in this box, and go right back to work. If you answer 'no,' then put a check in the box marked 'no,' and go right back to work." (Hallahan, 1979).

There is also an excellent program called the "Attention Training System" (Rapport, 1982) in which the teacher may award or deduct points via a remote control device to a child who has a receiver on his or her desk. This is an excellent means of training a child to discriminate among behaviors. These devices are inexpensive, relative to what they can do. The purchase of even one per school can be tremendously beneficial for this population. This system avoids stimulus generalization which may occur when the teacher is continually verbally interacting with the ADHD child. It also offers immediacy, or continuous reinforcement, which is essential in bringing about change for these students.

Textbooks on Tape

Many states have programs designed for those with print disabilities, reading disabilities, or others in which the students' textbooks may be placed on audiotape. For ADHD/LD students this can be particularly valuable. It will extend the length of time that the student will attend to the material. It will reduce the length of time required to obtain competency of the material. By following along with the tape, the student will not get "bogged down" with pronunciation difficulties associated with reading the material. Thus overall reading comprehension will increase. Many students with reading problems fail subjects, not because of an inability to understand the concepts, but rather because of an ineffective means of teaching the material. Offering textbooks on tape for children who have attentional or reading disabilities is a very legitimate means of improving learning.

Reduction of Math Mistakes

There are many simple interventions to reduce mistakes in math. These include using graph paper to keep numerals in line, using calculators, circling the operation's sign, making a flow chart of the steps to be completed, highlighting to emphasize steps, and so on. Educators should emphasize the importance of acquiring the steps, rather than obtaining the correct answer. There are also many good programs which teach shortcuts in arriving at answers; these methods fall under the category of "if it works, use it."

Stimulus Reduction

I once went into an elementary classroom where the door had a picture of Batman which said, "Welcome Bat to School." Over each desk was a mobile of bat wings. The children loved it; however, there is little doubt that such visual displays inhibit the educational process. A good rule of thumb is that "nothing should be in the child's line of sight which is more interesting than the teacher." Bulletin boards in the front of the room should have examples of student's work or should be relevant to the lessons presented. Classrooms with windows need shades. Doors should be kept shut to reduce distracting noises. Classroom pets or aquariums should be kept away from the line of sight of the students.

Stimulus Enrichment

Since ADHD children are constantly seeking stimulation, we should look for ways that we can manipulate color, novelty, lighting, touch, sound, and so forth in order to improve learning. Several years ago, I noticed that many ADHD children sought out manipulatives to touch or play with to reduce restlessness. They may play with a paper clip, their pencil, or even something from their nose, but they will play with something. This sensation-seeking behavior is often interrupted by the teacher who says, "Give me that paper clip and get back to work." In an informal experiment, I met with a teacher and several ADHD students. We agreed that they could hold an object in their opposite hands while doing seatwork as long as it did not interfere with what they were doing. We gave them a choice of several items such as balls, silly putty, paper clips, and others. What we found was that these students actually stayed on task for longer periods of time with these items in their hands than they did without them. They described feeling more calm and less restless. They stated that having the object to touch helped them to concentrate better.

This taught me that we need to listen to kids more in our search for interventions. In taking away these objects, we often were increasing frustrations and shortening attention to task. I am continually amazed at how distracted many of these children appear to be and yet how much they are, in fact, learning. I once sat next to a child with severe ADHD symptoms during four nights of three-hour classes to prepare him for taking the "hunter safety exam." It was my impression that the child was not listening at all. His looking around the room, picking at his fingers, playing with his hair, tapping his feet, and changing seating positions convinced me that he would miserably fail the exam. To my surprise, he did quite well.

Thus, exhibiting hyperactivity may not influence the child's comprehension of material. There are many children who are given medication to reduce these restless behaviors when they are, in fact, learning quite well. Color has also been shown to increase attention to task (Zentall, 1985). This is not surprising. All of us would rather watch color television than black and white. The use of highlighters, overlays, color monitors on computers, and so forth all increase attention. Regarding novelty, there is excellent software that makes learning fun. For some reason, many teachers distinguish between learning and fun. We need to teach in such a way that kids never want to stop learning and turn this insatiable characteristic into a desire to spend their lifetime learning.

Physical Contact

Teachers need to move around the room. Proximity plays a major role in attention to task. Likewise, a soft touch on the shoulder of a child may be all that is needed to bring him back on task. Many teachers use verbal reprimands when a soft touch will work much better.

Music

This medium has been underutilized for years in classroom education, as well as in therapy and home behavior management. Music can pick us up or calm us down. In the past, elementary teachers knew the benefit of dimming the lights, having the students put their heads down and playing some soft music. The result of these short breaks is that mood, temperament, and attention is improved.

Sleep

Some 26% of ADHD children are described as having difficulty falling asleep or as sleeping restlessly. The result of this is that they are monsters to get out of bed in the morning, and until they get some stimulants in their system, they are extremely difficult to manage. Rather than stimulants, many of these children need medications to assist them in getting to sleep. All of us are inattentive and irritable after a night of restless sleep. I have seen many ADHD children who do not go to sleep until after midnight, and even then wake up frequently. By targeting these sleep disorders rather than the attentional disorder, there is often such an improvement in daytime behavior that stimulants are not even needed. For children with this type of difficulty, medications such as clonidine (hypertensive medication) have proven themselves useful in creating some drowsiness and helping the child to sleep. Other medications like Antivert, or some of the tricyclic antidepressants, may assist in this same manner.

Teach with Activity

There are so many different ways in which information can be taught with activity (e.g., group work, labs, drama, games, drills). We need to get kids away from their desks more often. I have spoken to many hyperactive kids who had gotten into trouble simply because they "couldn't sit still any longer." Teachers often seem to fear a loss of control of their class by letting students get up out of their seats. Granted, these activities will take patience and practice, but in the end, your students will love you for them.

Summer Tutoring

Research has demonstrated that, for many ADHD/LD students, special educational services during the school year alone do not help them to "catch up." Rather, the goal appears to keep them from getting further behind. Summer months allow these students to actually begin to catch up. This does not have to mean summer school, but rather may involve a few hours of individualized tutoring each week. Software which assists the student with deficits can be wonderful for these students. I have seen many students who have increased grade equivalency in specific areas by over one year due to these types of programs. For many of these students, there is a steep decline in the "learning curve," which means that they simply forget learned information over the summer. Involving them in a summer remedial program reduces the likelihood of this occurring. Almost all of these students learn faster in a one-to-one relationship. In group settings, they may feel incompetent and embarrassed to ask questions. This is overcome in a one-to-one tutorial setting. An individualized achievement battery may be helpful in identifying a baseline of the type of problems to focus on. This may involve tests such as the Weschler individual achievement test, third edition, the Peabody individual achievement test, revised, or the Woodcock-Johnson individual achievement test. If this type of testing is not available, even an item analysis of a group administered achievement test may be helpful.

Tape Recorder/Video Camera

This technology is available in most schools and may be beneficial in several ways. First, for the child who is acting disruptively, I have found that simply displaying a tape recorder and allowing the child to understand that his behavior is being recorded and may be played back to the principal or his parents is often enough to reduce or eliminate unwanted behavior. A video camera set up in the corner of the room to monitor the class may also accomplish the same purpose. It is remarkable the changes in behavior that occur when we know that we are being watched. It is also possible to use these devices to enhance learning and awareness. Coaches know very well the advantages of allowing an athlete to see himself perform. Likewise, to allow children with activity-level problems and distractibility problems to see themselves offers them a different frame of reference which may assist them in inhibition. Certainly, ADHD/LD children may benefit from lessons being taped simply for the purpose of repetition. To be able to slow down the lesson through pausing may allow the child to understand a concept that, through regular instruction, may have been presented too rapidly for their understanding.

Secret Signal

There are times when it is important to bring a child back onto task, yet to do so verbally often distracts other children in the process or may be embarrassing to the student. Similar to the signals of a baseball coach, a teacher may designate a secret signal between herself or himself and the student that, when given, is a warning to get back on task or correct behavior.

Earplugs

Inexpensive earplugs, such as the kind which "shooters" use, may reduce distractors during seatwork or reading time. Likewise, music played through headphones may also be helpful for some children to improve concentration and reduce boredom during seatwork.

Case Managers

Most of these children will benefit from a case manager checking with them each day to see that they are getting assignments written down, homework completed, getting along with peers, understanding concepts presented, and so forth. This person may also keep a good flow of communication between the school and the parents. There are many educators who see this as "babying" these children. These are individuals who obviously do not have a child with ADHD. These types of services simply help these children to succeed in the educational environment. They are what a secretary is to an ADHD adult. Many adults with ADHD can be highly productive, if they have someone to remind them of deadlines and keep them organized and focused. When I have seen this type of service removed from children, with the rationale that they are now old enough to do it on their own, it has typically resulted in failure. While failure often teaches valuable lessons, in this case it rarely does. Organizational/motivational deficits are a basic part of this handicapping condition and should be viewed as such, rather than seeing these children as simply "lazy."

Instruction about Word Processing

We now understand that it is certainly not necessary to wait until the high school years to teach keyboard skills. Computers are widely available and will continue to be more so. In the same way that calculators have not made us math illiterate, neither will word processors make us English illiterate. Rather, they will likely enhance our communication skills. For ADHD/LD students, these skills may result in lengthy assignments being completed. How many adults write research papers in cursive? Word processing is simply a tool to speed up the process.

Instruction and Supervision of Socialization

These are kids who frequently are rejected in social relationships by their same-age peers. This is because they exhibit developmental immaturity. They are frequently found with friends several years younger or older. Younger children cannot recognize the differences in maturity, while older children are probably more tolerant of immature behavior. It is important for educators and counselors to be involved in teaching behaviors that do not lead to rejection but to acceptance. For many children, factors associated with acceptance occur naturally. ADHD children, however, often do not recognize subtleties in nonverbal responses which other children perceive and then use to modify their behaviors.

Instruction of Core Subjects in the Morning

Typically, teachers will find that all children's attention and behavior will be at its best in the morning hours. This is particularly true for ADHD children. Following lunch, most of us get sleepy, and our attention decreases. We may also find that medication is likely to be more efficacious in the morning than in the afternoon.

Exercise

Periodic aerobic exercise seems to reduce activity level and results in a "calming" effect. Exercise may also help to reduce aggressiveness and irritability in some students. The explanation for this is not clear. Exercise possibly increases blood flow to the deeper regions of the brain, resulting from an increase of neurotransmitters or the release of endorphins (chemicals produced by the brain which help in stress reduction; they are theorized to produce the "runner's high" following exercise). As a long distance runner for much of my life, I often found that following a long run, I was able to concentrate better and was more reflective. I would suspect that many hyperactive children would experience improvement in their behavior following aerobic exercise which persists long enough to release endorphins.

Classroom Rules

One of the characteristics of ADHD children is that they have "deficient rule-governed behavior." One way to view these children is as if they are 20 to 30% developmentally younger in their ability to follow rules. Thus, the teacher should see the 10-year-old behaving more typically like a 7-year-old in his ability to follow instructions and act appropriately. It is very important to reinforce verbal instructions with visual instructions. The student may need a copy of the rules taped to his desk and may need to recite the rules which govern the activity in which he is beginning to participate. Keep in mind, however, that ADHD is not a problem in knowing the rules, but rather a problem in behaving relevant to the rules.

Discipline

ADHD children typically differ not so much in the kind

of behaviors exhibited as they do in the frequency of undesired behaviors. Thus, the educator should recognize that frequent discipline may be needed; however, this should be administered in balance with positive reinforcement. If punishment exceeds positive reinforcement, then the child's self-concept may become very negative and defeating. Since frequent discipline likely must occur, it is essential that the punishment not become severe. Increasing the severity of punishment will not cause a decrease in the behavior of these children, but rather will tend to evolve into abuse, either verbal or physical. Remember, this child did not wish to be born with this set of problems. Much of these behaviors are outside his "locus of control" and should be seen as such. To spank this type of child for an impulsive decision would be comparable to spanking a deaf child for not hearing.

Encourage Free Inquiry

ADD/ADHD students are notorious for interrupting and asking irrelevant questions. Helping this student to be able to turn this curiosity into research is essential. As educators, we need to begin teaching library and research skills very early. Many of these students seem to have a great talent for seeing the world differently. They may be wonderful writers, musicians, engineers, and so on. Singer/songwriter Harry Chapin wrote a wonderful song, *"Flowers Are Red"* (Electra/Asylum/Nonesuch Records, 1978) which seems to characterize these children. He described a young child who, when he painted flowers, wanted to use all the colors of the rainbow. However, his teacher would only allow him to paint with green and red. Eventually, the child's spirit was defeated and his creativity and love for learning was lost. May we never steal from these children the love for life which so enraptures them. I recall driving my ADHD son to school when he was in kindergarten and listening to his incessant questions such as, "How come some cows have spots?" or "How many leaves do trees have?" It seemed that he was interested in everything. We must see this curiosity as a strength, rather than a weakness.

Use of Humor

Let's face it. These can be very funny children. They

know how to have a good time. We can fight it, or we can accept it and use this characteristic to teach. Humor eases anxiety. Humor can motivate, excite, and even increase memory. Humor is grossly underutilized in teaching. If teachers are going to compete, maybe we need a course about teaching humor in the classroom. It has a place.

Physical Coordination

It is not uncommon to find that ADHD children have fine- or gross-motor coordination problems. They are frequently embarrassed by this weakness. As teachers, we need to be sensitive to this. All children do not write at the same pace. Many of these children need extra time or shortened writing assignments. A failure to modify in this manner will result in sloppy handwriting or unfinished work. Physical education instructors should also be a part of M-Teams to discuss the child's goals. (The M-Team is a multidisciplinary team composed of the student's parents, teachers, principal, school psychologist, counselor, and others, who meet to develop an Individualized Educational Plan for the student.) Frequently, I find that they are left out of M-Teams as if the child had no deficits in physical education. I wonder how often ADHD children are made to sit on the sidelines and watch the other children play because they did not remember to follow a rule. As excitement grows, these children often become even more impulsive. The physical education teacher may need to stay in close proximity to the ADHD child to assist in behavior control. The teacher may also do wonders for the child's self-esteem by placing him in leadership positions from time to time.

Recognition of Individual Learning Styles

ADHD children are not homogeneous. They have individual strengths and weaknesses. They also have preferred manners of learning. Only in the past decade have teaching strategies taken into account learning styles. There are many students who share characteristics of inventiveness and creativity or others who may enjoy risk and challenges or others who want group activities in which they work cooperatively. If we can identify these characteristics in children, then we can identify the motivational parameters which encourage the child to achieve. If we view ADHD children as having a motivational deficit, then it becomes essential that we identify the preferred teaching strategies. Too often in education we teach in a manner which is "comfortable" to us. As professionals, we must learn to adapt our presentation to the audience, and this means teaching to the whole class rather than just the A and B students who will probably understand the concepts regardless of how they are presented.

Values Training

While the teaching of values is primarily a function of the home, that is not to say that the educational system should not be involved. In fact, educational professionals are involved whether they like it or not. It is impossible to teach without teaching values. The question is which ones will be taught and how. For the ADHD child, it is vitally important that there be a support system in place which encourages the growth of a "conscience" as it is taught within the home. There are unarguably "core values" which have held together Western civilization as we know it. Who can argue with the teaching of honesty, truthfulness, sobriety, sportsmanship, compassion, empathy, kindness, courtesy, healthy living, human worth, and many others? We cannot assume that the ADHD child will somehow acquire these values by "osmosis," but rather they must be taught by both example and instruction through the home, community, church, and educational system.

Contracts and Reward Systems

Contracts are a means of identifying specific behaviors for change and agreeing upon the conditions which will lead to change. These conditions typically involve rewards for accomplishing the criteria and behavioral penalties for failing to do so. Contracts which are imposed are seldom effective; rather they should be written collaboratively. It is not uncommon to see children write contracts which are more punishing or difficult to accomplish than those written by adults. The adult should seek to assist in tempering the contract in a manner which will result in success for the child. The number of items for change should be limited to five or fewer, although it may be possible to place some items on the contract which the child is already doing, in order to encourage a positive outcome. Contracts should be goal-oriented, brief, and positively written. Reinforcers should be of high magnitude. Continuous reinforcement must usually be employed for ADHD children. Feedback must be frequent. Partial reinforcement or delayed rewards are typically ineffective. Contracts should be written in a manner which requires little time for record-keeping with rapid administration of rewards and/or consequences. While a goal for the child is to begin a new desirable behavior or extinguish an old undesirable behavior, it should be recognized that most ADHD children will need extrinsic motivators in order to first accomplish this task. Don't worry about making them materialistic or self-interested. They already are! Accept this about them, and move forward.

Make Yourself Loveable

We all listen to people that we like or love. When you interact with the ADHD child, treat him in a manner which says, "I care about you." Like all children, they will go a long way with someone they like, but will have little tolerance for someone who "puts them down" by humiliation or condemnation. More times than not, when I am involved with teachers who describe an ADHD child with an "attitude," there is a power struggle going on. These are not children who back away easily from threat or intimidation. If anything, they are bold and courageous. They will not run from a threat. They are indeed "mountain climbers" who will approach the highest peak unabated. They are the risk-takers among us. We must learn to love them for what they are, rather than try to change them into something that they despise.

Career Guidance

While this is a process that actually begins at birth, it is essential that the ADHD child be involved in career exploration throughout his school experience. The vision of someday being in a particular career is a long-term motivational parameter which affects us all. The child who does not have this often ends up feeling isolated and lost.

ADHD children frequently like jobs that involve activity, novelty, flexible work hours, excitement, and creativity. Their curiosity often leads them to having great insight into change. However, this must often be tempered by others. It has been said that ADHD adults need to have a good organizer or secretary to help them to be consistently productive. Through a program of career guidance, individuals with ADHD can launch careers that offer financial security and great productivity. Without this, they often fail to complete tasks, and go from job to job due to dissatisfaction with the work environment. When the ideal career is found, an ADHD individual must be careful not to become a "workaholic." Many ADHD adults fit this description. Work, too, can become an addiction.

If Your Child Comes Home with an F…

(1) Calm down. Getting angry will not help you or your child.

(2) Consult with the teacher. Try to determine what changes need to be made to pull your child's grades up.

(3) Consider a tutor. Many ADHD children need tutorial help, and with it can maintain or exceed grade-level work. A one-to-one teacher/student relationship for one hour a week can accomplish a tremendous amount.

(4) Communicate with your child daily. Discuss from your child's perspective what is difficult. Seek to understand his perspective on his strengths and weaknesses. Ask, "What changes do you believe that you can make which will help you to perform better in this class?"

(5) Contract for improvement. As has already been mentioned, contracts are a good way to agree upon a plan of action.

(6) Check homework. Frequently, ADHD children are performing well on tests; however, they are not turning in all of their homework. Discuss with the teacher the possibility of modifications of the amount of homework.

(7) Control outside activities. Frequently, ADHD children are simply watching too much television or spending

an excessive amount of time at play, rather than concentrating on their studies.

(8) Contribute positive reinforcement. Look for every opportunity to say to your child, "I believe in you!"

(9) Concern is the key. This suggests being involved. Take on a support role.

(10) Call for a support team. You may request a meeting with not only his teacher, but also the principal, guidance counselor, or school psychologist to discuss your child's current level of achievement and the need for modifications. Form a collaborative role of advocacy with the school personnel for your child. Avoid an adversarial role. This will help no one.

Chapter 5

Proposed Neurobiological Subtypes of ADHD-Spectrum Disorders

Proposed Neurobiological Subtypes of ADHD-Spectrum Disorders

Cognitively Impaired Subtype
Overaroused Subtype
Underinhibited Subtype
Attachment / Reward Insensitive Subtype

Four major groupings of ADHD children may exist. The fundamental problem in one group is that of **cognitive dysfunction** in the processor itself. The "computer" is not functioning at the level of efficiently processing information—it needs to be upgraded. These children are typically inattentive, but not necessarily hyperactive. They tend to be impulsive and disorganized; they are fidgety but not running around. They have difficulty accessing what they know, when this requires the ability to inhibit. They are prone to have learning disabilities and fine motor integration impairment. The onset of their symptoms occurs later than with the more hyperactive group. They are more likely than the hyperaroused group to be girls, and their problems are likely to persist into adulthood. Their neuropathology is primarily reflective of a functional dopamine deficit. Thus, they are more responsive to psychostimulants that have broad effects on selective and sustained attention, and secondarily enhance memory, coding, retrieval and organization.

A second group with **primary modulatory difficulties** might be considered over-aroused ADHD. Their primary deficits are evidence of increased basal brain arousal, likely to be noradrenergically mediated. This hyperarousal produces secondary cognitive flooding, resulting in information overload. This condition is probably mediated primarily by excess norepinephrine.

A third group has symptoms of ADHD secondary to a **failure of inhibition.** Instead of extreme hyperactivity, their

> **ADHD/ADD Symptoms**
>
> *Symptoms of ADHD/ADD can result from disturbances in several brain systems.*

> **Attention Failure**
>
> *Failure of attention may be due to cognitive dysfunction, inability to modulate arousal, or a failure of inhibition or reward.*

major symptoms reflect increased touching and talking. When upset, these children are overwhelmed with emotional dependency or irritated with rage. Their symptoms reflect this failure of behavioral inhibition. This pattern, closely linked to aggression and antisocial behavior, is more responsive to medications like psychostimulants that enhance input to the prefrontal cortex and may be responsive to low doses of serotonergic antidepressants.

The fourth subtype of ADHD may be described as **reward deficient** or **reward insensitive**. This group typifies those who appear to have a chronic course characterized by a lack of goal-directed behavior and a relative lack of empathy. This group often appears to have motivational deficits characterized by the need for intensive concrete rewards in order to complete tasks. They experience rapid boredom and reward satiation occurs quickly. They appear impervious to rewards and consequences. Parents and teachers often describe a sense of helplessness in changing this individual's behavior patterns. They are the most globally impaired and thus the most difficult to treat. Diagnosis may move towards more serious disorders such as borderline personality disorder or intermittent explosive disorder. Treatment frequently involves multiple medications and intensive psychotherapy with strong family and educational support.

All ADHD children appear underinhibited for reasons described earlier. But this subgroup is underinhibited even when they are not overactive. Their cognitive abilities may be intact. They cannot effectively transmit information to the prefrontal cortex lobe. They are not extremely hyperactive, but they cannot stop themselves once they get going. They touch, talk, or fidget; they are easily irritated, or very explosive. They are not exploding, however, from a high baseline of arousal and activity, but from a base of normal or low arousal through a flimsy ceiling of impaired inhibition.

Validation of This Clinical Model for Neurobiological Subtypes Tests and Validation

Clinical
Pharmacological
Neurochemical—Challenge
Brain Imaging

Clinical studies can phenomenologically review how the components of symptoms interrelate. We recognize that children who are highly overactive and overaroused may have all of the symptoms of all of the other disorders—until they are calmed down on medication. Then they can be evaluated for separate deficits in cognition and inhibition. The differential course of these subtypes can be empirically studied; differences in associated symptoms in subjects and family members can be determined.

Pharmacologically, these hypotheses can be validated by testing medication response in these subgroups. The question is not whether psychostimulants would "work" in these subgroups (since they have such broad effects), but whether they are preferentially beneficial in the more hyperactive/aggressive group.

Psychophysiological studies using computerized power spectral analysis of EEG and evoked potential may also provide an index of cortical activation and inhibition.

Neurobiological studies, including challenge studies such as the yohimbine challenge, may be helpful. Yohimbine acts the opposite of clonidine and acutely releases norepinephrine, producing a pulse of norepinephrine lasting about 15 to 30 minutes. We hypothesize that, when administering yohimbine to ADHD children who appear behaviorally hyperaroused, norepinephrine (NE) response to a

---

Measures of Brain Functioning

Neurochemistry
1. *Blood and urine studies*
2. *CSF studies*
3. *Acute neurochemical challenge studies*
   - *Clonidine*
   - *Yohimbine*
   - *l-DOPA*

EEG and Evoked Potential
1. *Power spectral analysis*
2. *Evoked potential*

Brain Imaging
1. *MRI*
2. *SPECT scan*
3. *PET scan*

yohimbine challenge will be greater than in children whom we consider to be overaroused.

Brain imaging provides a method of assessing active brain metabolism. The PET scan allows visualization of regional brain metabolic activity. It has been utilized to demonstrate decreased prefrontal cortical activity in adults with residual ADHD. Unfortunately, the basal brain and locus coeruleus are less easy to visualize because they are so deep. Use of radio-labeled ligands for dopamine and norepinephrine in these populations may be paired to SPECT or PET scanning methods to assess arousal.

ADHD children may have primary difficulties with cognitive processing. For some of our ADHD children, their attentional and behavioral difficulties reflect an elevation in arousal that alters their sensitivity, or responsivity, to their internal and external environments. Children also can have variations in their responsiveness due to failure of inhibition, and even in a more complex manner, due to a failure of reward systems. These changes in modulatory systems impact information processing as well as behavior, and affect regulation. These differences in neurobiological mechanisms are relevant to understanding brain chemistry and selecting medication treatment. They are even relevant to defining our psychosocial interventions.

Subtype I—Cognitive Processing Deficit

For these ADHD children, the major deficit is in information processing. Their hyperactivity consists primarily of restlessness and fidgetiness. Their impulsivity derives from inadequate cognitive analysis. Concurrent cognitive deficits can often not be identified until excessive arousal is diminished.

Cognition: They primarily exhibit attentional disturbances and are highly distractible and underinhibited. Their primary deficit in stimulus filtering impairs selective attention. They may also have deficiencies in information processing related to perception, analysis, memory encoding, and retrieval.

Activity: This subtype is usually less active than the hyperaroused subtype, but their activity is often off-task. They are frequently restless, fidgety, and noisy—and appear to not be paying attention.

Impulsivity: These ADHD children are prone to impulsive behaviors due to difficulty in actual cognitive assessment. They may fail to engage cognitive strategies that they possess. They do not self-cue or prompt themselves to think of consequences before acting. Their impulsivity may also reflect a difficulty with analytic processes and avoidance of the added effort of appropriate amnestic retrieval and abstraction.

Social: This subgroup of ADHD children has poor social judgment, partially due to failure to perceive social cues and inadequate or faulty analysis of interpersonal significance. For example, they may not notice the incongruence between verbal content and facial expression in a peer, or not recognize the rising frustration of an angry parent.

Aggression: Less severely aggressive, this subtype is likely to fight defensively if they misperceive a threat or opportunity, or if they are unable to think of an alternative response.

Learning Difficulties: Their cognitive deficits are often associated with modality-specific learning disabilities in reading or math. They may have specific deficits in cross-modality association, visual-motor integration, memory, or abstraction.

Onset: Symptoms may not be apparent until the child enters school and significant attentional focusing is required.

Course: This primary attentional disturbance often appears pernicious and continues into adulthood.

Differential and Associated Diagnosis: Learning disabilities; mental retardation.

Neurofunctional Systems: Posterior cerebral sensory integrative centers involved in stimulus analysis; hippocampus in identification of change; nucleus accumbens in gating of new versus ongoing stimuli; prefrontal cortex in judgment and response selection.

Neurochemistry: This may be primarily a dopaminergic deficit.

Pharmacological Treatment: The major therapeutic agents for this subgroup are the psychostimulants that narrow the range of attention and increase the focus on a stimulus.

Subtype II—Excessively Aroused ADHD

The behavior of these children is characterized by extreme hyperactivity, impulsivity, and explosiveness. Their primary abnormality is one of excessive arousal that overwhelms attentional filters and overrides inhibitory processes.

Cognition: Their high degree of arousal increases the percentage of stimuli requiring further processing. In addition, these children often experience associated aggression and affective disorders.

Activity: The highly aroused ADHD group is characterized by very high levels of activity.

Impulsivity: Their high energy state increases activity. They react intensely and quickly, allowing little time for reflection. The high arousal overwhelms functioning of the behavioral inhibition system.

Social: Their intensity and irritability often offends people.

Aggression: This subgroup of ADHD is predisposed to impulsive aggression that is often "incidental." In their high level of activity, they may "run over" or collide with others, much as a tornado destroys obstacles in its path. They may have considerable affect associated with their aggression.

Learning Difficulties: These ADHD children often have difficulty learning due to their high degree of distractibility. When calmed down, they usually do not exhibit a formal learning disability.

Onset: The onset of excessive activity is usually pronounced by age two to three years.

Course: As these children enter adulthood, their high degree of arousal may spontaneously diminish and be partially compensated for by a maturing behavioral inhibition system.

Differential and Associated Diagnosis: Mania; aggressive conduct disorder.

Neurofunctional Systems: Locus coeruleus, reticular activating system.

Neurochemistry: Norepinephrine, which is highly involved in arousal processes, may be excessively released or activated in this subtype. Increased noradrenergic firing within the locus coeruleus may increase the number and strength of stimuli that need to be filtered and screened, requiring cortical information processing.

Pharmacological Treatment: This group of patients appears to respond best to the alpha-2 noradrenergic agent clonidine which reduces norepinephrine-dependent arousal.

Subtype III—Impaired Behavioral Inhibition System

This subtype of ADHD appears to be a primary deficit in the functioning of behavioral inhibition systems essential to response analysis and selection. Though less hyperactive, they cannot stop talking, wiggling, and touching. Their attentional deficits reflect an inability to inhibit or delay responding. Their common characteristic is severe impulsivity and inability to inhibit impulses. The specific symptoms or behaviors expressed depend on which impulses are unveiled. This group can often not be identified until excessive arousal is diminished.

Cognition: These ADHD children have difficulties in cognitive analysis because they act before thinking. They do not access alternatives or delay responses long enough for appropriate analysis or response selection, although they have this cognitive ability.

Activity: This subtype is usually less active than the hyperaroused subtype, but they are often unable to inhibit or control restless, fidgety movements that are not goal-directed. They are often over-responsive to stimuli or stress.

Impulsivity: This subtype is prone to impulsive behaviors due to difficulty in actual cognitive assessment and avoidance of the added effort of appropriate amnestic retrieval and abstraction.

Social: These individuals act before they think. They frequently engage others to meet their endless dependency needs or provoke them to gain sustained attention. They require considerable structuring and monitoring from adults to be able to stay organized and direct their activities. Those children who lack the ability to adequately inhibit their anger will exhibit aggression. Others who cannot dampen their neediness will constantly seek affection.

Aggression: Less severely aggressive, this subtype is likely to fight impulsively, not because they are overly energetic or misperceive stimuli, but because they cannot delay their response or consider alternative actions. They are easily overwhelmed by stimuli and emotions. They react quickly, excessively, but usually briefly.

Learning Difficulties: The underinhibited subgroup has learning difficulties secondary to its impulsivity. These children often respond before thinking and become very frustrated when attempting to check or re-evaluate their work. If they can force themselves to reconsider before answering or acting, they often are able to reason and problem solve.

Onset: Although this subtype of ADHD may be evident by an early inability to calm himself or herself, or manage frustration, the problem may be more specifically limited to cognitive processing and be evident later.

Course: During maturation, inhibitory processes increase parallel to a decreasing intensity of arousal. This subgroup may be expected to improve with age.

Differential and Associated Diagnosis: Developmental delay; borderline personality disorder; intermittent explosive disorder.

Neurofunctional Systems: Prefrontal cortex involved in analysis, delay, response selection; caudate and thalamus in gating internal versus external orientation.

Neurochemistry: This failure of inhibition is postulated to reflect a disturbance in serotonin functioning. Dopamine may be relevant to response selection.

Pharmacological Treatment: Theoretically, serotonergic agents with net pharmacological effects opposite to clomipramine might increase "obsessionality" and behavioral inhibition. No medication is yet available that clearly does this.

Subtype IV — Deficient Reward Systems

These ADHD children seem schizoid—emotionally aloof and socially remote. Their hyperactivity reflects a lack of goal-directed behavior; their difficulty directing attention reflects their lack of internalized interests. They often seem less responsive to rewards and punishments. While they may be better classified as having atypical personality development, they often meet the overt diagnostic criteria of ADHD.

Cognition: This subgroup may exhibit unusual associative patterns and less human investment. Their attentional impairment reflects a lack of meaning and personal goal direction.

Activity: They are fidgety, restless, and off-task—but usually not severely hyperkinetic. They may have significant, irregular bursts of activity and irritability, frequently characterized by their lack of predictability, consistency, and meaningful direction.

Impulsivity: These individuals are highly impulsive and unpredictable, primarily due to their lack of a sense of consequence.

Social: These ADHD patients are the most socially impaired. Their inattention appears to reflect emotional indifference. They seem relatively indifferent to their emotional impact or involvement on others—a deficit in attachment and empathy. They may be better classified as having atypical personality development due to their interpersonal aloofness

Aggression: They seem impervious to rewards and punishments, and are affectively flat or dysphoric. Their aggressiveness often reflects a lack of empathy and human implication or significance.

Learning Difficulties: These ADHD variants may have peculiar associative patterns and learning difficulties due to their lack of meaningful engagement in any cognitive problem. They seem unable to experience the joy of discovery and understanding.

Onset: Although onset is probably congenital, these patients may seem impervious to rewards or punishments and rather indifferent to praise or pain at an early age. The effect on attention may not be evident until middle childhood, and then consists of inappropriate, unfocused activity and thought.

Course: Although social skills and improved cognitive habits can be partially learned, this subgroup may have a chronic course characterized by relative lack of empathy and goal-directed behavior.

Differential and Associated Diagnosis: Developmental delay; borderline personality disorder; intermittent explosive disorder.

Neurofunctional Systems: Limbic system in affect regulation; postcentral cerebral associative centers and prefrontal cortex in cognitive analysis and integration.

Neurochemistry: Anatomically, this capacity involves the limbic system and associative linkages among cognitive systems. For those ADHD children who seem impervious to reward and punishment, and who are unable to form adequate close emotional attachments, a deficit in endorphin functioning may be present.

Medication: Unknown. They are the most globally impaired and difficult to treat. Neuroleptics may decrease their cognitive diffusion.

Section 2

Chapter 6

**Pharmacological Diversity—
Medication Types and Effects**

Pharmacological Diversity - Medication Types and Effects

Three major categories of medications are commonly utilized in the treatment of ADD-spectrum disorders. These include the psychostimulants, antidepressants, and arousal-modulating medications.

The **psychostimulants** include methylphenidate, amphetamine, and magnesium pemoline. The psychostimulants are the most frequently prescribed and the best studied. They have powerful effects on focusing and sustaining attention, and may enhance memory storage and retrieval. Their effects on reasoning and problem-solving are under investigation, but may increase secondary sustained attention. Psychostimulants improve regulation of activity and increase the focus and effectiveness of action. They enhance fine-motor control relevant to reading, writing, and speaking. They have significant antiaggressive effects in subjects who are not severely aggressive.

The **antidepressants** include tricyclic antidepressants (such as imipramine, amitriptyline, and desipramine), other antidepressants (bupropion, monoamine oxidase inhibitors), and the newer selective serotonin reuptake inhibitors (SSRIs—fluoxetine, sertraline, paroxetine). The antidepressants have the advantage of being administered twice daily, and these enhance mood while calming anxiety. Since depression itself may impair attention and reasoning, antidepressants may improve thinking. However, they appear to be less potent in focusing attention and diminishing distractibility. Some of these medications are more cardiotoxic, and often the tricyclics are uncomfortable.

The **arousal-modulating medications** act specifically to diminish the release of norepinephrine. These medications,

---

Major Medications for ADHD and Comorbidities

Psychostimulants
- Ritalin (methylphenidate)
- Dexedrine (dextroamphetamine)
- Adderall
- Cylert (magnesium pemoline)

Antidepressants
- Tricyclics:
  - Elavil (amitriptyline)
  - Tofranil (imipramine)
  - Norpramine (desipramine)
- MAOIs:
  - Nardil (phenelzine)
  - Parnate (tranylcypromine)
- Selective Serotonin Reuptake Inhibitors (SSRIs):
  - Prozac (fluoxetine)
  - Zoloft (sertraline)
  - Paxil (paroxetine)
  - Anafranil (clomipramine)
  - Celexa (citalopram)
- Luvox (fluvoxamine)
- Effexor (venlafaxine)

Other Antidepressants
- Remeron (mirtazapine)
- Wellbutrin (bupropion)

Antihypertensives/Arousal Modulating
- Catapres (clonidine)
- Tenex (guanfacine)

Anticonvulsants
- Tegretol, Carbatrol (carbamazepine)
- Depakote (valporic acid)

Neuroleptics
- Haldol (haloperidol)
- Thorazine (chlorpromiazine)
- Risperdal (risperidone)
- Zyprexa (olanzepine)

clonidine and guanfacine, reduce activity and appear to decrease aggression. They enhance frustration tolerance and minimize withdrawal side effects from the psychostimulants.

The relevance of this pharmacological diversity to understanding ADHD subtypes is that these medications have distinctly different mechanisms of action. They also differ in their capacity to improve specific components of ADHD. Their effect on varied dimensions of the ADHD spectrum may provide a window into the underlying neurobiology and neurophysiology of ADHD and help define specific chemical subtypes.

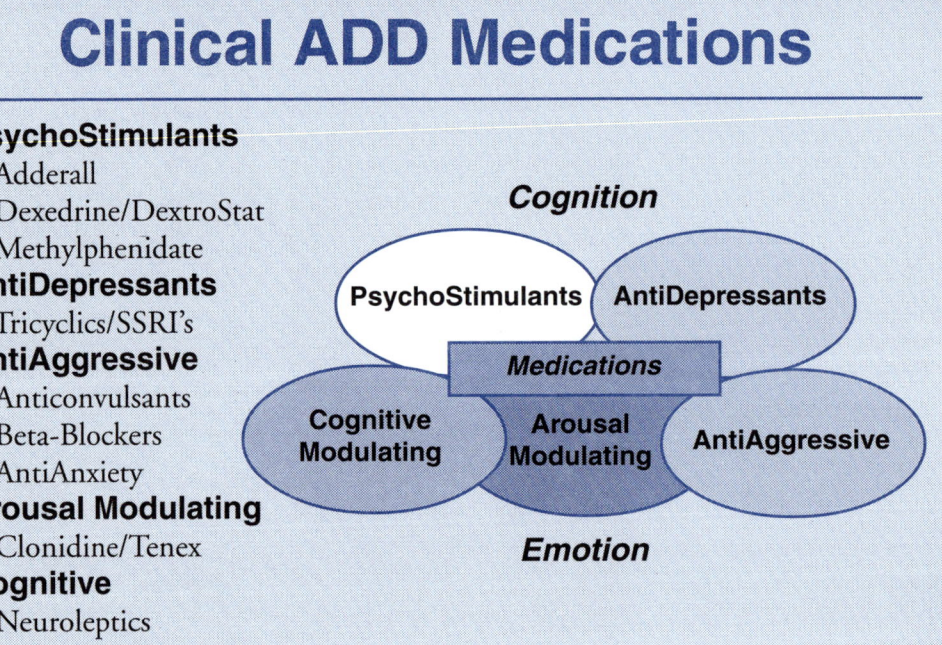

Medication

Risk/Benefit

Chapters 6 thru 12 will examine medications from the relationship of benefit versus risk. **They are in no manner to be used as clinical guides in medication management.** Reference literature such as the *Physicians Desk Reference, 1999* should be consulted regarding the use of any medication prescribed to individuals. Rather, this is a summary of the major medications used in the management of ADHD along with an outline of their benefits, mechanism of action, side effects, warnings, and so on. With any medication, there is a degree of risk. However, with proper management, some of those risks can be minimized or accepted.

Treatment Effectiveness

While research does not support the conclusion that medication as a sole form of intervention is effective in the long run, nonetheless its efficacy for change when used as a part of a multimodal treatment system is well established. It was in the year 1937 that Charles Bradley discovered that, in administering "amphetamine sulfate" (Benzedrine) to hyperactive children, their ability to inhibit improved (Bradley,1937). This discovery went relatively unnoticed for several years, but finally caught on. Today, while stimulant medications are still the primary medications of choice in treating ADHD, there are numerous others which have now been shown to be effective in treating specific symptoms or subtypes of ADHD. This is not an attempt to document all of these, but rather an introduction to some of the more commonly used. The reader would be advised to consult a physician regarding these medications and their appropriateness for treating ADHD.

> **Treatment Effectiveness**
>
> *The value of medication treatment must be compared against the risk of non-treatment, not just to side effects elicited.*

Clinical Variability and Subtypes

Because there are many subtypes of ADHD, it is not surprising that there are multiple medications which play a

> **Clinical Variability and Subgroups**
>
> *Different subgroups of ADD and their associated problems respond to different medications.*

role in treating this disorder. These may include the categories of stimulants, antidepressants, antihypertensives, neuroleptics, and antiseizure medications. While research on stimulants in the treatment of ADHD has been around since the 1940's, such is not the case for many of these other medications. Discretion needs to be used. Because many of these medications operate on different functions, they may at times be administered concomitantly.

The use of medications to assist in behavior or learning improvement is controversial. With each passing year, these medications seem to be used in greater frequency (Safer & Krager, 1988). They should not be used as a quick and easy solution to behavior control, but rather as one part of a multimodal, multidisciplinary approach to intervention.

Biederman, 1998, notes that there is increasing scientific recognition that attention deficit hyperactivity disorder (ADHD), a heterogeneous disorder that carries a high risk of comorbidity, continues past childhood and adolescence and in many cases, into adulthood. It may be underidentified in girls.

The etiology of ADHD is unknown, although evidence from family studies of ADHD suggests a genetic origin for some forms of this disorder. A variety of pharmacologic agents are available in treating ADHD: stimulant medications remain the first-line treatment for noncomorbid ADHD, whereas tricyclic antidepressants and bupropion are recommended for stimulant nonresponders and patients with more than one psychiatric disorder. Complex cases of ADHD, however, may require rational use of combined pharmacotherapy.

Preparation for Medications
Before Medication Is Used, One Should Ask...

> **Effective Use of Medication**
>
> *Effective use of medication requires an adequate assessment, a therapeutic alliance, and monitoring of response.*

Has there been a comprehensive *evaluation* through a differential diagnostic approach, which confirms the existence of ADHD in a form severe enough for which medication is warranted? This evaluation should include data gathered from parents, teachers, physicians, psychologists, and possibly specialists, such as psychiatrists or neurologists.

Have the care providers received *education* regarding the behavioral management of this disorder, and have other interventions been tried?

Are there *contraindications* to specific medications, such as epilepsy, tics, heart problems, other medication interactions, the age of the child, alcohol or drug abuse, and so forth?

How does the *child* feel about taking medication? Has someone explained to him or her the purpose of the medication?

Can the family *afford* medication?

How do the *parents* feel about the use of medication for their child? Are they knowledgeable of the benefits and risks associated with its use?

Will the parents and physician *monitor* the medication effectively?

Pharmacologic Treatments for Alcohol and Drug Abuse

As our view of alcoholism is changing from an environmental learning perspective to that of a sociobiological view, there has been a corresponding change in the manner in which pharmacologic agents may assist the individual in fostering and maintaining sobriety. For over twenty years, physicians have used medications such as the benzodiazepines (Librium and Valium) to treat alcohol *withdrawal*. These medications were used primarily to avoid seizure and prevent "delirium tremens" during the withdrawal phase of treatment. Later on, medications such as lorazepam (Ativan) and oxazepam (Serax) were also used as shorter-acting agents to reduce the urge to use alcohol (Liskow & Goodwin, 1987).

Disulfiram (Antabuse) has been used since the 1950's to treat alcohol *abuse*. It increases blood acetaldehyde when alcohol is consumed, resulting in extreme nausea. This aversive response hopefully will encourage sobriety; however, it is dependent on the individual's compliance in self-administering the Antabuse.

The most interesting phenomenon in recent years has been the use of newer *antidepressants* that are serotonin

> **Pharmacologic Treatment**
>
> *Medications used to treat substance abuse may complement medications used for ADD.*

reuptake inhibitors. Medications such as Prozac (fluoxetine hydrochloride), and similar medications such as Paxil and Zoloft (which are classified as antidepressants), are reported to be effective in reducing the urge to drink. While these medications are primarily utilized in treating major depression, clinical experience suggests that they may be helpful in reducing alcohol and drug use, particularly in reducing the anxiety which is common in early withdrawal. In addition, these medications typically elicit few side effects, allowing them to be tolerated better than most of the older *tricyclic antidepressants* such as imipramine and Norpramine.

Bupropion (Wellbutrin), another antidepressant which is unrelated to the tricyclics and appears to be a weak blocker of the uptake of serotonin and norepinephrine along with inhibiting the neuronal reuptake of dopamine (*Physicians Desk Reference,* 1999), also has gained attention as being of help in both ADHD and in the treatment of alcoholism. It appears to demonstrate effects similar to that of the stimu-

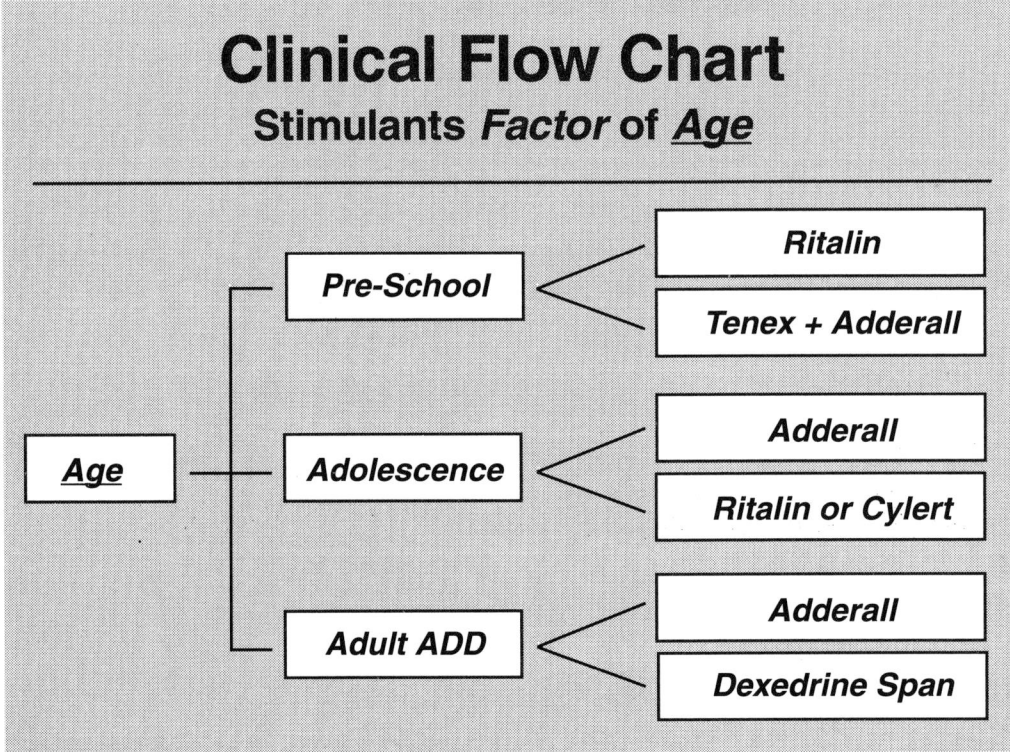

lants and to traditional antidepressants. Most of the studies have focused on adults as opposed to children. Bupropion, however, has been shown to increase the risk of seizure at approximately four times the rate of other commonly prescribed antidepressants. However, this can be reduced by keeping the daily dosage under 450 mg per day and single dosages under 150 mg.

Another medication thought to inhibit the reuptake of serotonin is clomipramine hydrochloride (Anafranil). This medication, classified as a tricyclic antidepressant, is used primarily to treat obsessive-compulsive disorder (*Physicians Desk Reference*, 1999). Many individuals with ADHD, and also many alcoholics, appear to have characteristics common to obsessive-compulsive disorder. Verbal expressions of "I have too…" or "I must…," or ritualistic behavior patterns such as obsessional alcohol usage, may suggest that this is a medication which could be helpful to this population.

Chapter 7

Psychostimulants

Specific Medications for Treating ADHD

Stimulants - Overview

Medications can provide significant salutary effects for children and adolescents with ADHD. Due to their well-established safety and efficacy, psychostimulants are generally considered first-line pharmacotherapy for most young patients with ADHD.

Since psychostimulant treatment often requires frequent dosing and may be associated with unacceptable side effects and risks, other classes of medication have been studied as possible treatment alternatives (Findling & Dogin, 1998).

The most extensively researched nonstimulant medications are the tricyclic antidepressants. In addition, alpha-2 agonists have also been shown to reduce symptoms of ADHD. Newer antidepressants such as bupropion and venlafaxine may hold promise as treatments for ADHD.

Psychostimulants

Without question, Ritalin is the most commonly prescribed medication for ADHD.

It is relatively safe when properly prescribed and managed. Benefits are achieved rapidly, but they do not last long.

Mechanism of Action and Behavioral Effects of Psychostimulants

The psychostimulants have a broad spectrum of clinical effects. They clearly improve attentional focus and enhance both selective filtering and sustained attention. They decrease distractibility, and increase attachment to stimuli. In an overall clinical summary, the psychostimulants increase the strength of the signal:noise ratio. This enhances filtering

---

Mechanism of Action and Behavioral Effects of Psychostimulants

Psychostimulants have behavioral and cognitive effects.

of information coming in, and strengthens the efferent signal directed out to the nerves and muscles. This improvement in attention and information processing often enhances memory encoding and retrieval processes. Via inputs into the prefrontal cortex, psychostimulants enhance the ability to delay response and exercise judgment. This inhibitory ability enables more selective and appropriate social functioning, more appropriate reading of incoming cues, and more enhanced selection of self-emitted behaviors. ADHD children become less provocative, irritable, and aggressive. They become more able to introspect.

We have discussed the relative effects of psychostimulants, antidepressants, and clonidine in ADHD (Hunt, et al., in submission). The medications that have greatest effect on activity are those that act principally on norepinephrine systems, while those that have greatest effect on distractibility in ADHD children act primarily on dopaminergic systems (Hunt, et al., 1991).

Clinical Effects of Psychostimulants

The public debate, characterized as the "Ritalin controversy," reflects the concern for appropriate selection and utilization of medication in children (Cowart, 1988). Extensive research has defined and reviewed the behavioral efficacy of psychostimulants in ADHD (Dulcan, 1990; Hunt, et al., 1987; Barkley, 1988).

Behavioral Effects of Psychostimulants

Nearly a hundred studies have demonstrated that psychostimulants are therapeutically effective in improving both behavior and attention. Methylphenidate has been shown to decrease and focus activity in ADHD (Porinno, et al., 1984), to improve visual-motor coordination, and reduce impulsive, aggressive behavior (Pelham, et al., 1985). Activity levels are reduced by psychostimulants, and movements become more efficiently goal-directed. Social functioning and impulsivity improve during treatment with methylphenidate (Henker, et al., 1988).

Although methylphenidate is very effective in decreasing distractibility, our preliminary data suggests that methylphenidate may be less effective than clonidine in treating the hyperactive and aggressive components of severe ADHD.

Behavioral Effects of Psychostimulants

Stimulants improve task performance, impulsivity, and aggression.

Cognitive Effects of Psychostimulants

A large number of studies have demonstrated improvement from methylphenidate in selective and sustained attention in ADHD (Kupietz, et al., 1988). Both selective and sustained attention are increased as measured by cognitive tasks (Rapport, et al., 1990). Psychostimulants increase the "strength" of the stimulus. In addition, both long- and short-term memory have been improved with psychostimulant medication (Swanson, 1976). Improved performance in classroom learning and grades, however, has been much less documentable. A three-year, multimodal study demonstrated that combined therapy of medication, education, and psychotherapy improved most areas of reading and math (Satterfield, et al., 1981). Studies have documented short-term gains in academic learning from treatment with methylphenidate (Pelham, et al., 1985; Famularo, 1987).

Methylphenidate improves the rate and efficiency of processing and diminishes impulsivity (Rapport, 1987; Pelham, 1985). Prior studies have shown that most ADHD patients respond to methylphenidate, but may experience significant short- or long-term side effects including instability of response, anorexia, insomnia, and a possible increase in tics and explosiveness. The predominant effects of psychostimulants are on attentional focusing; methylphenidate may be less efficient in reducing excessive hyperactivity (Hunt, et al., 1990).

There is a complex relationship between the dose-response evident for control of attention and control of behavior. Sprague and Sleater, 1977, suggested that optimal performance of a pattern-matching task occurred at a lower dose, while control of hyperactivity required a higher dose of a psychostimulant. While most subsequent studies have not found this dissociation of dose-response effect, different components of cognition may be variously affected by Ritalin. Most attentional studies have utilized stimulus-bound tasks—tasks in which the subject must respond directly to a stimulus on the screen—by reacting to it, matching it, or memorizing it. These tasks do not correlate well with classroom learning. Furthermore, they do not assess the role of attention in the more complex components of cognition—reasoning, problem solving, and abstraction.

> **Cognitive Effects of Psychostimulants**
>
> *Stimulants enhance selective and sustained attention and can improve storage and retrieval from memory.*

Perhaps Ritalin narrows the attentional field and increases the strengths of the "signal" being processed. It is less clear whether Ritalin enhances processing competencies required to abstract or reason—processes that often require ignoring external stimuli in preference to inner contemplation. This component of contemplation and reasoning may correlate more highly with classroom learning in later grades. Other medications that strengthen frustration tolerance may facilitate this form of classroom learning and efficient problem-solving.

Treatment of ADD Adults
Response to Stimulants

Clinical Efficacy
- Children: 85%
- Adults: 70%

Psychopathology
- More Comorbidity
- Habits
- Identification with ADD
- Personality

Dose
- Varies with Age
  —*Size*
  —*Metabolism*
  —*Energy*
- Varies with Task
  —*Differences by Adults*
  —*Adaptations*
- Timing

Compliance

Comparative Effects of Psychostimulants

Comparative Effects of Psychostimulants

Psychostimulants increase the strength of the signal going into and coming out of the brain.

Compared to other medications used in the treatment of ADD, the psychostimulants are the best researched and globally the most effective. However, the effects of the psychostimulants are not homogenous in ADD. Although they improve most symptoms of ADHD, their predominant effect is on attention focusing and behavioral inhibition. Clinically, they have less effect on activity and aggression than does clonidine, and less effect on mood than do the antidepressants.

Pliszka (1998) reviewed the use of psychostimulant medications in pediatric patients. Psychostimulant medications have a long history of safe and effective usage in the treatment of ADHD and remain the drugs of first choice in this condition. Because of their effectiveness and the differences in response between different psychostimulants, Pliszka believes that children with ADHD should be aggressively treated with at least two different classes of psychostimulants before moving to nonpsychostimulant agents. As long as side effects are not troublesome, higher dosages may be used to adequately control the ADHD symptoms, and such high dosages do not impair learning. No evidence shows long-term effects of psychostimulants on growth.

Neurochemical Effects of Methylphenidate

Psychostimulants increase the release of dopamine. Both of those mechanisms produce an increase in available dopamine within the synaptic cleft. There is a slight difference between the effects of dexedrine and methylphenidate. Dexedrine is slightly more dopaminergic; it has a more direct effect on postsynaptic dopamine receptors and a little more effect on inhibition of monoamine oxidase and serotonin. Some antidepressants block the reuptake of neurotransmitters into the presynaptic neuron. Antidepressants have a similar behavioral effect, but act primarily by blocking reuptake. In contrast, drugs like clonidine diminish the release of norepinephrine by stimulating presynaptic autoreceptors.

The psychostimulants that act primarily to release dopamine appear to have their most powerful effects on attentional filtering and focusing. They improve reliability or rate of memory encoding and retrieval processes. They also facilitate behavioral inhibition.

Mechanism of Action of Methylphenidate

Methylphenidate acts primarily by release of reserpine-sensitive presynaptic stores of dopamine and norepinephrine (Clemens & Fuller, 1979). Stimulant medications affect noradrenergic, dopaminergic, and serotonergic sys-

> **Neurochemical Effects of Methylphenidate**
>
> *Stimulants primarily increase dopamine release and concentration in the synapse.*

Mechanism of Action of Methylphenidate

Methylphenidate (Ritalin) increases release of stored dopamine and affects norepinephrine.

tems and activity of the enzyme monoamine oxides (Ferris & Tang, 1979). Chronic treatment with methylphenidate may diminish postsynaptic noradrenergic receptor sensitivity, as evidenced by reduced growth hormone response following a single oral dose of clonidine given during treatment with methylphenidate (Hunt, et al., 1984). Methylphenidate may alter the disposition of dopamine primarily by reducing catecholamine reuptake (Ross, 1976). Methylphenidate binds with relatively high affinity to a site in the brain that is associated with the dopamine transport complex (Janowsky, et al., 1985). Methylphenidate may also diminish the availability of norepinephrine in certain brain regions, such as the rat hippocampus, via a reduction in the synthesis of dopamine (Lawson-Wendling, et al., 1981).

Studies on the Effect of Methylphenidate on Catecholamines in ADHD

Acute administration of methylphenidate produces a transient rise in norepinephrine and epinephrine and growth hormone, while chronic administration has little effect on growth hormone release (Greenhill, et al., 1980; 1981; Joyce, et al., 1984). A single acute dose of methylphenidate increases plasma growth hormone in children with ADHD (Shaywitz & Hunt, et al., 1982).

The effects of chronic methylphenidate treatment on urinary 3 methoxy-4 hydroxy-phenyethylene glycol have been conflicting (Zametkin, et al., 1985; 1988), although we have found that another psychostimulant, d-amphetamine, does reduce urinary 3 methoxy-4 hydroxy-phenyethylene glycol excretion (Brown & Hunt, et al., 1981; Shekim, et al., 1983; Zametkin, et al., 1985). Treatment-induced elevations in norepinephrine, normetanephrine and dopamine were noted in an initial, but not in the follow-up, study (Zametkin, et al., 1985; 1988). Another study reported that a large sample of nonresponders had significant decrease in urinary 3 methoxy-4 hydroxy-phenyethylene glycol, but used a flurometric assay not sufficiently sensitive (Yu-Cun & Yu-Feng, 1984). Large baseline differences in this sample, and that of Shekim (1977; 1979) and of Brown, Hunt and others (1981), require further clinical correlation. We anticipate that methylphenidate treatment will have no

Studies on the Effects of Methylphenidate

Stimulants can affect growth hormone and neurotransmitter metabolites. These changes are not clinically useful for monitoring treatment effectiveness.

It has also been shown to increase cerebral blood flow and may increase glucose metabolism in the orbital-limbic regions (Lou, 1989).

effect on urinary and plasma levels of 3 methoxy-4 hydroxy-phenyethylene glycol, but may reduce platelet alpha-2 receptor binding and possibly increase diastolic blood pressure.

Methylphenidate Hydrochloride (Ritalin)

Methylphenidate (Ritalin) is available in varied doses. The regular release usually lasts 3 to 4 hours. The sustained release lasts 3 to 6 hours.

Dosage: Beginning dose is usually 5 mg in the morning. After three days, increase the dose to 5 mg in the morning and at noon. Gradually increase as tolerated while monitoring response to:

- Low dose: about 10 mg in the morning, 5 mg at noon and 5 mg at 4:00 p.m., equaling 20 mg per day (about 0.3 mg/kg/d).
- Medium dose: about 15 mg in the morning, 10 mg at noon and 5 mg at 4:00 p.m., equaling 30 mg per day.
- High dose: about 30 mg in the morning, 20 mg at noon and 10 mg at 4:00 p.m., equaling 60 mg per day (about 1.0 mg/kg/d).

Side Effects: Appetite suppression, insomnia, headache, stomachache, and increase blood pressure.

Benefits: Decrease in activity level (with low doses), improved frustration tolerance, reduced impulsivity, improved attention—sustained selection and vigilance, improved emotional lability, improved visual-motor coordination, more goal-directed, improved ability to delay gratification, immediate change, increased productivity, improved socialization.

Contraindications: (Not comprehensive) seizure disorder, Tourette's syndrome.

It has also been shown to increase cerebral blood flow, and may increase glucose metabolism in the orbital-frontal-striatal-limbic regions (Lou, 1989).

Research suggests that cognitive gains occur with slightly lower doses than do behavioral gains (Sprague & Sleator, 1976). Therefore, if one is dosing to reduce hyperactivity, for example, there is a possibility of overdosing relative to learning. As the individual matures into adulthood, lower doses may be effective due to increases in brain maturity,

---

Dosage of Stimulants

Dosing of stimulants may depend on the relative degree of behavioral or cognitive disorganization.

Stimulant Treatment

Stimulant treatment in ADD can reduce the risk of substance abuse.

decreasing body metabolism, and greater ability of the individual to adequately inhibit. On high doses, individuals may "rebound" with a deterioration of behavior below baseline for a short period of time after the medication has been metabolized out of the system.

The advantage of this medication for individuals with alcohol and drug problems has been that it has enabled them to read literature about alcohol and drug abuse and participate in the educational and support group processes. In addition, stimulants often reduce the underlying anxiety that prompts addicts to use alcohol and marijuana. Stimulants in ADD often reduce the stimulation craving that prompts cocaine abuse.

Effect of Dose Response: In order to assess the effects of varied doses of methylphenidate (totaling 25, 50, or 75 mg per day), researchers studied the behavioral and social response of 46 adolescents using a placebo controlled double-blind crossover design. The results showed that (a) the dose-response is influenced by the measurement method, (b) the majority of adolescents exhibited improved social behavior when treated with methylphenidate, (c) the bulk of the positive effects of methylphenidate were achieved at the lowest dose, and (d) there appears to be diminishing positive effects and an increased risk of negative effects with successively higher doses (Smith, et al., 1998.)

Is Ritalin an Addictive Drug?

While there is an addictive potential for Ritalin, it is rarely seen in pill form and is evidenced in significantly higher doses than would be commonly prescribed. One exception to this has been the recent phenomenon of "snorting" Ritalin. This abusive practice is rapidly growing with adolescents. When Ritalin is administered orally in prescribed dosages, the risk of serious injury is minimal; however, when it is snorted so that most of this drug enters the blood system rapidly, there is great risk of serious injury or death. Parents and school personnel need to exercise more control over accessibility of this drug. Parents should not allow their adolescent to carry their own medication to school to self-administer. Schools should establish policies in which all prescription medications should be administered within the school office. ADD patients do not experience a "buzz" or "high" from Ritalin.

Alcoholics we have worked with who were prescribed Ritalin have often been able to maintain sobriety much more easily, and have seen improvements in their ability to maintain healthy relationships in their families with their spouses and children. We have not seen this drug abused by ADD alcoholics. For those who have a history of stimulant abuse such as cocaine, Ritalin would likely be entirely inappropriate.

> **Ritalin Addictive Risk**
>
> *The risk for abuse of stimulants is greater in individuals without ADHD/ADD.*

Use of Stimulants in Substance Abusers

The relationship between attention deficit hyperactivity disorder (ADHD) and psychoactive substance use disorders (PSUD) in siblings of ADHD and normal-control probands was assessed using DSM-III-R structured diagnostic interviews through a four year follow-up of siblings. Both ADHD and male gender predicted higher rates and an earlier onset of PSUD after adjusting for high-risk status, other psychiatric disorders, and for age. The risk was particularly high if the siblings had ADHD plus conduct disorder. Results highlighted the importance of drug and alcohol prevention in ADHD youth and their siblings, particularly those with comorbid conduct disorder (Milberger, et al., 1997).

Methylphenidate for Substance Abusers

In patients with combined ADHD and substance abuse, considerable debate exists regarding the relative benefit versus risk of treating these individuals with a psychostimulant. In general, researchers find that treatment with stimulants during active cocaine abuse does not improve outcome nor reduce the cocaine abuse. However, stimulant treatment of the ADHD after a three to six month interval of being substance abuse free does reduce the risk of relapse (Wilens, personal communication, 1999).

In an open 12-week trial of 12 patients with adult ADHD and cocaine dependence, Levin, et al. (1998), found that sustained-release methylphenidate (40 to 80 mg/d) when combined with received individual weekly relapse prevention therapy reduced cocaine use evident by urine screens. Self-reported cocaine use and craving decreased significantly. These preliminary data suggest that under close supervision, the combined intervention of sustained-release methylphenidate and relapse prevention therapy may be effective in treating individuals with both adult ADHD and cocaine dependence.

Dextroamphetamine sulfate (Dexedrine)

Our clinical experience and research demonstrates some differences between Ritalin and Dexedrine. Dexedrine is more activating than Ritalin. It has more antidepressant effect. In contrast, Ritalin is more inhibiting and quiets hyperactive behavior in younger children.

This clinical variation reflects differences in mechanism of action. Dexedrine releases recently-synthesized dopamine, and has more direct postsynaptic effects and more serotonergic effects.

Dexedrine may have a few more side effects, producing jitteriness and nervousness. Because it is more potent, a lower dose may often be utilized. A liquid form is also available. For treating ADD, the benefits are similar to those of Ritalin. Dexedrine is often chosen by physicians as an alternative to Ritalin in adults. The spansule has a longer duration and is more predictable than sustained-release Ritalin.

Methamphetamine Hydrochloride (Desoxyn)

Desoxyn is an amphetamine which is rarely used in treating ADHD due to its high potential for addiction and significant side effects of anorexia. When used, it must be monitored carefully. The anorectic effect of this drug may decrease with low dosages as tolerance is built. It is available in 5, 10, or 15 mg for oral administration. As with any stimulant, when used it should only be taken as an integral part of a total treatment program which includes psychological, educational, and social measures (*Physicians Desk Reference*, 1999).

Dexedrine

Dexedrine is somewhat more activating than Ritalin.

Magnesium Pemoline (Cylert)

Cylert is a longer-acting, less potent stimulant. It generally has less behavioral effect but good cognitive-attentional effect.

Due to its slower release, Cylert has less euphoric and less addictive potential. Therefore, Cylert is often used in patients with addictive histories. Its longer duration of action, 12 to 18 hours, provides some advantage in adolescents and adults.

In a two year follow-up study of 40 college students taking Cylert, Heiligenstein, et al. (1996), found that 70% improved by clinicians global ratings. They recommended Cylert for college students, especially those who might be at risk for addiction.

Cylert has the advantages of being longer acting than methylphenidate or d-amphetamine and of being less rigidly controlled. It is generally considered to have less effective behavioral control, but is effective in helping focus attention. Due to its highly dopaminergic effect, Cylert is somewhat more likely to produce stereotypic (repetitive) movements in animals and possibly more tics (rapid, jerking movements) in humans. The problem with Cylert is that it can produce severe and sudden liver toxicity. This can usually be recognized through blood studies of liver enzymes, and generally improves when the medication (Cylert) is stopped. It has a higher incidence of (hepatic) liver toxicity, with 13 patients either dying or requiring liver transplants. This risk prompted the FDA to determine that Cylert should only be used as a second-line treatment for specific indications. It is occasionally prescribed to stimulant-resistant adolescents or to individuals with a substance abuse history, since it appears to have less addictive potential. Liver enzymes can be monitored routinely (about every 2 to 3 months) to reduce, but not eliminate, the serious risk of liver damage.

> **Cylert**
>
> *Is longer acting, has less behavioral effects, but is more likely to produce liver toxicity and motor tics.*

Adderall

Adderall is an amphetamine that is approved by the FDA for treatment of ADHD.

Adderall to Dexedrine

Both are amphetamines that improve attention and reduce hyperactivity and impulsivity in children and adults with ADD or ADHD.

Differences Between Adderall and Dexedrine

Chemically, Adderall is bound to a different vehicle that appears to sustain a longer release—salts consisting of saccarate and aspartate. More importantly, Adderall contains both isomers of amphetamine, dextro (d-AMPH) that is 75% and 25% levo (l-AMPH). This chemical difference may be clinically important because the dextro has more effect on dopamine; the levo has greater effect on norepinephrine.

Adderall

Consists of both d- and l- isomers of amphetamine.

Medication Management
Adderall

Dosing
- Children: 15-20 mg in AM; 5-10 @2PM = 20-30 mg/d
- Adults: 20-30 mg/10-15 mg = 30-50 mg/d
- Increase: Begin 5 mg in AM; increase by 5 mg q.3rd d.

Side Effects—usually transient
- Common: decreased appetite, headache, nervousness, insomnia, stomachache, taste
- Rare, but significant: aggression, anger

Comparative Trial
- Clinical trial of Adderall, Dexedrine, Ritalin and placebo

Adderall Versus Ritalin
Open Trial
Scores: DSM-IV Items (Hunt, et al., 1996)

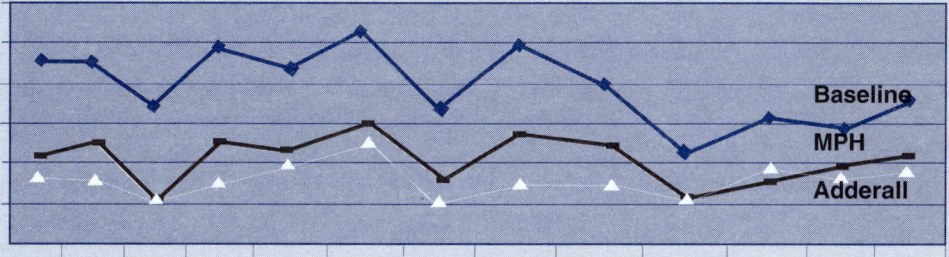

Baseline, Ritalin, Adderall—DSM-IV Items
Effect of No Meds, Ritalin & Adderall

Response better on Adderall to 11 of 14 items
Significant differences on 3 items

The Clinical Significance of the Longer Duration of Action of Adderall

In our experience, Adderall is usually effective for about six hours. This usually means that children do not have to take a dose of medication at school. This avoids the embarrassment and the logistical and administrative hassles of approval and administration of a school dose. That means less paperwork for the physician, less disruption for the teacher, and less embarrassment for the child. In total, compliance appears to increase.

Compared to Ritalin, Is There Any Advantage in Clinical Effects from Adderall?

We completed an open trial comparison of 13 patients with ADHD in whom we compared the response to no medication and clinically significant doses of Adderall and Ritalin administered in random sequence. Results were measured using DSM-IV behavior ratings, completed by parents or adult patients.

Adderall

Adderall is longer acting and frequently "more natural" than other stimulants.

Adderall Preference

About 70% of patients preferred Adderall; 20% only responded to Adderall.

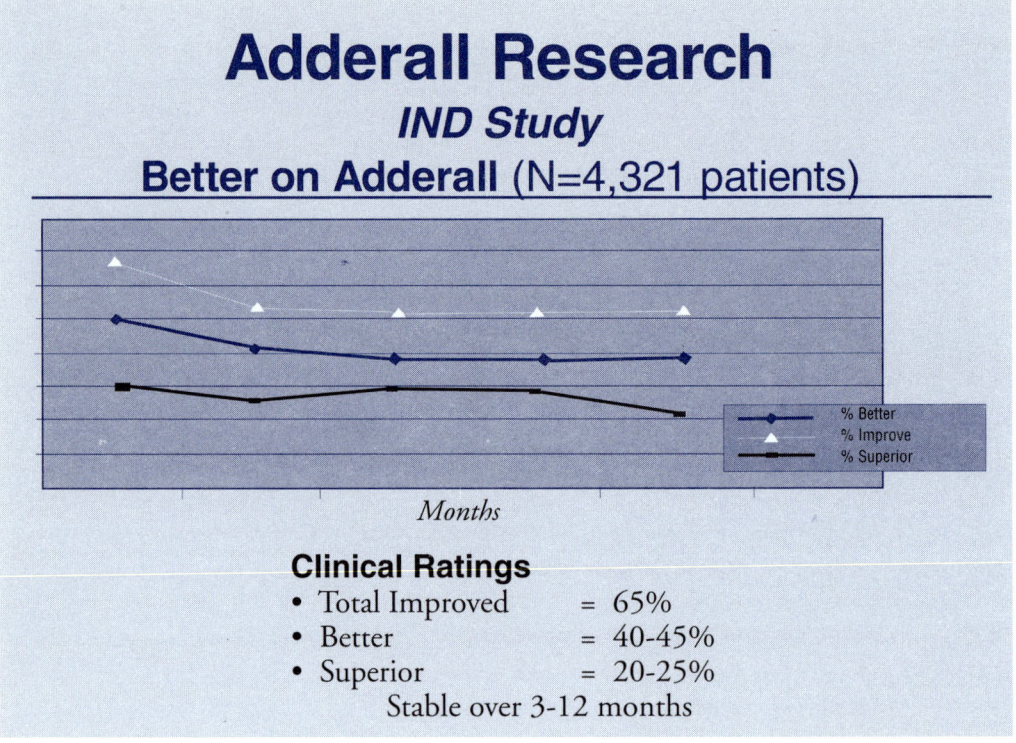

It was no surprise that both medications were better than no medication. We were impressed that the degree of response to Adderall was greater than from Ritalin in most items.

Favoring Adderall, three items were statistically significant: attention, mood, and irritability. Ten items showed a trend favoring Adderall. The only item in which Ritalin was better than Adderall was in "acts smart."

Patients' Preferences to Adderall

Eleven of the 13 elected to stay on Adderall; one preferred Ritalin. What they described was that they felt more natural, even, and comfortable on Adderall. Subjectively, they characterized Adderall as being "smoother."

Differences in Side Effects

In this study there were relatively few side effects, and the differences did not reach clinical significance. However, we have treated about 500 patients with Adderall. Many have reported that they experience less abrupt onset and stopping of Adderall and less "withdrawal" side effects on Adderall than other stimulants.

In the "IND" study, physicians were asked to compare the response of patients treated with Adderall to their response on other prior psychostimulants (Ritalin—60%, Dexedrine/Cylert—30%). Physicians reported the response of 4,321 patients to Adderall. Twenty-five percent were rated as "superior" on Adderall, 40% were scored as "better." Thus 65% of patients did better on Adderall than other stimulants, and this effect continued stable for one year.

Question: What have you learned from other clinicians using Adderall?

Dr Hunt: We performed a questionnaire survey of 13 physicians who have treated collectively nearly 1500 patients with Adderall. They reported that about 70% of their patients preferred Adderall. What was even more interesting is that 20 to 30% of patients report having a selective response to Adderall; it is the only stimulant medication that works for them.

I have had the opportunity to talk to over 300 physicians about their experience with Adderall through telesessions in which we discuss treatment of ADD. Those who have used Adderall report a very good response—and in some cases, find a selective response in about 20% of the cases.

Swanson, et al. (1998), studied 29 ADHD elementary school children, comparing their response to a single a.m. dose of Ritalin (the dose prescribed by their physician), a dose of Adderall (5, 10, 15 or 20 mg), or placebo. These children attended a special class for ADHD students in which they were rated every 1.5 hours up to 7.5 hours for attention and behavior. They also completed a math test every 1.5 hours up to 7.5 hours.

Results showed that:
1. At 1.5 and 3.0 hours, Adderall 10 to 20mg and Ritalin (about 20mg) were similar.
2. The behavioral effects of Ritalin ceased after 3 hours, the cognitive effects of Ritalin stopped after 4.5 hours.

Adderall

Adderall is often described by patients as being "smoother," longer acting, and more natural.

Adderall Effects

The cognitive effect from a single dose (10 to 20 mg) lasted 7.5 hours, the behavioral effect lasted 6 hours.

3. Adderall at higher doses lasted longer. The 20mg dose of Adderall improved behavior for 6 hours, the 10 to 20mg dose improved attention for 7.5 hours.
4. Higher doses of Adderall lasted longer.

This data suggests that a single 15 to 20mg dose of Adderall in the morning would improve attention throughout the entire school day. No in-school (lunch time) dose would be required. A second, smaller, 5 to 10mg dose could be given after school to aid behavior and homework.

Clinical Experience: Comparison of Adderall to Ritalin

We have treated over 600 patients with Adderall and several thousand with Ritalin. Compared to Ritalin, Adderall is smoother and longer-acting. Ritalin is more inhibiting. Although the inhibiting effects of Ritalin may benefit children who are very hyperactive and talkative, many patients

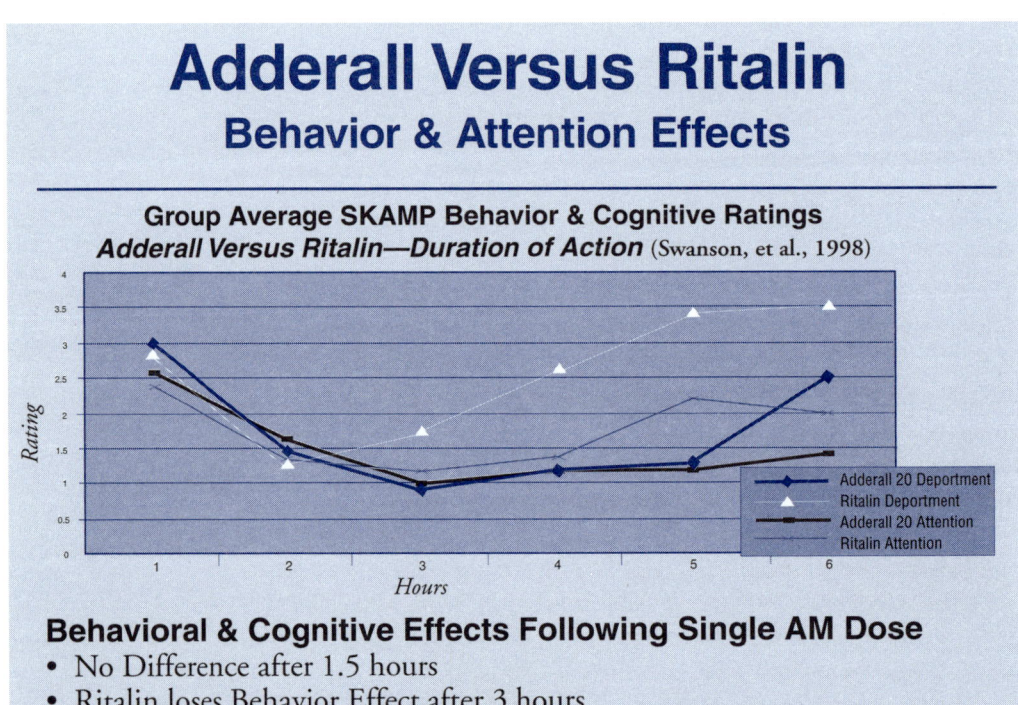

feel overly constricted on Ritalin. Because Ritalin is shorter-acting and more abrupt, it can produce a dysthymic irritability. Many patients on Adderall feel more natural and smoother and appreciate only needing to take medication twice daily.

Adderall has some of the advantages of the longer, smoother effects of Cylert, with less liver toxicity.

Adderall Withdrawal

Adderall has less withdrawal side effects.

Clinical Experience: Comparison of Adderall to Dexedrine

We have had about 80 patients on both Adderall and Dexedrine. Our clinical impression is that Dexedrine is more activating. That may have an advantage for adults with depression and ADHD. However, Dexedrine makes many patients anxious and nervous. We have seen less of this jitteriness on Adderall.

Recommendations for Use

We use Adderall as a first-line treatment for ADD. Generally, we suggest that patients try a controlled comparison of each of the major stimulants—Ritalin, Adderall, and Dexedrine, in therapeutic doses given in random sequence for a month each. We use behavior ratings and cognitive tests on SmartSoft-ADD to measure clinical effect.

Question: **What dose of Adderall is most common?**

Dr Hunt: Our common dose is 15 to 20 mg in the morning; 10 mg at two or three p.m. This usually gets students through school. We have little difficulty with insomnia at this dose.

For patients starting on Adderall who are not taking a stimulant, we begin at 5 mg in the morning, then increase it by 5 mg every third day, alternating morning and afternoon doses. For patients on a stimulant, we may shift abruptly to Adderall, or phase one medication down while increasing the Adderall. An advantage to Adderall is that it is scored in quarters, making it easy to titrate the dose. Many patients seem to reach and maintain a stable dose of Adderall more quickly.

Adderall Dosing

Begin with 5 mg in the morning and increase by 5 mg every third day.

Adderall Common Doses

Children: 15 to 30 mg/d
Adults: 20 to 50 mg/d, depending on tasks.

> **Adderall Twice Daily Dosing**
>
> *Most of our patients receive a higher dosage in the morning, and a second dose after school. No school-time dose.*

Stimulants in Adolescents and Adults

Stimulant medication is equally effective with children and adolescents with ADHD if they engaged in similar activities. Treatment providers should rigorously examine environmental causes to problems before prescribing higher doses of stimulants to adolescents with ADHD who exhibit a worsening in functioning.

Adult ADD

The validity of ADD in adults has been challenged in the media due to concern about outcome, criteria, and treatment response. However, the diagnosis of ADD meets the core criteria for a medical or psychiatric diagnosis:

- There are definable symptoms that constitute a valid cluster for identification.
- There is a predictable course to the disorder with identifiable patterns of outcome.
- There is a genetic pattern to the disorder evident in familial studies and now in molecular genetic studies.
- There exists a brain dysfunction that is identifiable.
- Treatment can be defined that has predictable effects.

These criteria are clearly met by ADD in childhood and continuing into adulthood. Spencer, et al. (1998), reviewed the empirical evidence to date regarding the validity of the diagnosis of ADHD in adults and its consistency with the childhood syndrome. Evidence of descriptive, divergent, predictive, and concurrent validity were examined.

The available literature provides evidence that adult ADHD can be reliably diagnosed, and that the diagnosis confers considerable power to forecast complications and treatment response. Studies of genetic transmission, specific treatment responses, and abnormalities in brain structure and function in affected individuals are also consistent with studies in childhood ADHD.

There is converging evidence that adult ADHD is a not-rare, valid clinical diagnosis. In addition, studies show that adult and child patients with ADHD may share a similar treatment-responsive, underlying neurobiological substrate.

Long-Term Effects of Amphetamine

Gillberg, et al., (1998), studied the effects of amphetamine on symptoms of ADHD over a longer period than had been reported in previous studies. Sixty-two children, aged 6 to 11 years, meeting DSM-III-R symptom criteria for ADHD, participated in a parallel-group design, randomized, double-blind, placebo-controlled study of amphetamine treatment. Some children with comorbid diagnoses were included. In the amphetamine group, children received active treatment for 15 months.

Amphetamine was clearly superior to placebo in reducing inattention, hyperactivity, and other disruptive behavior problems, and tended to lead to improved results on the WISC-R IQ Test. Treatment failure rate was considerably lower and time to treatment failure was longer in the amphetamine group. Adverse effects were few and relatively mild.

The results of this long-term, placebo-controlled study of the central stimulant amphetamine in the treatment of ADHD indicate that there are remaining positive effects of the drug 15 months after starting treatment.

ADHD Spectrum/Pharmacological Diversity

The need for alternative medications in the treatment of ADHD is evident by the diversity of patients who present with core symptoms of overactivity, inattention, and impulsivity, and by the limitations of response to the psychostimulants alone. There is virtually no psychiatric disorder in which there is a direct correspondence between diagnosis and treatment. Especially early in development, patients present with symptoms that are less clearly differentiated.

Within the spectrum of ADHD, important pharmacological distinctions may be guided by the relative preponderance of hyperactivity versus distractibility and the presence of comorbid diagnoses such as learning disabilities, depression, anxiety disorder, intermittent explosive disorder or suggestions of underlying disorganization or thought disorder. The patient's age may affect the distribution of these symptoms and the selection and dose of medication.

Young children with severe hyperactivity are often

Factors Affecting the Selection of Stimulant Medication Include:

1. *Age of patient.*
2. *Relative degree of inattention, hyperactivity or impulsivity.*
3. *Presence of symptoms such as depression, anxiety or obsessive-compulsive disorders.*

> **Young Children & Psychostimulants**
>
> *May have an unstable response to psychostimulants.*

> **Stimulants**
>
> *May reduce appetite and sleep, and can increase motor tics.*

> **Stimulants**
>
> *Usually decrease aggression, but can make explosive episodes more severe.*

extremely aroused and have brittle response to methylphenidate. Adolescents may respond better to antidepressants that pose less risk for abuse. Although prepubertal children with externalizing symptoms are rather rarely depressed or anxious, the coexistence of these symptoms may respond better to an antidepressant than a psychostimulant. Patients with Tourette's syndrome often present a complex clustering of symptoms in which distractibility and tics respond to stimulants like the opposite ends of a teeter totter. Similarly, some patterns of aggression, thought disorder, or hypomania may become activated during treatment with psychostimulants. Ritalin may not be the optimal medication for children at these developmental stages or with these comorbid disorders.

An additional need for alternative medications is presented by the pharmacokinetics and side effects of the psychostimulants themselves. The short duration of action of psychostimulants can produce a roller coaster-like effect. Several times per day, the ADHD child may swing from being out of control to being well controlled, even excessively inhibited. Insomnia limits the use of medication in the evenings, often resulting in a loss of control or even a rebound hyperactivity in which the child who was calm at school becomes frenetic at home in the evening. Appetite suppression limits the use of psychostimulants in some children who are thin and may lose weight.

The basal-brain activating effects of stimulants, evident by insomnia, anorexia, and a slight increase in pulse, can lead to a breakthrough or activation of severe aggression or thought disorder in some children. The combination of basal brain activation and cortical inhibition produces a state of heightened arousal coupled with increased cortical suppression, somewhat similar to placing a lid on a pressure cooker. Some ADHD children appear to be overinhibited, unspontaneous, and overcontrolled on the doses of psychostimulants needed to control their hyperactivity.

Chapter 8

Antidepressants

Antidepressants

Antidepressant medication can be helpful in ADD—used either alone or in combination with psychostimulants.

The main beneficial effects of antidepressants are on mood and affect regulation. Not only do antidepressants relieve depression, but they can improve frustration tolerance and decrease irritability and anxiety.

Among the antidepressants are the "tricyclic" antidepressants that have been available since the 1960's and the selective serotonergic reuptake inhibitors (SSRIs) that were introduced in the late 1980's. The tricyclics improve the disruptive behavior of ADD in addition to enhancing mood. The SSRIs generally have fewer side effects, and decrease obsessive-compulsive symptoms as well. The antidepressants are less effective than stimulants in increasing the attachment or "sticking" of attention.

These antidepressants also have a mood-elevating effect. Patients often experience an overall calming and organizing effect and are relieved of irritability and depression. They may experience an increase in cognitive organization secondary to increased ability to modulate their mood and frustration. The effects on selective and sustained attention appear somewhat less.

Clinical Effects: The most effective tricyclic antidepressants in improving the behavior of ADHD patients appear to be those whose predominant effect is on norepinephrine reuptake. The effectiveness of desmethylimipramine in ADHD has been demonstrated in two studies (Biederman, et al., 1988; Donnelly, et al., 1986).

Neurochemical Effects: Desipramine blocks the reuptake of norepinephrine leading to an increase of norepinephrine concentration in the synapse. Clinical improvement correlates with the decrease in norepinephrine turnover, evident by diminishing levels of urinary norepinephrine, 3 methoxy-4-hydroxy-phenylethylene glycol and vanillymandelic acid (VMA).

The main mechanism of effects of antidepressants is to block reuptake. Among the varied antidepressants, some have a preferential effect on norepinephrine (such as Norpramine),

---

Antidepressants in ADHD/ADD

Antidepressants improve mood and frustration tolerance, thereby enhancing task completion.

Antidepressants

Antidepressants vary in their mechanisms of action.

> **Desipramine (DMI)**
>
> *Desipramine, the most effective tricyclic in ADHD, alters norepinephrine.*

others on dopamine (Wellbutrin), and others on serotonin (SSRIs, for example, Prozac). This blockade leads to an increase in available neurotransmitters in the synapse.

Noradrenergic antidepressants such as desipramine achieve a similar effect by a slightly different mechanism.

The serotonergic antidepressants appear to have some preferential effect on disthymic mood and irritability (Hunt, in preparation). The serotonergic antidepressants relieve the disthymic mood, irritability, and anxiety that often plagues ADHD patients.

Antidepressants in ADD
Tricyclics in Children

Examples: Elavil, Tofranil, Norpramine, DMI

Action: Increase neurotransmitter by blocking reuptake

Duration: 6-24 hours

Side Effects: Dry mouth, constipation, cardiac side effects

Clinical Indications and Benefits:
- More effective for childhood ADD (70%) than depression
- ADD with depression or aggression, impulsive behavior
- Less direct attentional effect than stimulants

> **Tricyclic Antidepressants**
>
> *The tricyclic antidepressants are often helpful in reducing depression, anxiety, and hyperactivity in ADHD. They can improve frustration tolerance and increase problem solving and task performance.*

Tricyclic Antidepressants

The recognition in the 1970's that imipramine was effective in the treatment of attention deficit disorder with hyperactivity raised fundamental questions about medication and diagnostic specificity. While phenomenological diagnosis became more empirically precise through greater definition of symptomatology, pharmacological treatment suggested that a few basic neurophysiological symptoms must underline a broad spectrum of disorders. The recent addition of serotonergic antidepressants and clonidine to the possible repertory of psychopharmacological treatment of ADHD provides an opportunity for a better understanding of how different facets of ADHD may be medicated by intersecting brain mechanisms. As evident by this book, much has been learned about the effectiveness of methylphenidate for various components of attention, activity, aggression, and socialization in ADHD. The link between psychopharmacological response and neurochemical actions is informing our understanding of basic brain mechanisms in ADHD.

Antidepressant Drug Therapy and ADHD

Introduction:

Recent studies have evaluated the use of antidepressant drug therapy in the treatment of ADHD, in the search for an effective and safe alternative to stimulant drugs. Possible advantages of antidepressants over stimulants include:
1. A longer duration of action, due to once-daily dosing without symptoms of rebound or insomnia.
2. Greater flexibility in dosage.
3. The readily-available option of monitoring plasma drug levels.
4. Minimal risk of abuse or dependence (Biederman, et al., 1989).

Medications studied in the recent literature include imipramine, desipramine, nortriptyline, bupropion, and monoamine oxidase inhibitors. Of these antidepressants, desipramine may be the most effective.

Tricyclic antidepressants have been used in ADHD since initial studies by Rapoport and Quinn, 1974, documented their usefulness. More recent studies have focused on the desmethylated metabolite, desipramine, that appears to have fewer side effects. The behavioral effects may be more pronounced than the cognitive effects, although this may reflect the limitations in the type of cognitive tasks employed (Swanson, 1985). The most effective tricyclic antidepressants for ADHD may be those that affect the noradrenergic system. Antidepressants have a longer duration of action than Ritalin, and may concurrently improve mood. However, they require monitoring of blood level and ECGs for cardiovascular safety.

Imipramine Hydrochloride (Tofranil)

Mechanism of action: Presumed to block the reuptake of norepinephrine at nerve endings, causing potentiation of adrenergic synapses. It may enhance the dopaminergic system as well.

Usual dose: 1-3 mg/kg per day with maximum of 5 mg/kg per day. (A maximum of 2.5 mg/kg should not be exceeded in childhood without careful monitoring of blood levels.)

Benefits: Imipramine has been used primarily in the treatment of depression and childhood enuresis. Its use with ADHD has been predominantly with those who responded poorly to stimulant medications, and who often manifest mood lability. It has been somewhat effective in treating aggression. When effective, it often prevents the roller coaster effect which is common with the stimulant medications. There is some concern, however, that the drowsiness often produced may impair cognitive functioning within the academic environment.

Side effects: Drowsiness, dry mouth, blurred vision, slowed intracardiac conduction, tics.

Warning: Extreme caution should be exercised when using this medication with any patient with cardiovascular disease (*Physicans Desk Reference, 1999*).

Children are sometimes more sensitive to an acute overdose than are adults. A baseline EKG and periodic monitoring may be appropriate, especially for young children who are near the maximum daily dose.

Research studies: Imipramine, a long-acting antidepressant, was recognized to be an effective treatment for ADHD in the mid 1970's. Several controlled studies found it to improve symptoms of hyperactivity, but reservations remain in suggesting it for wide spread use due to the high frequency of side effects.

Many studies were conducted in the 1970's on imipramine, including studies by Huessy and Wright (1970), Gross (1973), Gittleman-Klein (1974), and Greenberg, et

---

Imipramine Compared to Stimulants

Both imipramine (Tofranil) and stimulants (Ritalin, etc.) improve impulsivity and hyperactivity. Stimulants have greater attentional effect. Antidepressants are more calming.

al. (1975). Early studies also included a comparison of amitriptyline and methylphenidate and found both to be effective (Yepes, et al., 1977).

A study by Rapoport and Quinn (1974) compared imipramine, methylphenidate, and placebo in 76 hyperactive boys. Both medications were found to be superior to placebo.

Method: The subjects were 76 middle-class boys, ages 6 to 12 (x=9), all of whom had been symptomatic for two or more years, had an IQ of 80 or above (x=98), and had no known neurological disorder. They were administered imipramine (maximum dose=150 mg; x=80), methylphenidate (maximum dose=30 mg; x=20), and placebo twice a day in a double-blind, noncrossover design.

Conners' Parents Symptom Questionnaire (CPSQ) and Conners' Teachers Ratings Scales (CTRS) were completed at baseline and at six weeks. Parents also completed four-day diaries recording hourly activities and behaviors at home. The Wechsler Intelligence Scale for Children and Kagen Matching Familiar Figures tests were administered before and after treatment. Physicians' global ratings of improvement (National Institute of Mental Health) were made at baseline, and after three and six weeks.

Results: Parents reported significant improvement in symptoms of impulsivity and hyperactivity (p<0.01) on the Conners' Parents Symptom Questionnaire and significant improvements in activity (p<0.01) and negative interactions (p<0.01) from their four-day diaries. Teacher rating scales showed improvement in classroom hyperactivity (p<0.05), but no significant change in conduct or inattentiveness. Physicians' global ratings after six weeks demonstrated methylphenidate was clearly better than placebo (p< 0.001) and slightly better than imipramine (p<0.02).

Side effects were more pronounced with imipramine than with methylphenidate. They included decreased appetite, sedation, and increase in diastolic blood pressure. The increase in blood pressure necessitated the withdrawal of three children from imipramine. No cardiological or liver function abnormalities were noted.

While both medications were rated superior to placebo by all examiners, methylphenidate was clearly favored over

Response to Medication

This was measured by rating scales and diaries at home and at school.

On Imipramine

Activity and social functioning improved at home. Hyperactivity was reduced at school, but attention did not improve.

> **Clinical Results: Imipramine Versus Ritalin**
>
> *One year later, both medications decreased hyperactivity and distractibility and improved classroom behavior in those students who continued treatment.*

imipramine. The authors suggest that this was possibly due to the relatively low dose of imipramine used in this study.

One Year Follow-up: Quinn and Rapport (1975) then compared baseline and outcome measures in a one-year prospective follow-up study of the same 76 hyperactive boys.

At the end of the initial six-week drug trial, the placebo group was randomly assigned to one of the treatment groups and another six-week trial was performed. Drug therapy was then continued for a year. The mean daily dose of methylphenidate was 20.65 mg +/- 8.56, and the mean daily dose of imipramine was 65.4 mg +/- 19.2.

Method: On re-evaluation at one year, the patients were divided into three groups: (1) those continuously receiving methylphenidate (n=23); (2) subjects continuously receiving imipramine (n=13); and (3) subjects who discontinued medication after less than four months of treatment (n=12). Conners' Parents Symptom Questionnaire and Conners' Teachers Ratings Scales were completed along with Wechsler Intelligence Scale for Children and global clinical ratings.

Baseline measures of hyperactivity and behavior ratings were not different among the three groups. After one year of treatment, Conners' Parents Symptom Questionnaire ratings did not differ significantly among the three groups.

Results: Parents reported an **overall decrease** in hyperactive and distractible behavior as compared to baseline in all three groups. Teachers' ratings documented significant improvement in both treatment groups in their classroom behavior ($p<0.05$ and $p<0.02$ for methylphenidate versus placebo and imipramine vs. placebo, respectively), while those who discontinued treatment exhibited no improvement. Those who responded well to methylphenidate and those who responded well to imipramine did not differ in any measure at one-year follow-up.

This study found that those who maintained treatment demonstrated similar and significant improvements in their classroom behavior ratings at the end of one year, regardless of whether the drug was methylphenidate or imipramine. It is notable, however, that while there was improved behavior over baseline, classroom ratings of the two groups were still

ADHD in the Classroom, Effects of Imipramine

In a study by Waizer, et al. (1974) involving 19 hyperactive boys with serious classroom behavioral problems, imipramine therapy was found to be effective in improving hyperactivity as well as defiance, inattentiveness, and sociability.

The subjects ranged in age from 6 to 12 years (x=9.2). All scored 1.5 or higher on the hyperactivity factor of the Conners' Teachers Rating Scale and had received a diagnosis of "hyperkinetic reaction of childhood" according to DSM-II.

Following a one-week, drug-free period, subjects completed eight weeks of imipramine treatment and four weeks of placebo treatment. Imipramine dosage was 100 to 200 mg a day (x=173.7 mg). Subjects were rated at baseline and thereafter by child psychiatrists, parents, and teachers. Psychiatrist ratings were based on direct observation as well as data obtained from parents and teachers. Parents completed a 27-item hyperactivity list in addition to the Conners' Parents Symptom Questionnaire. Teachers completed the Conners' Teachers Ratings Scale.

Results: On comparing imipramine at eight weeks versus baseline, child psychiatrist ratings demonstrated significant improvement ($p<0.01$). Parents reported significant decrease in hyperactivity at home following imipramine treatment ($p<0.01$). These scores remained improved over baseline even after placebo treatment ($p<0.01$). Comparison of imipramine versus placebo on CPSQ factors revealed no significant differences. Conners' Teachers Rating Scale showed there to be significantly improved scores in the areas of hyperactivity ($p<0.05$), defiance ($p<0.05$), sociability ($p<0.05$), and inattentiveness ($p<0.01$) after imipramine therapy. Following placebo treatment, hyperactivity, defiance, and sociability scores returned to baseline, while inattentiveness remained significantly below baseline level ($p<0.01$).

The most prominent side effect produced by imipramine

Imipramine Effectiveness

Imipramine improved activity, attention, and social behavior at home and school in those who continued treatment.

Imipramine Side Effects

Imipramine decreased weight and produced mild insomnia and drowsiness.

> **Imipramine Effectiveness**
>
> *Imipramine may be less effective in ADHD patients who do not respond to Ritalin.*

therapy was weight loss (seen in 78% of the subjects). The average amount lost over the eight weeks was 0.9 kg. Recovery was quickly achieved on placebo, with an average increase of 1.3 kg in four weeks. Other symptoms noted in the group included mild anorexia, insomnia, and mild drowsiness.

Classroom: Imipramine therapy proved to be effective in improving overall classroom behavior in this population of hyperkinetic children. Although this change deteriorated during placebo treatment, there is some evidence of sustained improvement over baseline, possibly attributable to the long-acting property of imipramine.

Imipramine in Ritalin Non-Responders

In a study of ADHD children known to be unresponsive to methylphenidate, imipramine was also ineffective in improving behavior (Winsberg, 1980).

Ten children were administered imipramine and placebo on a double-blind, crossover basis. Treatment lasted for five weeks in each condition, with the average daily dose of imipramine being 3.7 mg/kg. Response measures included Conners' Behavioral Rating Scales and the Continuous Performance Task. No benefits were observed from imipramine therapy.

While it is frequently hoped that children who do not respond to stimulants will respond to imipramine or another tricyclic, this study suggests that patients may cluster more as global responders or as non-responders to both medications.

Summary of Imipramine

Most studies suggest that both psychostimulants and imipramine are more effective than placebo. Generally, a slight therapeutic advantage has been attributed to the psychostimulants, and they generally remain the medication of first choice. *Behavioral* response to imipramine is nearly equivalent to that seen with stimulant use, but *cognitive* attentional improvement is less robust. One advantage of imipramine is that it is long-acting and therefore does not have to be given at school. Imipramine may be helpful in those ADHD patients with concurrent mood disturbance.

> **Imipramine Compared to Stimulants**
>
> *Similar behavioral effect, improved mood and frustration tolerance, and less attentional improvement.*

Cardiac side effects must be monitored and may constitute an important limitation in the use of imipramine.

Desipramine Hydrochloride (Norpramine)

Mechanism of Action: Desipramine (DMI) is presumed to restore normal levels of neurotransmitters norepinephrine and serotonin through blocking their reuptake in the central nervous system. It is the most noradrenergic of they tricyclics.

Norpramine's rate of metabolism by the liver varies greatly from individual to individual and therefore may need special attention in management. Like imipramine, discontinue action should be done gradually over a 10 to 15 day period.

Tricyclic antidepressants act substantially by enhancing functional availability of catecholamines and indoleamines by blocking presynaptic uptake. Antidepressants vary significantly in their relative effect on norepinephrine, dopamine, serotonin, and other neurotransmitters. Desipramine is the tricyclic antidepressant with the most selective effects on norepinephrine reuptake and activity at alpha-1 adrenergic receptors. Desipramine has relatively low affinity at muscarinic and histaminergic receptors and only moderate affinity at alpha-1 adrenergic receptors; it is a very weak agonist of alpha-2, beta adrenergic, and dopaminergic receptors.

Usual Adult Dose: 100-200 mg per day.

Primary benefits: Norpramine is used primarily in the treatment of depression. Early studies indicated excellent benefits for adolescents and adults with ADHD.

Side effects: Same as imipramine: drowsiness, dry mouth, rash, dizziness, cardiac conduction.

Desipramine is associated with lesser risks of adverse effects than amitriptyline, clomipramine, doxepin, and imipramine (Biederman, et al., 1989). However, cardiac toxicity can be most severe. Six patients have died from desipramine—in part taken during exertion, dehydration, at high dose, or in association with prior cardiac problems.

However, its use has declined due to the "sudden death" of three children who were being treated with this medication. Clinical studies of these accounts suggested that one

Desipramine (DMI)

Desipramine is the most noradrenergic of the tricyclics and the most effective for ADHD.

Rare Side Effects of Desipramine

Desipramine has been associated with rare cardiac fatalities and requires monitoring.

child had a family history of sudden cardiac arrest, and another child died while running laps at school. This child's mother died of congestive heart failure after his birth. The third child was an eight-year-old male (18 kg) who had an "acute collapse" and "sudden death" after having been treated with Norpramine for approximately two years. Therefore, it is not recommended for use with young children, and ECG should be monitored.

Several recent studies have focused on desipramine, the desmethyl metabolite of imipramine that has more specific effect as a noradrenergic presynaptic uptake blocker, and is often less sedating than imipramine (Garfinkel, et al., 1983; Gastfriend, et al., 1984).

Desipramine Compared to Placebo— Clinical and Neurochemical Response

In a study of 29 ADHD boys, desipramine was found to be more effective than placebo in improving behavior (Donnelly, et al., 1986).

Desipramine was administered to 29 males, mean age 8.8 +/- 1.5 yrs. All patients scored two standard deviations above normal on Factor IV of the Conners' Teachers Ratings Scale (39-item) for ADHD and met DSM-III criteria for ADHD in two settings. Eight boys had coexistent conduct disorder, two had oppositional disorder, and seven had developmental disorder. Nineteen had no prior treatment with psychostimulants; ten had been previously treated. All were medication-free for 14 days prior to the study.

Treatment was administered on a double-blind non-crossover basis: 17 subjects received desipramine; 12 were treated with placebo. The dose was increased by 25 mg per day to 100 mg every a.m. The mean final dose equaled 3.38 +/- 0.78 mg/kg. Desipramine blood levels obtained at day 3 were 21.9 +/- 14.6, and on day 14 were 92.3 +/- 61.6 mg/ml. Patients were evaluated in a day hospital with assessments at days 3 and 14.

Baseline assessments included the Diagnostic Inventory for Classification Assessment and PANNESS, a Wechsler Intelligence Scale for Children—Revised, Peabody Individual Achievement Test, the Bender Gestalt Test, and projective tests. Response measures included the Conners'

Desipramine Versus Placebo

Desipramine was compared to placebo in elementary ADHD children using behavior ratings and an additional task.

Although hyperactivity improved rapidly, attention did not increase significantly.

Desipramine acts by decreasing norepinephrine.

Abbreviated Behavioral Rating Scale performed daily; the Continuous Performance Task was performed at baseline and days 3 and 14. Cognitive tasks included a revised version of the Rosveld Continuous Performance Task using a specific two-letter sequence (A-X) and the Buschke Prompted Recall Serial Learning Procedure. Motor activity was monitored using a truncal motor accelerometer. Patients were placed on a low monamine diet for three days prior to collections of plasma desipramine, and urinary catecholamine and metabolites were measured at days 3 and 14.

Results: Behavioral hyperactivity was significantly improved on days 3 and 14 ($p=0.003$) during treatment with desipramine, while placebo produced no behavioral change. However, there was no facilitation on the cognitive tasks. There was no correlation between medication level and behavioral response. Neurochemical changes constituted an important correlate of behavioral change. On the 3rd and 14th treatment day, urinary 3 methoxy-4-hydroxy-phenylethylene glycol and norepinephrine all decreased in the responsive patients. Standing plasma norepinephrine and 3 methoxy-4-hydroxy-phenylethylene glycol also decreased during treatment.

Side effects showed no significant change in Survey for Treatment Emergent Side Effects; however, desipramine prompted an increase in heart rate and an increase in diastolic blood pressure. Desipramine elicited behavioral, but not cognitive, improvement in ADHD.

In this study, behavioral change occurred by the third day, more quickly than the usual affective response to antidepressants. A therapeutic blood level appeared essential to clinical improvement. In this small group, treatment response factored with change in norepinephrine metabolism, but did not correlate with blood level of medication.

Desipramine in ADHD Boys

Treatment of children with ADHD using desipramine has been evaluated in several studies by Biederman, et al. (1986, 1988, 1989). The effectiveness of desipramine was compared to placebo in a group of ADHD males (Biederman, et al., 1989).

The 62 subjects were ages 6 to 17 years, with about two

> **Behavior Patterns**
>
> *Patients behavior improved in symptoms of ADHD at home and school.*

> **Desipramine Side Effects**
>
> *Heart rate and blood pressure increased, but did not correlate with the plasma level of the medication.*

thirds prepubertal and one third adolescent. Patients came from the 3.1-3.2 SES; 43 (69%) had previously responded poorly to psychostimulant treatment. All but two patients met DSM-III criteria for ADHD in two settings (home, school, clinic) and scored > 15 on the Conners' Abbreviated Questionnaire by parents and teachers. The clinical diagnosis was confirmed using the DICA-P. Some patients had other diagnoses, including learning disabilities (n=48), conduct disorder (n=24), and oppositional disorder (n=32).

Treatment: The treatment group (n=31) received desipramine which was gradually increased over the course of six weeks to a mean dose of 4.7 mg/kg, producing a final mean serum level=156 mg/ml. Another group (n=31) was randomized to treatment with placebo using a double-blind, parallel group design. Response in an outpatient setting was measured using the Conners' Abbreviated Parent and Teacher's Questionnaire, Clinical Global Impression Scale (physician), and the Children's Depression Inventory (patient and mother). Cognitive assessment was performed using the Continuous Performance Task and the Paired Associate Learning Task.

Results: The results of this study showed an overall response rate of 68% (desipramine daily dose 4.6 mg/kg), over a 10% response rate of the placebo control group. Of those treated with desipramine, 68% were "much" or "very much" improved, while only 10% of the placebo group improved (p=0.001). However, on the cognitive tests, there was no significant change. Mood showed a nonsignificant trend towards improvement in depression ratings (p=0.05), even though these subjects were not initially clinically depressed.

Side effects: Dry mouth (32%); decreased appetite or headaches (29%); abdominal discomfort or tiredness (26%); dizziness or insomnia (26%).

This study produced several significant findings: desipramine was clearly more effective than placebo in the treatment of ADHD; the behavioral improvement appeared more prominent than the cognitive effects; side effects were primarily anticholinergic and generally well tolerated.

The cardiovascular side effects of desipramine were examined in a separate report from the same study in which

Effects of Desipramine

The effects of desipramine given to a large number of boys was measured at home and school for input on mood behavior and cognition.

Behavior significantly improved in two-thirds, and mood was slightly improved. Attention did not change.

31 desipramine-treated subjects were compared to 27 placebo-unresponsive subjects.

In this active treatment group, the mean desipramine dose was 4.6 +/- 0.2 mg/kg. The blood levels showed considerable variability (mean=227.0 +/- 27 mg/ml; median 152). Higher serum levels were noted in the older subjects (adolescents) who also exhibited greater improvement. The cardiovascular side effects consisted of a clinically unimportant, but statistically significant, increase in diastolic blood pressure, heart rate, and EKG conduction. Desipramine-treated patients showed higher incidence of sinus tachycardia and intraventricular conduction defects consisting of the right bundle branch block.

Treatment with doses of 3-5 mg/kg may be necessary in some cases of childhood ADHD, and careful monitoring of serum drug levels and EKG should be used in pediatric populations. Since cardiac side effects from antidepressants do not correlate closely with blood level, EKG monitoring is necessary to identify emergent intraventricular conduction defects.

Desipramine in ADHD with Associated Tics

Several clinical problems present special cases for use of antidepressants, for example, children with concurrent tics and ADHD. The effect of desipramine treatment in ADHD associated with tics was studied in seven boys (Riddle, et al., 1988).

Seven boys, aged 7-11 yrs, who met DSM-IIIR criteria for ADHD and also had Tourette's syndrome or chronic multiple tics (possibly exacerbated by stimulants), were treated with desipramine. Four had been previously treated with methylphenidate, three had not.

Desipramine was gradually increased to 50 to 100 mg/d as an open trial, and patients were followed for 6 to 52 weeks in either in- or out-patient settings. Response measures included the Conners' Parent and Teachers Questionnaires. Inpatients were assessed using the Yale Clinical Inventory to monitor activity, impulsivity, conduct, socialization, and aggression. Physicians completed the Clinical Global Impression on all patients.

Results: A beneficial treatment response was noted

> **Desipramine Tics**
>
> *Two studies have shown that desipramine decreases tics in ADHD patients. In this study, 70% improved globally. Tics did not change.*

in 71%, who were rated as moderately or markedly improved on the CGI.

The main side effects included tachycardia which developed in four patients. One patient experienced an increase in diastolic blood pressure; one had increased sedation. **None of the patients had an increase in tics.**

Although this study is limited by being small and uncontrolled, the authors note that desipramine appears to be safe and effective in children with ADHD associated with tics. While the results of the desipramine study were similar to prior studies with imipramine, desipramine's precursor, there was a significant decrease of adverse effects due to the greater selectivity of desipramine.

Summary of Desipramine

Desipramine appears to be effective in treating ADHD. Because of its more specific action on norepinephrine, it may have some advantage over other neurotransmitters in treatment of highly active children—however, direct comparative studies between antidepressants have not been performed. Most studies have been relatively brief, and the long-term effectiveness requires further confirmation. The lack of change on cognitive tests suggests that desipramine's effects may not occur at the level of these concrete tasks—but desipramine may improve task performance by modulating affect and frustration. Multimodal studies that monitor the effect on classroom grades and learning would be helpful.

These studies suggest that desipramine is a reasonable alternative in cases where psychostimulants have failed, or when ADHD is associated with depression or anxiety, or when associated with tics.

Nortriptyline (Pamelor/Aventyl)

Nortriptyline is a potent, activating antidepressant, thought to inhibit the activity of serotonin and acetylcholine, and increasing the pressor effect of norepinephrine.

Nortriptyline has been studied in 60 ADHD adolescents and found to have positive effects (Saul, 1985).

Sixty patients with ADD ranging from 9 to 20 years of age were treated with nortriptyline. Children who rated more

> **Nortriptyline**
>
> *Nortriptyline has broad neurochemical effects on serotonin, acetylcholine, and norepinephrine.*

than 9 points on a scale of 0 to 54 on the Kovacs Children's Depression Inventory prior to treatment were started on nortriptyline. Patients who scored less than 9 were placed on psychostimulants initially. Stimulant-treated patients who responded poorly or had substantial side effects were switched to nortriptyline. Dosage was begun at 10 mg at night for two weeks, followed by 25 mg twice a day for two weeks.

Results: 54 of the 60 patients improved in symptoms of attention deficit as shown by home and school evaluation forms. Teacher reports documented improvement in attitude, increase in attention span, and most significantly, a decrease in impulsivity.

Clomipramine Hydrochloride (Anafranil)

Anafranil is a tricyclic antidepressant that is used primarily to treat obsessive-compulsive disorder. There is considerable comorbidity among ADHD, addictive illnesses, and obsessive-compulsive disorder. Therefore, this medication may play a role in overall treatment when the patient is displaying obsessive-compulsive behaviors which are interfering with his social, academic, or occupational functioning.

Mechanism of Action: Presumed to affect the serotonergic system through inhibiting reuptake.

Dosage: Anafranil is available in dosages of 25, 50, and 75 mg for oral administration. The initial treatment dose is 25 mg daily and is gradually increased, as tolerated, during the first two weeks to a maximum of 3mg/kg or 100 mg, whichever is smaller, for children and adolescents. Adults may be increased to a maximum of 250 mg daily.

Contraindicators: Anafranil should not be given in combination with monoamine oxidase inhibitors or other antidepressants within 14 days before or after their use. Nor should it be given to patients with a history of hypersensitivity to other tricyclic antidepressants. It is also contraindicated during acute recovery after a myocardial infarction.

Summary of Tricyclic Antidepressants

The tricyclic antidepressants have well-established effectiveness in ADHD, but do not yet have definitive indications. They may be most useful in ADHD patients with

---

Major Use of Clomipramine

Although it is a tricyclic antidepressant, the major use of clomipramine is in obsessive-compulsive disorders. It acts by increasing sertonin availabilty.

concurrent depression or anxiety (Pliszka, 1987).

Antidepressants are frequently utilized in adolescents to minimize the exposure to psychostimulants that may have potential for abuse. It is not clear that their effect on cognition is as potent as their effect on behavior. They may affect cognition indirectly through modulating excessive affective-arousal.

Desipramine has become the tricyclic antidepressant of choice in many patients due to its lower sedative and side-effect profile. Its noradrenergic effects suggest a role for this neurotransmitter system in some components of ADHD. Careful monitoring of cardiovascular response is needed above doses of 3 mg/kg.

Monoamine Oxidase Inhibitors

> **Monoamine Oxidase Inhibitors**
>
> *Monoamine oxidase inhibitors may be helpful in severe ADHD patients, but are limited due to side effects. Severe headaches may occur if taken with cheese, beer, or chocolate.*

In one study comparing two forms of monoamine oxidase inhibitors to d-amphetamine and placebo in 14 prepubertal children, clorgyline and tranylcypromine appeared clinically effective (Zametkin, et al., 1985; Rapoport, et al., 1986).

Subjects of this study consisted of 14 boys (x=9.2 yrs) with severe, persistent hyperactivity as determined by referring teachers' Conners' scales (mean item scores: 1.53 +/- 0.59 for factor I/conduct problem and 2.54 +/- 0.60 for factor IV/hyperactivity). Each was treated with clorgyline (12.5 mg/d) or tranylcypromine (10 mg/d) and amphetamine (13.2 mg/d). All forms of the active medication were administered for four weeks each, using a double-blind crossover design, separated by a two-week placebo washout. Parent and Teachers' Questionnaires were used to monitor response weekly, and a modified Continuous Performance Task was given during placebo week 2 and treatment week 4.

Results: Teacher ratings demonstrated immediate clinical improvement from all medications, but not from placebo. Staff could not distinguish effects of the two monoamine oxides inhibitors from each other or from d-amphetamine. Parent ratings (Conners' Questionnaire) were less positive. Improvement on the Continuous Performance Test occurred.

Both monoamine oxidase inhibitors appeared to be as efficacious as d-amphetamine and were safe when dietary and multi-drug restrictions were followed. The main side effect from monoamine oxidase inhibitors was mild sedation that persisted into the third or fourth week.

Summary of Monoamine Oxidase Inhibitors

Monoamine oxidase inhibitors appear to be clinically effective in this sole, small study of ADHD. Given the risks inherent in dietary control, these medications should be used with extreme caution in impulsive children. Under well-controlled conditions, they may have value in otherwise refractory patients. The multineurotransmitter mechanisms of action of monoamine oxidase inhibitors suggest that combined neurotransmitters are needed for clinical effect.

New Antidepressants

Bupropion (Wellbutrin)

Bupropion is a recently approved antidepressant. It is a weak blocker of neuronal uptake of serotonin and norepinephrine, and possibly is a weak dopamine agonist. Data from animal studies indicate that bupropion is not associated with the alteration of central nervous system receptors often implicated in the action of other antidepressant drugs. In two published studies, bupropion appears promising for some symptoms of ADHD.

> **Wellbutrin**
>
> *Wellbutrin is a highly energizing antidepressant that greatly improves motivation. It has some improvement of attention.*

Bupropion Study

In an outpatient study of 30 prepubertal children, a modest beneficial response was noted by clinicians and teachers (Casat, et al., 1989).

Outpatient children were selected who met DSM-III criteria for ADHD with parent and teacher ratings > 1.5 on the Conners' Questionnaire for Impulsivity-Hyperactivity or Restlessness Immaturity and on the teacher's ratings of the hyperactivity factor. Twenty-six had never been previously treated with stimulants; four had prior treatment with methylphenidate. All were randomized to treatment with placebo or bupropion. The dose schedule was gradually increased to 6 mg/kg/d over the course of a month. Blood levels of bupropion ranged from 2.1 - 212.1, mean = 37.9 mg/ml.

Behavior was rated using the Conners' Parent and

> **Wellbutrin Study**
>
> *In prepubescent children, Wellbutrin improved overall merit ratings and classroom hyperactivity, but not behavior at home. Cognitive functioning did improve.*

Teacher Questionnaire. Physician ratings included the Brief Psychiatric Rating Scale and the Clinicians' Global Improvement. Cognitive testing performed at baseline and on day 28 included the STMI and the Continuous Performance Test.

Results: Response on the Clinical Global Impression was considered positive for 18/20 as rated by clinicians. There was significant reduction of classroom hyperactivity as reported by teachers (p=0.016), but no difference was noted between active drug and placebo groups on Conners' Parent Questionnaire hyperactivity ratings nor on Conners' Parent Questionnaire and Conners' Teacher Questionnaire conduct ratings. Parents noted no behavioral change from bupropion, and no improvement was detected in measures of cognitive performance.

The main side effects consisted of a skin rash and periodic edema that occurred in only one child.

In this short-term placebo comparison of bupropion in 30 prepubertal ADHD children, clinicians rated a significant improvement, while teachers showed only a modest positive trend. Cognitive testing demonstrated no improvement. Bupropion appears to be safe, but not very effective. It may reduce hyperactivity in the classroom but have less effect at home.

Study of Bupropion on Preadolescent Males

A second study of bupropion assessed effectiveness in 17 preadolescent males, and reported significant behavioral improvement in 12 patients (Simeon, et al., 1986).

Subjects were 7 to 13 years old (x=10.4), 14 of whom met Diagnostic Statistical Manual-III criteria for ADHD. Eight also had comorbid diagnosis of compulsive disorder; two had coexistent overanxious disorder. Three subjects had compulsive disorder unassociated with ADHD. Six had been previously treated with psychostimulants.

After one week of being drug-free, patients were treated for 14 weeks—consisting of a baseline placebo period (4 weeks), bupropion therapy (eight weeks), and post-drug placebo (two weeks)—in a single-blind uncontrolled design. Bupropion was given for 8 weeks in an escalating dose,

Wellbutrin

Improved hyperactivity, depression, and aggression, but not cognition.

resulting in 50 mg twice a day by the third week.

Behavioral measures included the Conners' Parents and Teacher Questionnaires; physicians completed the Clinical Global Impression; children completed the Beitchman Children's Self-Report Scale. A sleep questionnaire was utilized and cognitive testing was performed.

Results: Behavioral hyperactivity was significantly improved ($p<0.001$). A positive bupropion response was noted to be marked in five subjects and moderate in seven. Patients reported some improvement in symptoms of neurotic anxiety and depression ($p<0.03$). Aggression also improved with a decrease in hostile, uncooperative behavior ($p<0.03$). No significant improvement in performance of cognitive tasks occurred when practice effects were considered. After the bupropion was discontinued, behavioral deterioration occurred within two weeks ($p<0.03$).

The major side effects were mild nausea, stomach discomfort, increased appetite, and nausea and vomiting.

Although this was an uncontrolled trial, the results suggest that bupropion may be effective and safe for treatment of hyperactivity, especially if associated with conduct disorder.

Medication Management
Wellbutrin (Bupropion) for children

Indications: *(not all FDA approved)*
- Depression, Oppositional Aggression
- Low Energy, Poor Motivation, Smoking

Benefits: Increased energy, calmer, some increase in attention (especially in teens)

Dosing:(SR) AM HS Total
- Children: 100-150 mg 0-150 mg = 100-300 mg/d
- Adults: 150-300 mg 0-150 mg = 150-450 mg/d
- Increase: Begin 100 mg in AM; increase by 100 mg q. 3rd day

Side Effects: headaches, sedation, irritability

Recommendations: slow increase

Summary of Bupropion

Collectively, these two studies of bupropion are inconclusive. In the larger but better controlled study, less consistent clinical improvement was noted. In the smaller, less controlled study, there was a more significant effect, with the suggestion that bupropion may have concurrent anti-aggressive and antidepressant effects.

Selective Serotonergic Reuptake Inhibitors Antidepressants (SSRIs)

> **SSRIs**
>
> *Several SSRIs exist that reduce depression, anxiety, and obsessiveness. They may reduce these symptoms in ADHD/ADD patients.*

These antidepressants have potential for treatment of ADHD, but their effectiveness and specific indications are not yet defined. Monoamine oxidase inhibitors appeared effective in a small study, but have potential side effects that limit their utility. Bupropion has a modest effect that may prove significant in a well-characterized ADHD subgroup.

These newer antidepressants act primarily by blocking reuptake of serotonin, thereby increasing the concentration of this neurotransmitter in the synapse.

Medications in this category include:
- Prozac (fluoxetine)
- Paxil (paroxetine)
- Zoloft (sertraline)
- Luvox (fluvoxamine)
- Celexa (citalopram)
- Effexor (vanlafaxine) shares serotonergic effect, but also alters norepinephrine.

Rameron (mirtazapine) combines the effect of increasing serotonin and norepinephrine while decreasing histamine (H1).

All of these medications have a spectrum of clinical effects that reduce irritability and depression, generally improve energy, and decrease anxiety and obsessiveness. These meditations have a role in treating many of the frequent comorbidities associated with ADHD and with substance abuse, including depression, agitation, and anxiety. Ruminative worry and obsessional thinking also respond to most of these medications.

Medication Management
Effexor (Venlafaxine) for children

Indications: *(not all FDA approved)*
- Depression, Oppositional Aggression
- Obsessive-Compulsive, Anxiety

Benefits: Calmer, pro-social, enhanced mood

Dosing: (SR)

	AM	HS	Total
Children:	37.5-180 mg	37.5-150mg	= 75-300 mg/d
Adults:	75-225 mg	75-225mg	= 150-450 mg/d

- Increase: Begin 37.5 mg in HS; increase by 37.5 mg q. 3rd day

Side Effects: headaches, sedation, irritability

Recommendations: slow increase

Our clinical experience has included over 100 patients treated with Prozac, Paxil, Zoloft, Effexor and 50 patients with Celexa. We are currently performing a placebo-controlled cross-over comparison of several SSRI's utilized in combination with Adderall.

No single medication emerges as categorically superior. These medications are more similar than different. However, Paxil has developed the clinical reputation of being preferentially effective in anxiety disorders; Zoloft as being very well tolerated and less sedating; Effexor and Luvox as having an antiaggressive profile. Medications differ in their extent of chemical effects on metabolic enzymes, with implications for differences in drug interactions with other meditations that share the same metabolic pathway. However, it is not clear how clinically relevant these chemical differences are in actual clinical practice. Several hypotheses have been advanced, suggestive of future studies. Zoloft is the most dopaminergic, and may have some selective benefit on attention. Paxil may have more effect on anxiety and obsessiveness. Effexor's noradrenergic effect may preferentially reduce hyperactivity and attendant aggression.

SSRI Antidepressants

Difference between various SSRIs are still being defined in children. Clinical experience suggests some possible distinctions.

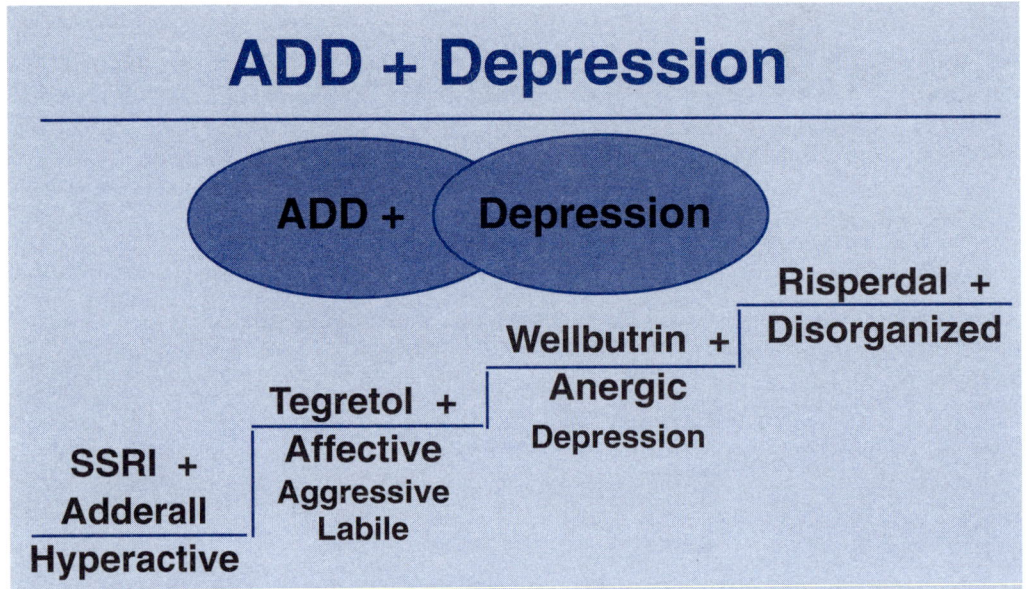

Clinical validity of these constructs, especially in children, requires further controlled study.

Fluoxetine Hydrochloride (Prozac)

Mechanism of Action: Prozac appears to inhibit the neuronal uptake of serotonin.

Benefits: Prozac is used primarily for treatment of depressive illnesses. It has found some usefulness in treating obsessive-compulsive disorder, eating disorders, and attention deficit hyperactivity disorder.

Side Effects: Approximately 4% of patients develop a rash with almost one-third evidencing systemic signs along with the rash requiring discontinuance. Insomnia, headache, anxiety, and nervousness are commonly reported side effects, but are usually transient in appropriate dosages. Weight loss may also occur.

Contraindications: Prozac should not be administered in combination with monoamine oxidase inhibitors or within a 14-day period of discontinuing a monoamine oxidase inhibitor, nor should an monoamine oxidase inhibitor be administered within a 5-week period of discontinuing Prozac.

Dosages: Average adult dosages begin at 20 mg per day and should not exceed 80 mg per day.

Antidepressants
Paxil: Depression + Anxiety; OCD

Broad Spectrum:
- Useful for depression, anxiety, obsessive-compulsive disorder, social withdrawal (as school refusal)
- Fewer other drugs required (anxiolytics; sedative hypnotics) (PSA (BC/BS) retrospective review of 117,000 patients)
- Decreases agitation and anxiety without impairing psychomotor functioning (Boyer & Blumhardt, 1992)

Early onset: 3 weeks, quicker than Prozac (Schoen & Ludwig, 93)

Short half life—implications in children

Comments on Use of Antidepressants

The overall findings of clinical research support the utility of antidepressants in ADHD. Studies have not adequately defined which clinical subtypes would preferentially respond to antidepressants compared to psychostimulants. Psychostimulants still remain the medication of first choice. Failure to respond to psychostimulants may be a negative predictor of response to antidepressants.

The relationship of clinical response to dose and blood level of antidepressants suggests a similar treatment profile as that used for depression. While antidepressants are generally well tolerated and can be administered twice daily, monitoring of cardiovascular side effects is essential. Further research may also validate the duration of treatment effectiveness and the stability of dose and blood levels over time.

Patients with concurrent depression or anxiety and ADHD may be the specific subgroup most likely to benefit from antidepressants. However, further research in such a comorbid population is necessary to validate this presumption. In addition, patients with ADHD and tics may respond to antidepressants. While clinical use has favored antidepressants in adolescents, further studies should compare psychostimulants and antidepressants throughout development of ADHD.

The cognitive effects of antidepressants require further exploration. Several studies have suggested less effect of antidepressants on classical measures of stimulus-bound attention, e.g. Continuous Performance Test. Since these laboratory tests do not correlate closely with classroom learning or grades, there may be significant improvement from antidepressants in applied learning that is not reflected in these concrete measures of attention.

Chapter 9

Arousal Modulating Medications

Arousal Modulating Medications

Antihypertensives (Catapres/Tenex)

Dr. Robert Hunt (Hunt, Minderaa, & Cohen, 1985) pioneered the research on clonidine (Catapres). When compared to the stimulants on rating scales, clonidine appeared to have primary benefits of reducing hyperactivity and impulsivity. Parents often reported that temperament was more in control and frustration tolerance improved. For children with difficulty sleeping, clonidine has been helpful because it may create some drowsiness as a side effect. However, it should be administered near bedtime to assist with this. While stimulants may create anorexia, clonidine appears to stimulate appetite. Clonidine has gained increasing acceptance as an alternative medication to stimulants and antidepressants for treatment. Clonidine may be particularly helpful for children who have difficulty with oppositional behavior and aggression. Clonidine comes in either a transdermal patch or a pill form. Obviously, since this is a hypertensive medication, blood pressure must be monitored carefully and normalized.

Mechanism of Action: Reduces and normalizes norepinephrine and thereby reduces arousal.

Usual Dose: 0.15-0.3 mg/kg/day titrated upward over several weeks.

Side Effects: Hypotension, sedation, dry eyes and mouth, appetite stimulation.

> **Arousal Modulating Medications**
>
> *Have a calming effect in ADHD patients.*

Clonidine in ADHD

Introduction

Clonidine is an imidazoline derivative, used for over two decades as an antihypertensive agent. In the 1980's clonidine was used in child psychiatry to reduce the activation or arousal component of attention deficit hyperactivity

> **Clonidine and Tenex**
>
> *Clonidine and Tenex normalize noradrenergic activity in the brain. They reduce blood pressure in the heart.*
>
> *Behaviorally, they have a calming effect on hyperactivity, aggression and tics, and traumatic anxiety.*

disorder, Tourette's syndrome, and aggression. Clonidine is not specific for all the symptoms of any diagnosis (Cohen, et al., 1980). Preliminary studies suggest that clonidine effectively reduces arousal in very hyperactive children. It appears useful in patients with aggression associated with highly aroused ADHD. For patients with combined hyperarousal and distractibility, clonidine given concurrently with Ritalin may be optimal. When administered in a transdermal (skin patch), clonidine is the first psychotropic medication for children that maintains a constant and effective blood level for about five days. This form is preferred by many children, since no "pills" are required.

Clinical Indications

Preliminary studies and clinical experience suggest that clonidine may be useful in ADHD children with the following associated conditions:
- Very highly aroused/overactive ADHD
- ADHD with oppositional/conduct disorder
- Motor tics
- Growth impairment
- Poor response to psychostimulants

Clonidine is not useful for treatment of distractibility in ADD without hyperactivity.

Therapeutic Efficacy

Clonidine Versus Placebo

Initial studies assessed the effectiveness of clonidine in ADHD through comparison with placebo, and then in relation to methylphenidate in samples of ten children each. Clonidine was found to be significantly better than placebo in effects on behavior as rated by parents, teachers, and clinicians in a double-blind study (Hunt, et al., 1985).

Ten boys, ages 8 to 13 years (x=11.6 +/- 0.54 yr) met DSM-III diagnostic criteria for ADHD. Their behavior at baseline was evaluated using the Child Behavior Checklist and the Conners' Questionnaires completed by parents and teachers. Subjects were >1.5 standard deviation above normal on the Hyperactivity Index as rated by both parents

> **Clonidine Versus Placebo**
>
> *Effects of clonidine versus placebo was studied in ADHD children as rated by parents, teachers, and clinicians.*
>
> *Clonidine improved hyperactivity, conduct, inattention, and learning.*

and teachers. The diagnosis was confirmed using the Diagnostic Inventory Classification Assessment interview of both parents and children. Baseline ratings were obtained during a two-week, drug-free period.

Coated placebo was administered for two weeks prior to and following active clonidine. Clonidine dose was gradually increased over ten days to a therapeutic level of about 4.5 mg/kg/d, constituting an average daily dose of 0.23 mg/d usually administered as 0.05 mg four times a day. Active treatment was continued for two months, and then tapered with return to placebo. Behavioral response was monitored by parent, teacher, and clinician ratings every two weeks. Parents and teachers completed the Conners' 48-item and 28-item behavior rating scales, respectively. Clinicians rated the children utilizing a quantitative adaptation of the Diagnostic Statistical Manual-III diagnostic criteria for ADHD and also made global assessments of improvement during treatment. Neuromaturational assessment of visual-motor coordination occurred monthly.

Results: Clonidine was found to be significantly more effective than placebo as rated by teachers, parents, and clinicians. Teachers noted significant improvement in overall behavior ratings ($p=0.001$), hyperactivity index ($p=0.001$), conduct ($p=0.4$), and inattention ratings ($p=0.5$); parents also reported improvements in overall ratings ($p=0.003$), hyperactivity index ($p=0.004$), conduct problems ($p=0.01$), and learning problems ($p=0.007$). Clinicians noted overall improvements in the treated group on total score of cardinal DSM-III symptoms of ADHD, with three subjects having >25 % improvement, and in areas of inattention, impulsivity, and hyperactivity. Based on the criteria of > 50% improvement in at least two settings, 70% of ADHD children were improved. Upon tapering of clonidine and return to placebo, behavioral control quickly deteriorated to pre-treatment levels.

The major side effect was sedation, occurring about one hour after administration of clonidine and lasting about 30 to 60 minutes. This sedation decreased to minimal levels or discontinued within three weeks in all but one child. There was no evidence of psychomotor retardation on the behavioral ratings, athletic participation, or the visual-motor

Clonidine

Clonidine can reduce hyperactivity, aggression, and tics in ADHD patients.

Clonidine

Teachers, parents, and clinicians reported behavioral improvement in ADHD symptoms.

Side Effects of Clonidine

Side effects of clonidine were sedation and decreased blood pressure. Performance on motor tasks was not diminished.

components of neuromaturational assessments. Blood pressure was reduced by about 10%, and was clinically nonsignificant. One child with prior symptoms of depression became more depressed on clonidine; children who had no prior symptoms of depressive disorder did not exhibit emergent symptoms on treatment.

Even in this small sample size, using a well-controlled, double-blind study, very significant improvement was evident from clonidine in contrast to pre- and post-treatment placebo. The medication was well tolerated and often preferred by parents and children in subjects previously treated with Ritalin.

Clonidine Versus Methylphenidate

The next problem was to compare clonidine to methylphenidate. A separate population of ten ADHD children was treated with clonidine, methylphenidate, and placebo using a cross-over design. Clonidine and methylphenidate were equally effective and significantly better than placebo as rated by parents and teachers (Hunt, 1987).

In a similar fashion as above, ten boys, ages 8 to 13 years (x=11.6+/- 0.56 yr) were selected who met DSM-III diagnostic criteria for ADHD. Subjects were > 1.5 standard deviations above normal on the Hyperactivity Index as rated by both parents and teachers. The diagnosis was confirmed using the DICA interview of both parents and children. Patients were rated by teachers, parents, and clinicians at baseline and every other week.

Treatment included clonidine (gradually increased to 5 ug/kg/d), low-dose (0.3 mg/kg) and high-dose (0.6 mg/kg) methylphenidate (given in divided doses, two thirds in the morning), and placebo (q.i.d.). Teachers did not know the treatment condition. Clonidine was administered for eight weeks while each dose of methylphenidate was administered for one week—in random sequence separated by a two-week placebo washout.

Results: Patients demonstrated significant response to both clonidine (p= 0.005) and methylphenidate (p= 0.05 and p= 0.01 for low-dose and high-dose, respectively) when compared to baseline and washout placebo ratings. Teachers expressed a slight preference for methylphenidate,

---

Ritalin Versus Clonidine

In a comparison with Ritalin and Clonidine, both medications were effective. Ritalin was better in school. Clonidine decreased the hyperactivity at home.

perhaps reflecting its preferential effect on distractibility. Parents rated a nonsignificant preference for clonidine, indicating that it improved hyperactivity, impulsivity, cooperation, and oppositionality on weekends and in the evenings.

This study and our subsequent clinical experience in large numbers of patients has substantiated a therapeutic benefit of clonidine that is slightly less effective than methylphenidate. However, clonidine is often preferred by parents because of its stabilizing effect, lack of evening and weekend withdrawal, and its absence of anorectic or insomniac effects. Teachers slightly preferred the effects of methylphenidate. A similar pattern and incidence of side effects has been noted.

Transdermal Clonidine

Clonidine is unique among pediatric psychotherapeutic medications in being available in a transdermal vehicle of administration. This form has significant potential advantages in a disorder in which taking medication can create significant embarrassment, and the relatively short behavioral half-life of clonidine and psychostimulants requires multiple doses producing a roller coaster pattern of behavioral control. The transdermal or skin patch preparation of clonidine can be worn for about five days. It is available in doses labeled: "TTS" (transdermal therapeutic system) "1," "2," and "3" that correspond approximately to 0.1, 0.2, or 0.4 mg/d, respectively. These doses can be further refined by cutting the patch to achieve intermediate dose levels. Children are usually begun on oral clonidine to verify response, and then shifted to transdermal, since absorption from the transdermal appears somewhat more variable. The patches adhere quite well, except during the summer in humid climates. Select a relatively hairless and inaccessible area, such as the lower back. Prepare the skin by washing the area with soap and water, then drying. Remove the plastic backing and attach like a bandage, placing the surface that was covered by plastic against the skin. A protective white adhesive covering about the size of a silver dollar can be worn optionally. We usually do not begin using this protective cover routinely, since it may increase the

Clonidine Skin Patch

The clonidine skin patch is longer lasting, smoother, less sedating than oral clonidine.

frequency of local dermatitis—erythema and itching. A topical steroid cream may reduce problems with local irritation. Although development of localized contact sensitization to transdermal clonidine may predispose to development of a generalized skin rash on subsequent return to oral clonidine administration, we have not seen this difficulty in our 50 patients who resumed transdermal clonidine. Transdermal clonidine was compared to oral using an open design in subjects who previously demonstrated good therapeutic response to oral clonidine (Hunt, 1987; Hunt, 1988).

In the prior group of ten ADHD patients, those who responded to oral clonidine (n= 8) were subsequently shifted to an open trial of transdermal clonidine, administered at an equivalent dose. This open design was selected in order to control for the effectiveness of transdermal clonidine separate from the effectiveness of clonidine alone.

After determining the optimal dose of clonidine for each subject (x=5.0 ug/kg; 0.23 mg/d) and for each patient (age = 11.4 +/- 0.6 yr), all subjects were shifted to transdermal clonidine and monitored for at least one month. Parent, teacher, and clinician behavioral ratings were obtained every two weeks.

Results: Results showed no significant difference in overall therapeutic response between transdermal and oral clonidine. The important difference was in tolerance and side effects. When the clonidine patches were comfortable, they were universally preferred by patients and parents. The children appreciated the privacy and consistency bestowed by the transdermal clonidine. The duration of clinical effect was five rather than seven days.

The main side effect of transdermal administration was local contact dermatitis, with associated pruritus and erythema. This occurred in about 40% of the patients treated.

Transdermal clonidine is often a preferred route of administration due to its consistency of effect and privacy. Subsequent clinical and research experience has supported these preliminary observations (Chen and Vidt, 1989; Hunt, et al., in preparation). Adherence of the patch is reduced during periods of heat and humidity. Further research is needed to clarify blood-level comparability of the oral and transdermal vehicles.

Differential Effects of Clonidine and Methylphenidate

The next issue was to attempt to differentiate the clinical response and the type of patients that optimally respond to clonidine verses methylphenidate. Our subsequent research has addressed differences in clinical effects of clonidine and methylphenidate. Clonidine is more effective in reducing high levels of activity and arousal that indirectly impede learning and may prompt aggressive behavior. Psychostimulants appear to have more direct effects on distractibility. Hence, these medications appear useful for distinct groups of ADHD children.

Methylphenidate narrows the attentional field and focuses attention, analogous to using a zoom lens. Methylphenidate is clearly superior for mild to moderately hyperactive children with primary attentional difficulties. Clonidine may be preferable for severely overactive, aggressive ADHD children, with generally intact cognitive functioning. The high level of arousal in the overactive group indirectly impairs attention, probably via cognitive flooding. In a highly aroused state, many routine or trivial stimuli are imbued with significance, and require excessive processing—leading to an overloading of functionally intact cognitive processes that impairs selective and sustained attention. The major effect of clonidine is to reduce excessive arousal in highly overactive ADHD children. The most responsive ADHD children appear to have an early onset, to be extremely energetic, and often exhibit associated oppositional or conduct disorder. In this group, clonidine improves frustration tolerance—often leading to an increase of task-oriented behavior, enhanced learning and effort, and improved compliance and cooperativeness. Clonidine has no direct effect on distractibility (Hunt, et al., in submission).

> **Effects of Clonidine**
>
> *The effects of clonidine and methylphenidate were assessed individually and combined. About 50% improvement in hyperactivity and in conduct problems occurred.*

Combined Clonidine and Methylphenidate

> **Clonidine and Methylphenidate**
>
> *Clonidine and methylphenidate used concurrently can reduce hyperactivity and aggression while also increasing focus of attention. The dose of Ritalin can be reduced by about half. Sedation and withdrawal side effects are decreased.*

> **Clonidine and Ritalin**
>
> *Clonidine decreases hyperactivity. Ritalin improved attention.*

Clonidine has been effectively utilized in conjunction *with* methylphenidate in ADHD children who are *both* highly aroused and very distractible. Used concurrently, the dose of methylphenidate could be reduced by about 40% and the net beneficial effects were increased. The response was smoother, less fluctuant or brittle, and the side effects of both medications appeared reduced (Hunt, 1989; Hunt, in submission).

Sixty-three ADHD patients were treated in random sequence with clonidine or methylphenidate alone, and with both together for four to six weeks in each medication condition. The average age was 10.3 yrs +/- 1.8, range 6 to 15 years. The mean school grade was 4.5 +/- 1.1. The dose of methylphenidate was initially increased to 0.5 mg/kg/d and then individually titrated using behavioral ratings, clinical interviews, and side effects. The dose of clonidine was elevated to a level of 4-5 ug/kg (about 0.2 mg/d). After three weeks, the final dose was clinically optimized based on clinical response. Dependent behavioral measures obtained during treatment included weekly parent ratings (Conners' Parent Questionnaire, Iowa Scale for ADHD and Aggression, and Revised Child Behavior Checklist (Quay)). Teacher behavioral ratings were also obtained weekly.

The final therapeutic dose of clonidine was 0.23 mg/d ±0.025. When administered alone, the mean methylphenidate dose was 27.3 mg (± 3.1 mg). When administered concurrently with clonidine, the dose of methylphenidate required to produce an optimal clinical response was significantly reduced by 40% (27.3 mg to 16.4 mg/d), with $p<0.05$.

Results: The Parent Questionnaire has provided the initial data for comparison of the effects of clonidine and methylphenidate. The changes in percent improvement on behavioral factors are similar for clonidine and methylphenidate when utilized alone. However, when given in combination, a significant improvement in the factor of conduct problems occurred (56% reduction, $p<0.05$).

Clonidine + Ritalin—Side Effects

Used in combination, clonidine and Ritalin have complementary effects on extreme hyperactive behavior (clonidine) and attention (Ritalin). Hunt, et al. (1988), reported a decrease in dose of methylphenidate required (by one-third) and a reduction of net side effects (sedation, agitation, blood pressure change) from this combination.

However, in the past three years, four deaths have been reported in patients using this combination of medications. These findings are difficult to interpret since two of these patients had preexisting cardiac problems, and one had no measurable blood level of clonidine. Yet, the fact that both of these agents are short acting and have contradictory effects on blood pressure and pulse creates a potential for conflict cardiac effects. Clonidine reduces blood pressure (and is still used as a hypotensive agent) while methylphenidate slightly increases blood pressure and pulse. Used in combination by individuals who are physically stressed or dehydrated, there exists the potential that one medication could be initiating or continuing its effect while another is stopping its effect—leading to an exaggerated rebound with potentially devastating blood pressure effects. Independent reviews by expert cardiologists and child psychiatrists suggested that this risk is very low, and may not exceed the natural rate of expected death in these populations. ECG monitoring, while often performed, does not effectively predict risk from these catastrophic moments.

In our judgment and clinical experience, these risks are likely to be reduced by combined use of longer-acting medications that have a similar effect: Adderall (versus Ritalin) and Tenex (versus clonidine), since these medications are less likely to have abrupt interface with rapid cardiovascular impact. We are monitoring blood pressure and ECG effects, but do not yet have enough long-term experience to predict rare events.

The patients who may benefit from the combined medication are those ADHD subjects who continue to have significant motor hyperactivity while on methylphenidate, or who have brittle clinical symptoms or severe withdrawal in the evening. We have also used clonidine and methylphenidate in some patients who did not tolerate methylphenidate alone due to aggression, irritability, weight loss,

> **Clonidine and Ritalin Side Effects**
>
> *Cardiac side effects from combined clonidine and Ritalin may be dangerous and require careful monitoring*

> **Other Medications**
>
> *Longer-acting medication may be more stable and safe.*

insomnia, or delayed growth. Clonidine-responsive subjects who remain distractible may respond to combined medication achieved by a gradual titration of methylphenidate added to a stable dose of clonidine.

Neurobehavioral Mechanisms of Action

The effect of clonidine in reducing the intensity of a variety of behavioral expressions of excessive arousal may provide an index of the role of locus coeruleus-based noradrenergic influence on behavior. The principal mechanism of action of clonidine is as an alpha-2 noradrenergic agonist. In the doses generally used in child psychiatry, clonidine reduces the endogenous release of norepinephrine by activating autoinhibitory effects of the presynaptic receptor. However, the behavioral patterns of many diagnoses reflect a continuum of multiple neurotransmitter effects. Norepinephrine may affect the responsivity of many behavioral systems and the sensitivity of other neurotransmitter systems. Clonidine may indirectly modify the expression of other neurotransmitters, such as dopamine, that may mediate the focus and breadth of attention in ADHD or the control of movements in Tourette's syndrome. Serotonin may mediate the capacity to inhibit thoughts or aggressive behaviors. Thus, the use of clonidine in child psychiatry may be helpful in defining the relative contribution of components of neurochemical systems in child psychopathology (Bunney and DeRiemer, 1982; Hunt, 1990).

Since the direct effects of clonidine appear to be limited to reducing the noradrenergic contribution to arousal-based symptoms, clonidine is frequently used as an adjunctive agent in those disorders in which other neurochemical systems are involved. For example, in ADHD, clonidine may be utilized concurrently with the dopaminergic releasing psychostimulants, such as methylphenidate or d-amphetamine, to increase attentional focus. In Tourette's syndrome, clonidine may be paired with dopamine blocking agents such as pimozide or haloperidol to reduce motor tics. In conjunction with these other agents, clonidine has a potentiating effect—probably by reducing the augment-

---

Clonidine Mechanisms of Action

Clonidine in therapeutic doses directly normalizes the release of norepinephrine. Secondarily, this may impact levels of dopamine and serotonin, neurotransmitters that impact movement, attention, and inhibition.

ing or amplifying role of norepinephrine in neurophysiology.

Much of clonidine's effect on specific behaviors or symptoms may be indirect benefits from reducing excessive arousal (Halliday, et al., 1989). For example, in ADHD, clonidine has no direct effect on distractibility, though it reduces activity and improves frustration tolerance, and thereby has powerful effects on task orientation—the ability to approach and complete demanding tasks. Similarly, in Tourette's syndrome, clonidine probably has little direct effect on dopaminergically-mediated motor tics (Cohen, et al., 1988; Leckman, et al., 1988; Goetz, et al., 1987). However, clonidine can reduce the anxiety and arousal experienced by many ADHD children that potentiates and exacerbates tics. As an antiaggressive agent, clonidine appears to be effective in reducing aggression related to hyperactivity, but is unlikely to be effective in controlling impulsive or premeditated aggression in nonaroused patients (Jouvent, et al., 1988).

Neurochemical Mechanisms of Action

Methylphenidate and clonidine have very different neurochemical mechanisms of action, probably reflecting differences in neurotransmitter and brain regional effects. Methylphenidate releases presynaptically stored dopamine and norepinephrine, producing an increase in basal brain arousal, evident by an increase in blood pressure and pulse and a decrease in appetite and sleep. However, methylphenidate also facilitates improved behavioral inhibition and cognitive selective attention—probably by activation of cortical dopaminergically-mediated inhibition systems.

Clonidine is an alpha-2 noradrenergic agonist that acts somewhat like exogenous norepinephrine (Hunt, 1988). In the doses prescribed for children, clonidine's preferential presynaptic effect reduces the firing of the locus coeruleus and inhibits the release of endogenous norepinephrine leading to a decrease in plasma and urinary norepinephrine and its metabolite, 3-hydroxy-4 methoxy-phenylethylene glycol (Hunt, 1984; Martin, et al., 1984). Alpha-2 norepinephrine receptors located on the platelet appear to be down-regulated after two to three weeks of clonidine treatment, leading to a buffering of response to activating stimuli. Clonidine inhibits norepinephrine release partially through presynaptic inhibition of locus coeruleus firing—thereby reducing basal brain arousal. Reduced arousal can diminish the background "noise" and reduce the amount of stimuli that must be processed (improved signal:noise ratio).

Pharmacokinetics

Oral Clonidine

The usual dose of clonidine is 0.15 - 0.3 mg/d which is about equivalent to 3 to 6 ug/kg/d. This dose level is reached gradually. Clonidine may be begun at night to facilitate sleep and enable tolerance to the sedative effects; then increase the dose of oral clonidine at a rate of 0.05 mg (1/2 tablet) every third day. The median dose for an 8- to 12-year-old ADHD patient is about 0.25 to 0.3 mg per day. A maximal dose would be about 0.4 to 0.5 mg/d, approximately 8 ug/kg. Oral clonidine is commonly given three to four times per day—with meals and at bedtime.

Pharmacokinetics

Clonidine is rapidly absorbed from the gut, achieving peak plasma level at 90 to 150 minutes. The excretion half-life in children is approximately 8 to 12 hours, with considerable cross-subject variability. The behavioral effects of clonidine last about three to five hours. Patients notice the most side effects (usually sedation) about 30 to 90 minutes after a dose, and may experience a loss of behavioral effect after four to six hours, depending on dose and severity of symptoms. Some clinical effect is longer lasting and may reflect gradual receptor down-regulation (Lowenthal, et al., 1988).

Therapeutic Blood Levels

Therapeutic blood level parameters have not yet been established for clonidine.

Clonicel

Given the side effects of sedation, hypotension, and the short duration of action of clonidine, Dr. H. Joseph Horacek worked with compounding pharmacists to create a longer-acting, oral version of Clonidine, Clonicel. Clinically, this lasts about 6 to 8 hours and has fewer sedative side effects.

Clinical Guidelines For Using Clonidine In ADHD

1. **Administration:** start and stop *gradually*

2. **Optimal dose:** 3 - 5 ug/kg/d

3. **Schedule:** 2 - 4 x / d.

4. **Monitor:**
   * Behavior: hyperactivity, inattention, mood

   * Physiology: drowsiness, blood pressure, weight

Starting Clonidine
Schedule for increasing dose: 1/2 tablet every third day.

Day	1	2	3	4	5	6	7	8	9	10	11	12
DATE	_	_	_	_	_	_	_	_	_	_	_	_
DAY	_	_	_	_	_	_	_	_	_	_	_	_
AM	---	---	---	X	x	x	x	x	x	x	x	x
NOON	---	---	---	---	---	---	X	x	x	x	x	x
PM	---	---	---	---	---	---	---	---	---	X	x	x
NIGHT	X	x	x	x	x	x	x	x	x	x	x	x

X = <u>Half</u> Tablet

Optimal Dose: Clonidine 3 - 5 ug/kg/d

Schedule: 2 - 4 x / d.

Side Effects of Clonidine

1. **Sedation:** May fall asleep for 20 minutes when inactive, alert when active.

2. **Blood pressure:** Decrease of about 10%, not clinically significant in children.

3. **Increase in appetite and growth.**

Monitoring Response to Clonidine

1. **Weekly measures:**
    - Conners' Parents Questionnaire
    - Conners' Teachers Questionnaire

2. **Observe for:**
    - **Attention span:** learning
    - **Need for supervision:** organization
    - **Frustration tolerance:** ability to perform tasks
    - **Social skills:** oppositionality, communication
    - **Mood:** irritability, depression, aggression

The Clonidine Skin Patch (Transdermal)

1. **Appearance**
    - Bandage-like, about 1 x 1.5 cm

2. **Doses**
    - 0.1, 0.2, 0.4, mg/d
    - Usually similar to oral dose

3. **Placement**
    - Hairless area, usually the back

4. **Application**
    - Wash with soap.
    - Peel off clear adhesive.
    - May use protective cover (3 cm dot).
    - Usually tolerates brief exposure to water.

5. **Duration**
   - 5 days (not one week).

6. **Side Effects**
   - Local irritation, itching, erythema (40%).

Proposed Relationship Between Symptoms, Neurochemistry, and Treatment

Clinical	Neurochemical	Treatment
Over-aroused ADHD *Behavioral Symptoms:* hyperactive, distractible, explosive *Physiological:* over-aroused, normal inhibited	↑ norepinephrine	clonidine/Tenex
Inattentive ADD *Behavioral Symptoms:* less hyperactive, distractible *Physiological:* normal aroused, under-inhibited	↓ dopamine	psychostimulants
Dysinhibited ADD *Behavioral Symptoms:* hyperactive, inattentive, disorganized, often explosive, aggressive *Physiological:* over-aroused, under-inhibited	↑ norepinephrine ↓ dopamine ↓ serotonin	both clonidine/Tenex and psychostimulants, SSRI's

Mechanism of Action of Medication

Neurochemical

	clonidine/Tenex:	**methylphenidate:**
Norepinephrine	decrease	increase release
Dopamine	No Acute Effect	increase release, direct

Physiological

	clonidine/Tenex:	**methylphenidate:**
Blood pressure	decrease	slight increase
Pulse	slight decrease	increase
Appetite	mild increase	decrease
Weight	mild increase	decrease
Growth	mild increase	decrease
Sleep	increase in ablity to fall asleep	decrease

Clinical Management of Clonidine in ADHD

Duration of Treatment: It usually takes about two weeks to see a specific response other than sedation, and about one month to see a significant clinical improvement. The sedation and tiredness often clear within the first month. Maximal effect may not be achieved for two to three months, since children seem to demonstrate a gradual maturation as their frustration tolerance is improved.

Long-Term Effects: ADHD children have been maintained on clonidine for up to five years without loss of effect nor significant change in dose. However, a few children do lose response or require a slightly higher dose during the first month. Occasionally, the dose must be increased after several months of treatment, but we have only seen this in about 20% of patients. We often continue children on clonidine during the summer, albeit at a reduced (two thirds to one half) dose. We discontinue all medications in virtually every child annually for a placebo-controlled trial to verify continued need for medication.

Adult ADHD: Clonidine has not been sufficiently studied in adult ADHD to allow for adequate assessment of its efficacy. However, since arousal tends to diminish with age, but distractibility may persist, clonidine may be less effective in adult ADHD than is methylphenidate.

Side Effects and Toxicity

Sedation: The most frequent and troublesome side effect is sedation, usually experienced as sleepiness. This is usually most pronounced during the first two to four weeks and commonly decreases thereafter. On four times a day doses, the most common time of sleepiness is 1:00 to 2:30 p.m. Sedation is more severe in the less highly active or aroused ADHD children. In about 15% of cases, this tiredness persisted at oral doses clinically required to decrease activity and enhance frustration tolerance.

After establishing a therapeutic oral dose, the clinician may shift to the transdermal route of clonidine administration, which produces less of a pulse of plasma level, and

---

Clonidine Dosage

Clonidine should be started or stopped gradually to decrease sedation or withdrawal.

hence is often less sedating. The tiredness may also decrease with combined treatment with methylphenidate. For a few children (about 10%), oral clonidine was discontinued due to tiredness.

Cardiovascular Effects: As an antihypertensive agent, clonidine may produce hypotension. While this is common in adults, hypotension in children is very rarely significant. In over 100 children systematically monitored for this, we observed about a 10% decrease in systolic pressure; this rarely produces clinical symptoms or discomfort. Acutely, clonidine mildly diminishes cardiac output (10 to 20%) and decreases peripheral vascular resistance. However, during long-term treatment, cardiac output returns to baseline, while peripheral resistance and pulse remain decreased. The frequency of symptoms suggestive of orthostatic hypotension is less than 5%. Clonidine does not alter renal blood flow nor glomerular filtration rate. Plasma renin and aldosterone excretion may decrease. Cardiac dysrhythmia with the use of clonidine has been reviewed by Dawson, et al. (1989).

Other Effects: Clonidine can induce depression. This has been observed in about 5% of our patients. All cases have been children with some definite depressive symptoms before treatment or with a prior history of depression themselves or in the family. Clonidine enhances sleep and appetite and may increase weight—which is often welcome if a child has been anorectic on psychostimulants. Clonidine is a potent releaser of growth hormone and may even facilitate growth. High dose, long-term clonidine has been noted to produce retinal degeneration in animals, due to concentration of medication in the choroid. Thus, most of the side effects of clonidine are opposite those of methylphenidate. When combined with methylphenidate, clonidine is usually well tolerated.

Tolerance: Tolerance has been noted in antihypertensive effect in adults. Clonidine should be gradually withdrawn. Sudden withdrawal from chronic, high-dose clonidine can produce nervousness, agitation, headache, and hypertension associated with increased catecholamine release.

Overdose: Acute overdose may produce hypotension, sedation, and somnolence. Treatment with gastric lavage or

Oral Clonidine Side Effects

Clonidine slightly decreases blood pressure. Cardiac output does not change over long-term treatment.

Oral Clonidine Versus Clonidine Skin Patch

Oral clonidine can produce sedation; the skin patch is smoother, long lasting, and less sedating.

Clonidine and Tenex

Increase sedation from alcohol, barbiturates, and sedatives.

tolazoline 10 mg intravenously every 30 minutes can reverse these effects.

Drug Interactions: Clonidine has been safely utilized in conjunction with other antihypertensive or diuretic agents in adults. Concurrent use of antidepressants may reduce the effect of clonidine and create a risk of corneal damage secondary to dryness effects of the eye. Clonidine may enhance the sedative effects of alcohol, barbiturates, or other sedatives, or potentiate mucus dryness of anticholinergic agents. However, anticholinergic effects (dryness, constipation, urinary retention) are much less serious in children than in adults. Initially, some headache, dizziness, and nausea may occur; glucose may be increased chronically.

Medical work-up and follow-up: In the baseline evaluation, the physician should consider:
- Blood pressure and pulse; CBC and urine analysis.
- Electrolytes, thyroid indices, fasting blood sugar.
- Liver function tests: alkaline phosphatase, SGOT, SGPT, bilirubin.
- ECG.

Summary: Clonidine acts primarily to reduce arousal in severely hyperactive ADHD children. The action of clonidine is to reduce norepinephrine release and basal-brain activation. Research to date suggests that it may be helpful in treating very active ADHD patients, especially those with early onset and arousal-dependent aggression. The calming effect of clonidine appears helpful in increasing on-task behavior, school performance, and reducing oppositionality. It may be helpful in patients with associated tics or growth impairment.

Administered in oral form, clonidine can be given throughout the day. It produces some initial sedation, facilitates sleep, and may slightly stimulate appetite and growth. Clonidine may be administered in a transdermal vehicle (skin patch) that can enable a steady therapeutic effect. Combined with methylphenidate, clonidine may reduce the dose of Ritalin required and minimize side effects. There is some cardiac risk from combined clonidine and Ritalin. Both medications concurrently may be helpful in ADHD children who are active, aggressive, oppositional, and distractible.

The main side effects are initial sedation and mild hypotension; depression occasionally occurs in individuals with a personal or family history. Slow initiation and withdrawal of dose diminishes side effects.

Additional multicenter research with behavioral, cognitive, and neurochemical monitoring is needed to validate these preliminary findings.

Tenex

Tenex is a guanfacine "cousin" medication that is similar to clonidine. However, tenex is longer-lasting, smoother, less sedating, and produces less hypertension. Our initial studies, (Hunt, et al., 1995) demonstrated significant effect of guanfacine compared to baseline on behavior ratings of attention, hyperactivity, aggression, and socialization. Tenex (guanfacine) is frequently preferred in treatment of outpatients with ADHD and continued hyperactivity or tics. It is then the drug of choice for young ADHD children.

Medication Management
Tenex (guanfacine)

Probable Indications:
- Young ADHD, Tourette's Syndrome, Aggression

Benefits:
- Calming, Longer-Acting, Smoother

Dosing:(SR)	AM	PM	HS	Total
• Children	0.5-1.0mg	0.5-1.0mg	0.5-1.5mg	=1.5-3.5mg/d
• Adults:	0.5-1.0mg	0.0-0.5mg	0.5-1.0mg	=1.0-3.0mg/d
• Increase:	Begin 0.5mg in AM; increase by 0.5 mg q. 3rd day			

Side Effects:
- Acute—Decrease blood pressure, mild sedation
- Chronic—Irritability, dysthymia

Recommendations: monitor blood pressure, pulse, ECG

Chapter 10

Anticonvulsant Medications

Anticonvulsant Medications

Carbatrol (Tegretol)

Tegretol is an anticonvulsant medication that is more often prescribed by neurologists when there is evidence of EEG irregularities, partial seizures (psychomotor or temporal lobe), tonic-clonic (grand mal) seizures, and symptoms associated with aggression, impulsivity, hyperactivity, and possible seizures. It is important in the assessment process that seizures be ruled out as a primary cause for ADHD behaviors. Tegretol is often useful in treatment of combined aggression or mood instability and ADHD.

Usual Dose: Children aged 6-12 begin at 100 mg twice a day and increase to a maximum of 1000 mg, adjusting the dosage to the minimum effective level, usually

Medication Management
Carbatrol (Tegretol)

Indications:
- Aggression (affective), Severe Temper
- Mood Instability or bipolar

Benefits:
- Calming, Longer-Acting, Smoother

Dosing: (SR)

	AM	HS	Total	Blood Level
Children	200-300mg	200-300mg	= 400-600mg/d	= 8-12 ng/ml
Adults:	200-400mg	200-400mg	= 400-800mg/d	= 8-12 ng/ml
Increase:	Begin 200mg at HS; increase by 200 mg q. 5th day			

Side Effects:
- **Acute**—Mild sedation, headache, stomachache
- **Chronic**—Blood dyscrasia, hepatotoxicity

Recommendations: Monitor CBC, SMA-12, blood level every 3 months

between 400 to 600 mg. For children and adults aged 12 and up, begin with 200 mg three times a day or four times a day with a maximum daily dosage of 1000 mg for those aged 12 to 15 and 1200 mg for those 15 years and up. A long-acting version of tegretol, Carbatrol, is useful in aggressive mood labile ADHD children since it can be given twice daily.

Mechanism of Action: Unknown

Primary benefits: Control of seizuring. Some ADHD children evidence abnormal EEG's, and treatment by neurologists may include the use of this medication.

Side Effects: Drowsiness, rashes, nausea, abnormalities in liver function, aplastic anemia, and agranulocytosis.

Contraindicators: Tegretol is inappropriate for individuals with a history of bone marrow depression or hypersensitivity to the drug (*Physicians Desk Reference, 1996*). Close blood and liver functioning monitoring is required.

Depakote (Valproic Acid)

Depakote (Valproic Acid) is another agent with mood stabilizing and antiaggressive properties. It can reduce sincere temper tantrums, irritability, and violent behavior associated with affective aggression.

Side Effects: Major side effects can include rash, sedation, blood cell and liver abnormalities, and hair loss.

Dosage: A typical dose in children is 250 mg three times a day with blood levels of 60 to 80 ng/ml.

Medications for Bipolar Disorder (Lithium)

Adolescents and adults with bipolar disorder have many symptoms in common with individuals with ADHD such as inattention, hyperactivity, and rapid mood changes. Bipolar disorder is generally considered to be more serious, with symptoms often appearing to be psychotic. Bipolar individuals may exhibit paranoid thought patterns and may be quite angry and aggressive. Lithium has proven itself to be quite effective with this population.

Lithium is rarely used to treat ADHD, but it may be tried when other medications have not been effective and when symptoms are progressing towards those of a diagnosis of bipolar disorder. Due to its potential for overdose, it must be monitored carefully with blood levels titrated frequently. It should not be accessible to individuals with suicidal characteristics due to its potential lethality.

Mechanism of Action: Lithium alters the sodium transport in nerve and muscle cells which results in a shift toward intraneural metabolism of catecholamines.

Usual Dose: 10-30 mg/kg/day divided twice a day to three times a day. Titrated to a serum level of between 0.6-1.2 mg/L.

Side Effects: Weight gain, tremor, diarrhea; may promote depression, daytime sleepiness, thyroid dysfunction.

Chapter 11

Neuroleptics

Neuroleptics: Major Tranquilizers

In some cases of ADHD that are refractory to methylphenidate and other stimulants, neuroleptic drugs such as haloperidol and thioridazine have been used as alternatives, or added to stimulant treatment. While there is some empirical observation of improvement in behavioral ratings of some ADHD patients, theoretical debate related to conflicting mechanisms of action has led to practical concern regarding the potential for developing tardive dyskinesia.

Clinical Efficacy: Several studies of neuroleptics in severely behaviorally disturbed children suggest that they are effective. However, many of these children are more disturbed than typical ADHD children, and may be excluded from the diagnosis because they have a pervasive developmental disorder or atypical personality disorder.

In the 1970's, clinical studies by Werry and Aman, (1975) with haloperidol, and Gittelman-Klein, et al., (1976) with thioridazine, found no changes in cognitive performance, but some improvement was noted in behavior as rated by teachers, parents, and physicians. Campbell, et al., (1983) noted that haloperidol and lithium were equally effective in decreasing the severe hyperactivity and aggression of hospitalized children, but the neuroleptics had greater sedative effects. However, compared to placebo, low dose neuroleptics improved social behavior and cognitive organization in children who were cognitively disorganized. Zahn, et al. (1975) found that neuroleptics had a cognitive blunting effect compared to placebo or d-amphetamine.

A study by Levy and Hobbes, (1988) investigated the effect of adding haloperidol treatment in ADHD boys already receiving methylphenidate. They found that haloperidol alone had a negative impact on cognitive performance, as measured by vigilance tasks, when compared with placebo. Pretreatment with haloperidol two hours before

Neuroleptics

Neuroleptics are medications used to treat psychosis. However, in low doses these medications can help organize complex ADHD children. These medications are useful in children whose ADHD is associated with speech, language, motor control, and social difficulties.

Haldol

Haldol, an older, potent neuroleptic, can be sedating and produce changes in muscle tone and tics.

> **Haldol**
>
> *Neuroleptics such as Haldol may blunt cognition and expressiveness.*

methylphenidate administration resulted in blockage of improvement on vigilance performance usually seen with methylphenidate alone. Since the haloperidol pretreatment seemed to block the effects of methylphenidate, the authors suggest that dopaminergic actions are important in the beneficial cognitive effects seen with stimulant treatment in ADHD children. These observations suggest that while the cognitive focusing effects of methylphenidate are mediated by dopamine, the behavioral effects may reflect multiple neurotransmitter systems. Unfortunately, this study did not address the subgroup of patients whose ADHD is refractory to stimulant treatment, in whom empirical observations of success have been noted after addition of neuroleptics.

Other reports have focused on the use of stimulant-neuroleptic combinations to control the attentional problems seen in adolescent schizophrenics. While these studies are not directly relevant to ADHD, many children who initially present as ADHD may have more severe disturbances.

> **Haldol and Lithium**
>
> *Haldol and Lithium both can improve behavior of highly disorganized schizoid children. However, Haldol is more sedating and can produce disturbance of movement and muscle spasm.*

In a case report, Rogeness and Macedo (1983) described an 11-year-old boy with schizophrenia whose behavior problems had been refractory to many drugs, including methylphenidate, thiothixene, and haloperidol. A combination of methylphenidate and chlorpromazine resulted in improved attention appropriate behaviors, and allowed for outpatient treatment to begin. Similarly, in a study of adolescent schizophrenic patients, Erickson, et al. (1984), observed the effects of neuroleptics on performance of the Continuous Performance Task. Thioridazine hydrochloride or thiothixene did not enhance performance on the Continuous Performance Task, and produced sedation.

Major Tranquilizers (Mellaril, Haldol, Thorazine)

These medications are rarely used in treating ADHD, but they may have benefit in treating ADHD individuals who are highly aggressive, exhibiting manic states, psychotic behavior, or having difficulty with sleep disturbance. Due to their sedating effect, they may inhibit cognitive functioning and thus interfere with learning. They are most commonly prescribed by child psychiatrists or neurologists in hospital settings. They are used more as a short-term intervention as opposed to long-term management. There are relatively serious potential side effects which may include tardive dyskinesia, which is a possibly irreversible tic disorder.

Thorazine is very similar to Mellaril, but somewhat more sedating. In general, the neuroleptics tend to be either more sedating, have greater decrease in blood pressure, and are less likely to produce tics or abnormal movements (for example, Mellaril and Thorazine), or are more potent, less sedating, but more likely to induce more abnormal movements (for example, Haldol). Some neuroleptics are approximately equal in these effects (for example, Trilafon).

> **Mellaril and Thorazine**
>
> *Are more sedating, but less likely to affect movement.*

Mellaril

Usual Dosage: 10-15 mg twice a day in children/ 10-25 mg in adolescents.

Side Effects: Increased appetite, daytime sleepiness, rash, increased depression.

Haloperidol (Haldol)

Usual Dosage: In children, the lowest possible dosage of 0.5 mg per day should be the beginning point. If required, the dose may be increased by increments of 0.5 mg at five to seven day intervals.

Warning: Tardive dyskinesia, a potentially irreversible, involuntary, abnormal movement.

Side Effects: In addition to sedation, the most serious concerns involve changes in movement from neuroleptic use in children or adolescents. The risks of developing extrapyramidal effects from neuroleptics remains high. These concerns have sparked much debate on this issue, including the concerns raised by Gualtieri and Hicks, 1985, who question whether or not neuroleptics provide any relief from ADHD symptoms.

Mechanism of Action: In the late 1990's several neuroleptic medications have been introduced that have fewer movement and motor control problems. The major examples are Risperdal (Risperidone) and Zyprexa (Olanzepine). These medications block mesocortical dopamine receptors involved in organization of thought, but have little effect on nigra-striatial dopamine pathways affecting

> **Haldol**
>
> *Most movement and sedative side effects disappear or subside after the medication is discontinued.*

> **Dopamine Receptors**
>
> *Different dopamine receptors are involved in the regulation of attention and movement.*

> **Neuroleptics**
>
> *Neuroleptics are useful in patients whose ADHD symptoms reflect a broader disturbance in regulation of thought and emotion.*

movement. There major side effects are sedation and weight gain.

The use of neuroleptics in combination with stimulants hinges on the theory that beneficial effects of stimulants are due to central changes in multiple neurotransmitters rather than a single transmitter. The dopamine-blocking effect of the major tranquilizers would seem to counteract positive stimulant effects on dopaminergic activity, if that were the only mechanism of pharmacological action.

In a review article, Zametkin and Borcherding (1989) discussed the role of dopamine and noradrenaline in ADD, and suggest that a network of neurochemical systems interacts to produce the behavioral and cognitive changes in ADHD patients. Well-controlled studies of neuroleptic effects on ADHD alone and in combination with stimulants would seem warranted to determine why positive changes are seen in the subgroup of patients described above.

It is clear that the risks associated with neuroleptics in these patients must be considered. However, these risks should be weighed against possible benefits in a carefully selected subgroup of ADHD patients whose symptoms are refractory to stimulant treatment alone. Certainly, careful selection is necessary, but judicious use of these drugs in certain patients might provide quite positive results.

Summary: Neuroleptics have a limited role in ADHD. The patients most likely to benefit are probably those with underlying thought disorder or personality disorganization. Although these individuals may have a broader-based disturbance than ADHD, they often present initially with symptoms of hyperactivity and distractibility. The decision to treat with neuroleptics must reflect consideration of the possible risk for tardive dyskinesia and conservatism in dose selection and monitoring.

Chapter 12

Dietary Intervention

Chapter 12 **Born To Be Wild**

Dietary Intervention

Introduction

Since Feingold introduced the concept that food dyes, preservatives, and colorizations may increase hyperactivity, many parents have utilized dietary restriction in their ADHD children. In spite of considerable testimonial evidence that this restriction decreases hyperactivity, initial, well-controlled studies have failed to find a consistently robust effect. This lack of response to dietary challenges occurred even in children whose parents presented dietary diary histories of negative effects of these foods.

In a comprehensive review of various Feingold diet studies, Wender (1986), found that of approximately 240 children evaluated in numerous diet studies, only 1% demonstrated any consistent behavioral change in the desired direction. Over 90% of the subjects showed no significant change when challenged with food colorings.

An early trial of the Feingold diet on 15 hyperkinetic children concluded that the diet reduced hyperkinetic symptoms, but the authors stressed that this conclusion was put forth with significant reservations (Conners, et al., 1976).

Fifteen children, ages 6 to 13 years (x=9.75 +/- 1.8) were placed on an experimental (Feingold) or control diet in random order for one month duration each. All children fit the diagnosis of hyperkinetic reaction of childhood according to DSM-II. Parent and teacher ratings were obtained at baseline and weekly thereafter for the duration of the experiment. Global assessment was completed by the investigator at the end of each diet period using the Clinical Global Impressions scale.

Results: The results of this study indicate that the experimental diet was significantly better than the control diet according to teachers (p<0.005), but not according to the parents. Clinical global impressions were rated as improved significantly more often on the experimental diet than on the control diet (p<0.01).

Dietary Intervention Debate

Considerable debate exists about the potential benefits of dietary intervention of ADHD.

Dietary Studies

Controlled studies of diets low in food dyes and additives showed little benefit.

Dietary Study Results

Improvement was noted by teachers, but not parents. The diet may have more cognitive than behavioral effects.

This trial of the Feingold diet suggests that a diet low in natural salicylates, artificial colors, and artificial flavors could lower the hyperactivity of some children. However, the authors expressed apprehension in accepting these conclusions too readily. They cited the small sample size of their study and the lack of complete consistency throughout their results (possibly due to the subjective measures of change) as reasons for their doubt. Behavioral effect of major dietary intervention was considered a factor as well.

Another test of the Feingold diet placed 36 hyperactive boys on experimental and control diets. No support for the Feingold diet was observed (Harley, et al., 1978).

The subjects were 36 boys, ages 6 to 13 years (x=9.5), who met at least two of the following criteria: (1) scored 15 or above on the Conners' Parent-Teacher Questionnaire, (2) a score of 15 or more as rated by the child's teacher, and (3) a primary diagnosis of hyperkinetic reaction given by the child's physician.

All medications were terminated for two weeks prior to a two-week baseline period. Subjects were then assigned in double-blind fashion to the experimental (Feingold) or control diet. The diets were designed to be indistinguishable in appearance, taste, nutritional value, and variety. Subjects were maintained on the diets for three weeks in the spring and again for four weeks in the fall of one year. Extensive procedures were undertaken to ensure dietary compliance.

Neuropsychological data and laboratory observation were completed at baseline and at the completion of each diet period. An average of three classroom observations per week made by a team of trained students was obtained throughout the study. Conners' Parent-Teacher Questionaires were completed weekly by the child's parents and teacher.

Results: No significant neuropsychological effects of the diet were found. Classroom observation yielded no significant change in classroom hyperactivity or disruptive behavior attributable to the diet or diet order. Conner's Parent-Teacher Questionnaire ratings by parents and teachers were rarely in agreement, with only four of the 36 children consistently rated as improved on the experimental diet. Analysis of variance of mean Conners' Parent-Teacher Ques-

---

Controlled Study

In a carefully controlled study using identical-appearing food, no effect of diet was found on behavior ratings or on neuropsychological tests.

tionnaire scores indicate improved behavior as rated by parents, but not by teacher ratings.

Results of this study show that though some positive diet effects were judged to be present by parents, they became greatly reduced in teacher ratings, and basically disappeared in objective observational data. One should keep in mind that parents' ratings have usually been found to be less reliable than teacher ratings.

Another challenge of the Feingold hypothesis was performed in 26 hyperactive children who were given Ritalin and placebo medication in combination with challenge and control cookies (with and without artificial food colors and additives, respectively). Stimulant medications were found to be substantially more effective than diet in reducing hyperactive behavior (Williams, et al., 1978).

> **Stimulants**
>
> *Stimulant medications were more effective than diet.*

The subjects of this study ranged from 5 to 12 years old, had been clinically diagnosed as hyperactive, and had been receiving stimulant medication to which they were responsive for at least three months.

The children were placed on a modified Feingold diet and then randomly assigned in double-blind, cross-over style to one of 24 possible orderings of treatment involving active drug (average daily dose 10 to 25 mg methylphenidate), placebo drug, challenge cookies, and control cookies. Behavior was assessed several times a week by parents and teachers using the Conners' 11-item, 40-item, and 96-item checklists. Daily diet diaries were kept by the parents to check for compliance with the Feingold diet.

Results: Contrasting effects of diet were noted between parent and teacher ratings. There were, however, consistent results showing more reduced hyperactive behavior while receiving stimulants than while receiving placebos, regardless of dietary status. Both parent and teacher ratings showed that there was some decrease in hyperactive behavior in response to the Feingold diet (p=0.1 (NS); p=0.025, respectively); this reduction was greatest when the children were not taking medication.

This study gives clear evidence to suggest that stimulant medication is more effective in treating hyperactivity than the Feingold diet. It also shows, however, that in a subset of hyperactive children, a modified version of the Feingold

Feingold Diet Versus Placebo

When the Feingold Diet was compared to placebo in ADHD students, no improvement was evident on video tape for hyperactivity or disruptive behavior.

This study did find behavioral improvement from a restricted diet, evident by being more manageable at home and school.

Child Food Allergies

Some children have food allergies or sensitivities.

diet seems to be effective, particularly in the absence of psychostimulant medication.

In a more recent study of the Feingold diet in 39 young adolescents with learning disabilities (half with concurrent ADHD), again no clinical benefit was observed from this intervention (Gross, et al., 1987).

The effect of dietary control compared to placebo on the behavior of hyperactive children was evaluated in 39 children, ages 11 to 17. While all subjects had learning disabilities, 18 exhibited hyperkinetic syndrome as rated by school psychologists. Seven had been previously treated with methylphenidate, five with other psychostimulants, and five with neuroleptics or anticonvulsants. They were placed on the Feingold diet, which is low in salicylates and tartrazine, and avoids preservatives, artificial flavors, or colors. These outpatients were monitored on videotape for motor restlessness and disruptive behavior. The authors' impression was that the Feingold diet appears to be distasteful for typical children. There seems to be no clinical advantage provided by these diets for most hyperkinetic children. In contrast, two recent studies have suggested some therapeutic benefit from dietary control.

In a study of 76 hyperactive children, many exhibited behavioral improvement while on a restricted diet. This improvement subsequently deteriorated when they were later challenged with a diet containing multiple additives (Egger, et al., 1985).

The hyperactive children were treated with an oligoantigenic diet (one containing only a narrow variety of foods). In those children who responded, the investigators identified the provoking foods by reintroducing them sequentially. These same foods were then reintroduced in a randomized, double-blind, cross-over, placebo-controlled manner to determine their effect on the development of overactivity. Overall, 62 (86%) of the children showed improvement on the oligoantigenic diet as evidenced by increased manageability at home and school, with 21 (29%) of them achieving a normal range of behavior. Of those who completed the cross-over, placebo-controlled trial (n=28), symptoms returned or were exacerbated much more often when the patients were on active food than on placebo.

In this study, 48 foods were identified as provoking overactivity, with artificial colorants and preservatives being the most common. Notably, no child was sensitive to these two alone.

Another study reported modest results from eliminating not only food colorings and additives, but any food felt to be provocative of undesirable behavior (Kaplan, et al., 1989).

The subjects of this 10-week study were 24 hyperactive preschool-aged boys with existing sleep problems or physical signs and/or symptoms (e.g, stuffy nose, stomachache). They were placed on a diet that eliminated not only artificial colors and flavors, but also chocolate, monosodium glutamate, preservatives, caffeine, and any other substance that the families thought might be affecting their child. Approximately 10 subjects (42%) exhibited about 50% improvement in behavior. Another 4 (16%) exhibited a 12% improvement with no placebo effect. The remaining 10 children (42%) were unresponsive to dietary intervention.

Summary: Dietary intervention was initially enthusiastically pursued by parents following Feingold's initiatives. However, most well-controlled studies failed to find objective benefit from restrictive diets, nor dyscontrol following dietary challenges with additives, preservatives, or food coloring. Several recent studies suggest there may be therapeutic benefit from restriction from multiple food "antigens" in some subjects.

Further research is needed to define which patients and food restrictions may be useful. The underlying mechanism of action of food responses and its putative relationship to allergic processes also requires further clarification.

Preservatives

Elimination of preservatives, chocolate, and caffeine helped about half of the "allergic" children improve their behavior.

Amino Acid Supplementation

Introduction

Since activity of catecholamines and indolamines has been implicated in the neuropathology of ADHD, the clinical effect of precursors to these agents has been studied. Disturbances in the release or uptake of the neurotransmitters serotonin, norepinephrine, and dopamine play a possible role in the pathophysiology of ADHD. As precursors

Phenylalanine

Phenylalanine, a precursor to catecholamine synthesis, improved mood but not attention in ADHD adults.

to these neurotransmitters, phenylalanine, tryptophan, and tyrosine in increased amounts could lead to increased levels of neurotransmitters. This suggests that phenylalanine, tryptophan, and tyrosine could theoretically be used as alternative treatments for increasing central nervous system catecholamine levels.

A trial was conducted using DL-phenylalanine in adults (21 to 45 years) with residual ADD (Wood, et al., 1985).

Thirteen subjects (5 male, 8 female, ages 21 to 45 years) completed a two-week, placebo, cross-over trial. The dose of phenylalanine was gradually increased from 50 mg three times a day to a maximum of 400 mg three times a day. Improvement was noted in symptoms of mood (depression and lability), but not in symptoms of distractibility or hyperactivity. Furthermore, patients who continued on the precursor supplementation after the two-week trial became refractory.

Amino acid supplementation has also been studied in prepubertal children (Nemzer, et al., 1986).

Dietary Tryptophan

Dietary tryptophan (a serotonin precursor) improved behavior ratings in some cases better than amphetamine.

The subjects were 14 children (x age = 9.3) who met DSM-III criteria for ADHD and scored above 15 on the Conners' Parent and > 40 on the Conners' Teacher Questionnaire. They were treated with tryptophan (100 mg/kg/d), tyrosine (140 mg/kg/d), d-amphetamine (5 mg/d if < 32 kg or 10 mg/d if > 32 kg), or placebo. During treatment, blood levels of both tryptophan and tyrosine were measured weekly. Tryptophan was better than d-amphetamine in 5 of 14 subjects, as rated by parents; tyrosine was not better than amphetamine. The main side effect of tryptophan was daytime sleepiness, problematic in one subject. The authors suggested that tryptophan might be useful during stimulant medication weekend holidays.

Summary: Dietary supplementation, although interesting, has not been universally helpful. Tryptophan may be beneficial in some patients if it is well tolerated. The negative report on DL-phenylalanine and tyrosine suggests they are not useful.

Conclusion

ADHD is a multifaceted disorder with several component features. The differential distribution of symptoms may reflect primary disturbances in selective neurotransmitter and neurofunctional systems. Although Ritalin remains the primary medication of choice for most patients, other medications may have a significant role in treatment of specific patients.

These medications may have their primary effect on affective or arousal components of the disorder in selected individuals.

Antidepressants have demonstrated utility in treatment of ADHD. Desipramine is frequently the most useful, due to its profile of modest anticholinergic side effects. Other medications that have been found effective in some studies include imipramine, amitriptyline, nortriptyline and monoamine oxidase inhibitors. However, their utility may be limited by side effects. Bupropion and other new generation antidepressants may also contribute to the treatment of selected ADHD patients. While these medications generally have the advantage of more stable administration and effect, their specific indications are not yet determined. Although antidepressants appear effective in ADHD patients who are not depressed, they may have special value in ADHD patients with comorbid affective disorder.

Clonidine appears useful in ADHD patients who are highly aroused, very hyperactive, and prone to secondary aggression, oppositionality or tics. Clonidine may be used in conjunction with Ritalin for patients with concurrent distractibility.

Dietary restriction and use of amino acid precursors have not usually been found effective. While there may be selected cases that respond, reliable predictors of response are not yet available.

The effectiveness of noradrenergic antidepressants and of clonidine suggests a role for noradrenalin systems in ADHD, in addition to the importance of dopaminergic effects on breadth of attention.

These studies suggest that important therapeutic alternatives exist for treatment of ADHD children who do not respond well to Ritalin, or whose treatment is limited by side effects. Further research may better define selected patient populations or symptom clusters that optimally respond to each medication.

> **Dietary Summary**
>
> *A spectrum of medication and dietary interventions exist that may be useful for selected adults and children with ADHD/ADD and related disorders. The challenge is to find the optimal fit for each individual.*

Summary

The use of medication is a highly sensitive issue. Parents deserve to have some understanding about the expectations and risks of medication use. As clinicians, we must not supercede our boundary in the decision-making process. It is absolutely essential that time be devoted to the education of parents regarding medication issues. This cannot be done in a 10 to 15 minute appointment.

The use of medication to assist with craving, sobriety, and temperament has been demonstrated thoroughly through research. Pediatricians and family practice physicians are becoming more and more involved in the use of psychotropic medications. Yet they must recognize their own educational limitations and know when to refer to the psychiatrist or neurologist for assistance. Frequently, the psychiatrist or neurologist may initially stabilize the patient on medication and may be able to return the patient back to the primary care physician for follow-up care. Excellent communication is vital for excellent care.

With improved early identification, assessment, and treatment of special needs children, the comorbid risks associated with ADHD and other behavior disorders diminish significantly. Too often, however, we are intervening too late, when the child is in middle school or high school and personality is less resistant to change. It is at this point that psychotherapy becomes less effective in reducing the risks of school failure and mental health problems. The current laws of special education have become much more explicit in this search process to try to prevent these kids from "falling through the cracks" of the system. It becomes increasingly important to bring together the medical, psychological, and educational communities into the collaborative treatment process. The question of who should pay for services continues to be an issue. As states move towards utilizing the same body of funds for education and health care through the consolidation of children's services, this will become less of an issue.

Improved Functioning

Improved functioning depends not only on selection of the optimal medication, but on collaborative monitoring of response.

Early Intervention

Early intervention improves outcome. Medications must be combined with educational and psychotherapeutic intervention tailored to the needs of each individual.

Section 3

Chapter 13

Addictions, AA, ADHD Adults, and Answers

Chapter 13 Born To Be Wild

Stimulus Seeking

Imagine a 7-year-old ADHD child walking into a candy store with a pocket full of coins and no parent around. What do you think would happen?

Imagine a 13-year-old ADHD adolescent walking into a video game room with a pocket full of quarters. What do you think would happen?

Imagine a 25-year-old ADHD adult walking into a casino with his cashed paycheck in his billfold. What do you think would happen?

What would happen? They would probably all leave broke. However, would they repeat their mistake under similar circumstances? Not only would they repeat their mistake, they would likely dream about it until they could do it all over again! What are the variables? Each of these settings offers an immediate reward with high stimulation and delayed consequences. ADHD individuals are highly prone to rapidly forming addictive behaviors whenever these variables are present. Parents of these children often feel that they would like to shelter them from all of the "temptations" of the world. This drive to seek more and more stimulation and to avoid dull, boring environments leads the individual into an addictive pattern of living.

> *"Oh, the worst of all tragedies is not to die young, but to live until I am seventy-five and yet not ever truly to have lived."*
> Martin Luther King, Jr.

Positive Addictions

Parents often seek to involve their child in "positive addictions." *Positive addiction* may be described as an activity which is engaged in on a frequent basis and which offers stimulation for which there is value. Positive addictions may be sports such as tennis, golf, running, fishing, or may be hobbies such as carpentry or automobile repair. Many positive addictions have the potential to become careers.

Many ADHD adults are described as "workaholics" because they spend so many hours in the activity which they enjoy. These individuals are often described as "perfectionists," wanting their work to be done exceptionally well. Spouses often grow frustrated due to the amount of time they spend at their hobby or work.

If the ADHD child does not find a positive outlet for his energy, he will often seek out other excitements, which may come in the form of alcohol and drug abuse, promiscuous behavior, or other vices. Parents need to encourage the development of positive addictions at a young age. Probably the most common statement heard by parents of ADHD children is, "I'm bored." This boredom is real, and to the ADHD child, it is often intolerable. It is what oftentimes leads to excitement-seeking in negative ways. Parents must not assume that, just because an adolescent knows the risks, he or she will not engage in the behavior. Many adolescents, for example, know the risks associated with drug abuse, but return to the drug. This is the nature of addiction. While balance is important in anyone's life and there can be "too much of a good thing," of greater concern, however, is "too much of a bad thing."

When these children finally move away from home without the restraint of parental authority, the risks are at an all-time high. With maturity should come the ability to inhibit. *Webster (1996)* defines inhibit as: "to repress, restrain, or discourage from free or spontaneous activity especially through the operation of inner psychological impediments or conflicts or of social and cultural controls." We expect individuals of adult maturity of normal intellect who have had proper parenting to inhibit, and when they don't, society views them as deviant. In worst case scenarios, they go to prisons or hospitals. One wonders just what percentage of our prison population, in fact, has had a history of ADHD in childhood. What a terrible tragedy it is for a restless, hyperactive individual to be placed in a small cell with little or no stimulation for years at a time.

Treatment or Punishment

Our court system has ignored the role of this disorder in rehabilitation. Psychiatric services and medical management are terribly lacking as an intervention. Judges must understand that counseling services alone **will not** likely change the outcome for this individual, nor will punishment be an effective deterrent. It is especially important for juvenile court judges to understand this. When psychological evaluations are ordered by the court, are they ever read? Are recommendations made with the psychological evaluation in mind? If so, are they followed? It is not enough to simply determine if the individual's intellectual capacity is sufficient to know the difference between right and wrong. Most serial murderers can distinguish between right and wrong. The most pressing question to answer is, "Does this person have the ability to adequately inhibit when he knows what is wrong, and to what degree?" Antisocial behavior follows a continuum; on one end of this scale may be lying, while on the other end may be murder. ADHD individuals frequently lie over incidental matters. They do this to the frustration of parents, friends, and psychologists, yet that does not mean that on more important issues they do not inhibit and tell the truth. One of the major goals of counseling is to keep a "cap" on these behaviors in order to assist the individual from progressing from one side of this continuum to the other. It can happen very rapidly! When treatment modalities are in place, then we can catch these behavior problems in their infancy and successfully intervene. Without treatment, however, we tend to be reacting from crisis to crisis.

Parents often grow frustrated over what they see as ineffective services, either through medication or counseling. However, what they need to realize is that these services are not going to "cure" this individual, but rather are simply a part of management. The value lies in preventing the migration of core symptoms to those associated with antisocial personality disorder, substance abuse, and so forth. When these services are doing what they are supposed to be doing, the individual may not be making A's in school, but he should not be failing either. He may not be conforming to all the "rules," but he will not be totally oppositional and defiant.

This author has, on several occasions, appeared in court to describe the developmental history of an ADHD adolescent. The story is almost always the same. There have been few or no interventions. Educational interventions were lacking, and he or she failed academically, often repeating several elementary years. He or she was described by the parents as oppositional and having made bad choices in friends and activities. Friends were usually older. He or she began alcohol and drug abuse at an early age. No medical management occurred. Often the adolescent had been placed in counseling for several months to several years with little or no positive outcome. Counselors sought to discover why the adolescent appeared angry, frustrated, and lacking in motivation. This is analogous to the opthalmalogist spending years trying to determine why a child is nearsighted, rather than just prescribing glasses. Assessment is important, of course, but not to the degree that we ignore basic interventions. The treatment often ignored the psychological data, and simply processed the adolescent as if he were just one more defiant child whose parents had not taught appropriate values.

Alcoholics Anonymous

Step One of AA states: "We admitted we were powerless over alcohol, that our lives had become unmanageable." The presumption is that, prior to the addiction to alcohol, their lives were manageable and that following sobriety they will become manageable again. Unfortunately, for 30 to 40% of alcoholics, this is not true. The individual's life was a mess before he ever took his first drink of alcohol, and even after obtaining sobriety, it often continues to be a mess. It is for this reason he often eventually gives up on AA.

AA claims to help approximately 50% of those who enter. What about the other 50%? Circular reasoning is often utilized by those in AA. "You're sick because you drink, and you drink because you're sick." Most in AA favor the disease concept of alcoholism; however, to suggest, as the founding fathers of AA did, that the problem of alcoholism centers around an "allergy" to alcohol is to perpetuate a myth. It may be better to say, "You are biologically predisposed towards addictive illnesses. This predisposition is genetically and neurologically linked. Your ability to manage your life and avoid the pitfalls of addictions will depend upon the use of a multimodal treatment program possibly involving medications, support group involvement, individual counseling, and family counseling."

There is considerable controversy within AA regarding the use of medication as a viable form of treatment. For years AA has suggested that the use of medication in maintaining sobriety is akin to "switching addictions." If a person can take an antidepressant and better control his impulsive-compulsive behavior patterns and thereby remain sober, how is that "switching addictions"? This dogmatic view of avoiding medication has prevented many from seeking psychological and medical services. AA insists upon the belief that alcoholism is a disease, yet ignores the use of medication in the treatment of this disease.

For many who are in AA, if the coffee pot was taken out, they would not stay themselves. Isn't it interesting that AA's philosophy discourages medications such as stimulants (Ritalin, Dexedrine, and others) and warns that the individual is switching addictions, yet at their meetings the amount of caffeine (a stimulant similar to Ritalin) ingested is likely equal to an average dose of Ritalin. What benefits are derived from the caffeine? People become less restless, more reflective, less impulsive, more attentive, and so forth. However, with caffeine will come a great many side effects, whereas with Ritalin there would be few. Nor should we forget about tobacco. Nicotine is also a stimulant which many who smoke suggest helps to reduce their fidgetiness and calms them. How many AA meetings end with a gray cloud over the participants due to the number of cigarettes smoked?

AA's benefit appears to be in the strength of conformity, understanding, support by those who have "been there," and its emphasis on restoring a moral consciousness within the individual. Its value is immeasurable. It is past time, however, for AA to mature in its thinking and its literature. Its education must no longer focus merely upon the social etiology of alcoholism, but on the hereditary etiology as well. As has been previously stated, not all forms of alcoholism or addiction are related to biological predisposition. Rather, to ignore the hereditary factors is to leave gaps in prevention and intervention, the result of which is to continue to fail many who are struggling with these difficulties.

ADHD Adults

As has been stated previously, ADHD is a disorder of the life-span, as opposed to a disorder of childhood. Only in the past five years or so has literature been available on the subject of ADHD adults. We now recognize that the problems do not go away. We frequently see economic underachievement, marital difficulties, addictions, and socialization failures associated with adults with ADHD. Medication is still a viable intervention for adults with ADHD. Recent research on medications, such as Wellbutrin and other serotonergic inhibitors, has yielded excellent benefits for adults. With brain maturity, often lower doses of medication are required than in childhood or adolescence. This may also be related to a slowing of metabolism with age. While children with ADHD may need case managers, ADHD adults frequently need either a spouse or even a good secretary to assist them in remaining focused on projects. The role of the psychologist with this population is to assist in self-management of the disorder. Due to more "freedoms" afforded them, adults with ADHD must be particularly careful about engaging in those activities which are highly exciting and potentially addictive. They must avoid becoming egocentric in their relationships. For families to interact positively, they must take a relational stance that everyone's needs are important within the family. ADHD adults often have difficulty seeing other peoples' "points of view."

Ten Keys to Managing ADHD in Adulthood

Acknowledge you have a disability

Denial of such is your greatest enemy. This disability is not curable, but is treatable. Grieve your disability. It may affect your life on a daily basis. Grieving encourages acceptance. Don't grieve for too long, however. Do not use your ADHD as an excuse for irresponsible behavior. This would become self-defeating.

Acknowledge your strengths

In all the world, there is no one like you. You are truly special! There is no one with your many talents. Use them! Use positive self-talk to encourage your day-to-day performance. Become goal-oriented. Become relentless in completion of projects. Read literature on success-building and use those concepts which are most meaningful to you.

Watch your appetite for thrill-seeking

Boredom is your number one enemy. Discuss your plans with friends before engaging in them. Seek constant feedback. On major decisions, delay for a short time if at all possible. This will reduce impulsive decision-making.

Develop positive addictions

These may include sports, music, art, or many others. They will be your salvation. Try to find something that you can do almost every day and that you never get tired of. If you find that you rapidly lose interest in one thing, move to another. Learn to play the violin or the guitar, sew, do photography, paint, and so on. There are so many wonderful things to do that will bring you great enjoyment. Go for it! Replace the negative behaviors with positive.

Become family and community oriented

Join groups such as the Lions Club or Exchange Club. Get involved in church. There you will find acceptance, support, and camaraderie. Church will promote your moral conscience and keep you focused on what really matters in life. It will help you to avoid an egocentric pattern of living. Seek to apply the application eternal principles of behavior such as the "Golden Rule." Practice being a "giving person." Get involved in your families' lives. Continue to "romance" your spouse. Develop your spiritual life. Seek out truth!

Constantly work on organization, goal setting, and how to be more productive

Obtain the tools you need, ask others how they became more efficient, watch and learn from those who have these skills, and imitate their behaviors.

Find a support group for ADHD adults or parents of ADHD children and attend

There is great benefit in understanding that others are fighting the same battles. Be involved in advocating for understanding of this disorder.

Learn to manage your moods

The moodiness of ADHD has been compared to someone having premenstrual syndrome every other day. Learn to recognize your frustration tolerance, symptoms of depression, manic behavior, and other signs. Learn to do those things which help you to feel better. Recognize that how you think may determine how you feel.

Manage your medication

Do not be lulled into the idea that if a little is good, then more is better. Nor should you begin to think that, after six months of success, you no longer need medication. Follow your physician's orders. Consult with him or her regularly.

Utilize counseling as needed

While a practical goal of the therapist is to reduce the need for counseling services, often the individual with ADHD frequently needs the services of the therapist to assist with management of the disorder. Most therapy should be oriented towards the "here and now." Behavioral and cognitive-behavioral strategies are frequently employed in working with ADHD individuals. The provider should be highly knowledgeable about ADHD. The approach should likely be collaborative.

Summary

Much has been written regarding the definition, identification, assessment and treatment of individuals with attention deficit hyperactivity disorder. Words are entirely inadequate, however, to express the feelings of those who have this disorder or of those who love them and care for them. The concept of "unconditional love" is truly put to the test in these families. Many parents hurt for their children daily. We have witnessed and shed many tears over these children, adolescents, and adults with ADHD.

All individuals are loveable, even though they may not be likeable. Such is the manner of those with ADHD. They are at times difficult to "like," but we must never stop loving them.

Chapter 14

Clinical Research and Developmental Diversity of ADHD

Clinical Research and Developmental Diversity of ADHD

Research into Clinical Typology

Epidemiological studies of ADD children have used factor and cluster analytic techniques to identify clinical patterns. These studies support the distinction of inattention and activity as the major dimensions of ADD. They reflect the comorbid characteristics found in subjects and their relatives that define differences in the frequency of associated problems. They confirm that some patterns of ADD symptoms are more situationally specific, others are more pervasive.

Cognition Versus Activity: The major subgrouping of ADD patients is into dimensions of hyperactivity and cognition. Although these dimensions emerge from factor analysis of both epidemiological and clinical populations, the current diagnostic boundaries of ADHD and ADD or undifferentiated ADD are not sufficiently homogenous nor distinct to define neurobiological homogenous nor treatment-specific groups (Cantwell & Baker, 1988).

Using factor analytic methods, Lahey and Carlson (1991) and Lahey, et al. (1988) found two dimensions of maladjustment: (1) inattention and disorganization, and (2) motor hyperactivity and impulsive responding that correspond to the DSM-III subtypes. Fergusson, et al. (1991) reported two distinct factors of attention deficit and conduct disorder that are highly correlated (r=0.88). Behavioral symptoms identified using the Conners' Teachers Rating Scale identified two relatively independent dimensions of inattention-overactivity and aggression (Loney and Milich, 1982). Barkley, et al. (1990) suggested that two types of ADD may be separate, distinct childhood disorders rather than subtypes of a common attention deficit— as evident by the disruption of their own symptoms and the symptoms noted in their relatives. Etiological differences

---

Clinical patterns of ADHD

1. ADD with Hyperactivity
   - More in boys
   - More activity

   Associated difficulties with ADHD
   - Conduct disorder (CD)
     - aggressive
     - oppositional
   - Oppositional defiant disorder (ODD)
   - Aggression

2. ADD without Hyperactivity
   - Fidgety—little gross-motor hyperactivity
   - Related learning and language difficulties
   - More evenly distributed across genders
   - More depression and anxiety disorders

   Associated difficulties with ADD
   - Learning difficulties
   - Mood and anxiety disorders
   - Social difficulties

   Pattern depends on:
   - Age
   - IQ
   - Personality
   - Environment

between these two major groups have been postulated by several investigators. Hynd, et al. (1991) speculate that the ADD-H group may suffer from a right hemispheric syndrome; the ADD+H group may have primary pathology in processes of arousal or inhibition.

Comorbidity of ADHD and ADD: The dimensions of hyperactivity and inattention tend to cluster with somewhat different associated symptoms in individuals and relatives. ADHD is more frequently associated with increased severity, conduct disorder, and aggression. It is more likely to be pervasive, and occurs predominantly in boys. Differences in comorbidity affect response to stimulant medication.

Barkley, et al. (1990) observed that the relatives of their ADHD subjects had a higher incidence of ADD+H, substance abuse, and aggression. Faraone, et al. (1991) found that the relatives of ADHD probands themselves had a high risk for ADHD (24%), and was highest among those with combined ADD+CD (38%). Children with pervasive symptoms are more likely to be overactive, impulsive, inattentive (ADHD), and be aggressive and oppositional (CD/ODD) (Schachar & Wachsmuth, 1990).

A large amount of literature supports the effectiveness of psychostimulants in improving attention, activity, and social skills within the population (Hunt, et al., in submission; Barkley, et al., 1981; Dulcan, 1990; Greenhill, 1991). However, medication response can be affected by the presence of comorbid symptoms (Halperin, et al., 1991).

ADHD—CD/ODD: ADHD often coexists with conduct disorder, aggression, and oppositionality (August & Stewart, 1982; Offord, et al., 1979; Loney, 1983). However, family factors may substantially contribute to the development of CD/ODD in families with hostile, punitive, or negligent parenting or antisocial modeling (Reeves, et al., 1987).

Biederman, et al. (1991) found considerable comorbidity of attention deficit hyperactivity disorder with conduct disorder, oppositional defiant disorder, mood disorders, anxiety disorders, learning disabilities, and other disorders. However, the distribution of these concurrent disorders is differentially distributed among ADHD and ADD-H subjects. Dykman and Ackerman (1991) defined three behavioral subgroups: 40% of the children had ADD with hyperactivity (ADDH), 30% had ADD with hyperactivity and aggression, and 31% had ADD without hyperactivity or aggression. The relatives of ADHD+CD probands were at increased risk for antisocial disorder if the probands had combined ADD+CD (34%) or ADD+ODD (24%), as compared to ADD alone (11%) or other psychiatric disorders (7.5%) versus normal controls (4%). Several investigators reported that methylphenidate treatment reduced aggression in ADHD + aggressive children, and was equally effective with both aggressive and nonaggressive subgroups (Klorman, et al., 1988). They also reported that it facilitated the development of self-control and prosocial strategies (Hinshaw, et al., 1989; Barkley, et al., 1990). However, the children in whom ADHD-associated aggression improve on methylphenidate are primarily outpatients who lack the severe extremes of aggressive behavior that can increase from methylphenidate treatment or during methylphenidate rebound. Clonidine appears to have substantial antiaggressive effects in our clinical experience and in studies of adults (Hunt, et al., in preparation).

ADD-H: A group of inattentive children with little gross-motor hyperactivity are more likely to have related learning and language difficulties. They are at higher risk for affective and anxiety disorders and suffer social rejection; yet they are less likely than the ADHD child to have aggressive conduct disorder, and are more evenly distributed across genders (Hynd, et al., 1991; Lahey & Carlson, 1991).

The symptoms of ADD-H may occur secondary to other psychopathological etiologies such as depression or anxiety disorder. The related classification DSM-III R term of "undifferentiated ADHD" misses a substantial segment of patients who were previously well characterized as ADD without hyperactivity, but who are excluded from DSM-III R because they are impulsive (Cantwell & Baker, 1988). This category includes not only children with primary cognitive impairment and inattention, but also a significant percent of children with depression, anxiety, or schizotypal personality disorders. Recent studies demonstrate that ADD patients with coexistent depression and anxiety are less responsive to methylphenidate (Pliszka, 1989; Biederman, et al., 1989; McBurnett, et al., 1991). Thus, Lahey, et al. (1988) criticized the Diagnostic Statistical Manual-III R term "undifferentiated ADD" for treating inattention as a separate dimension, since cluster analysis of factors from teachers' ratings found that the inattention occurred in three subgroups having distinctive levels of activity: hyperactive, normal activity, and sluggishness.

Our proposed subgroup of ADD patients most likely to exhibit a primary cognitive deficit should not be impaired secondary to depression, anxiety, or schizotypal disorder. However, their attentional difficulties might be associated with learning disabilities and/or mild hyperactivity (fidgetiness and restlessness) due to disorganization.

Situational Versus Pervasive ADHD: The other major framework for organizing the phenomenology of ADHD is according to the setting in which symptoms are manifested. When ADHD behaviors occur at home and school (pervasive), the symptoms tend to be more severe and to be associated with other comorbid diagnoses, such as conduct problems, emotional symptoms, and functional impairment.

In follow-up of the Isle of Wight study, Shachar, et al. (1981) noted that 2% of all ten-year-old children fit the pervasive hyperactivity criteria (both parent and teacher ratings), and 14% fit the situational hyperactive criteria (one setting). Pervasive hyperactivity was strongly associated with earlier onset, cognitive deficits (on the Matching Familiar Figures Test, or MFFT), more neurodevelopmental anomalies, greater overall behavioral disturbance, and poorer progress over a four year period. They are more likely to be aggressive and have greater problems with socially deviant behavior, have a more chronic course (Barkley, 1988) and are more difficult to parent (Paterson, 1980; Barkley, 1981). However, independent observers did not find differences between situationally and pervasively ADHD children (Costello, et al., 1991).

However, the distinction between pervasive and situational may often reflect a distinction based on severity. Some children identified in school alone may have mild forms of hyperaroused ADHD, but may not primarily be cognitively disturbed. We will determine whether children are predominantly pervasive or situational, but will not use this criteria alone to separate the groups.

Diagnostic Process

Only a few studies have compared diagnostic groups with each other (Werry, et al., 1987). The broader question is the degree to which symptoms are a general index of psychopathology, or are specific to a particular disorder. There is considerable doubt about the reliability of these subcategories (Quay, 1986). Livingston, et al. (1990) found that over half of ADHD children reported sufficient additional symptoms using the Diagnostic Interview for Children and Adolescents (DICA) to receive an additional diagnosis, with oppositional disorder and anxiety/mood disorders being the most frequent.

The diagnostic process in ADD is based on clinical history and symptoms (behavioral ratings) and supported by psychological and often educational and cognitive testing. However, the correlation among these components of the diagnosis is often low (Gittleman, et al., 1986). The diagnostic process affects classification and nosology. The relationship between "diagnosis" on behavior ratings versus standardized interviews shows a poor correlation.

Shekim, et al. (1987) compared dimensional and categorical approaches to the diagnosis of ADHD in 114 nine-year-old children using the DISC-P and the Clinical Behavior Checklist. While 14 met DSM-III criteria for ADD on the interview, only 2 were "diagnosed" on the Clinical Behavior Checklist. As with the Isle of Wight study (Rutter, et al., 1970), the parent interview is most sensitive to the presence of a disorder, while the child interview may identify differential components across disorders. Parent and teacher ratings tend to identify different children. Parents are more likely to present their children as hyperactive on the interview than on a general behavior rating due to ADHD appearing more prominently at school than home. However, statistical significance does not equal clinical significance (Gittleman, et al., 1986).

Developmental Aspects of ADHD

Developmental Changes
- *Irritable infants*
- *Tornado toddlers*
- *Finicky preschoolers (cannot entertain self)*

Elementary School
- *Hyperactivity*
- *Impulsivity*
- *Inattention*

ADHD in Middle School
- *Pattern becomes more fixed*
- *ADHD children are often in conflict with:*
  - *parents*
  - *teachers*
  - *peers*
  - *neighbors*

ADHD in High School
- *Demoralized and depressed*
- *Behind in learning*
- *More likely to:*
  - *become aggressive*
  - *use drugs*
  - *drop out of school*

ADHD does not simply extend uniformly into adulthood. Hyperactive children do not act like grown-up, ADD adults. They have not just gotten bigger, they have changed. There are developmental patterns to ADHD that metamorphose at different ages. This maturation of symptoms is the brain revealing itself to us in patterns that change at different stages of maturity. While the most hyperactive children are almost entirely boys, the adults with ADD are about equally men and women. Is there a sex change operation going on that we don't know about? Or does hyperactivity and aggression in childhood tend to diminish with age, while the core cognitive disturbance persists, manifesting itself in disorganization or difficulties with executive functioning? Does the cognitive disturbance persist, while the activity fades—even regresses to passivity?

Onset: In our clinical experience and in studies of early-onset ADHD, the symptom most apparent before age three is severe overactivity (Campbell, 1990; Hunt, et al., in press). The second group of ADHD symptoms are first apparent in elementary school (especially second and third grades), and are more cognitive, learning, and attentional deficits. These differences in clinical patterns are not equally apparent nor equivalently distributed across the developmental spectrum.

Early Onset: The children with earliest onset of ADD-spectrum behaviors present with severe hyperactivity and may be predominantly overaroused. This extreme arousal and activity tends to diminish with age. As adults, those with this pattern of childhood ADHD are usually restless and intense. The developmental transformation of ADHD reflects common processes of biological neuromaturation superimposed on the substrate of ADHD. The "tornado toddlers," whose symptoms begin at age two or three, appear to have an increase in drive or arousal. Given their high degree of energy, they are also prone to become aggressive.

Later Onset: Those whose symptoms are first evident in middle elementary school are most often recognized by their cognitive-attentional difficulties. They may stare blankly, appear bored, be disorganized, and fail to finish or hand in assignments. Although both groups appear disinhibited, some ADD children who are not highly active have an onset of symptoms of disinhibition in middle childhood. They cannot calm themselves down; they cannot resist impulses. While toddlers are entitled to such propensities, these characteristics rapidly lose charm and appropriateness in middle childhood. These symptoms briefly recur in normal adolescent development, but are problematic and high-risk features if they extend into adult life.

Outcome: Children whose symptoms are first discovered in third and fourth grade are more likely to have a primary cognitive or attentional deficit. When schoolwork becomes novel, more symbolic or abstract, their grades drop from A's to D's. When they are required to reason, their attentional dysfunction becomes apparent. Their cognitive difficulty was not evident earlier when they did not have to contemplate and learn complex new relationships—to build abstract concepts of sequences based on previously learned information. Many of these ADD children do not have a high level of sustained activity. They may be fidgety, or restless, but are not running and climbing. Many of them are girls. Those ADHD patients who grow out of ADHD in late adolescence and adulthood were primarily the more hyperactive. What remains problematic for them may be the cognitive disorganization that persists even when the high drive state decreases.

Adolescent Outcome: Follow-up studies of hyperactive children into adolescence and young adulthood indicate that similar symptoms persist in about 40 to 50% of those children (Gittelman, 1985; Hechtman & Weiss, 1986; Cantwell, 1985). Some differences exist in the expression of the disorder in adolescents, who may exhibit persistence of cognitive symptoms, disorganization, and academic failure. Others develop more impulsive antisocial behavior and experience subjective demoralization (Barkley, et al., 1990; Mannuzza, et al., 1991). Although psychostimulants continue to be effective in adolescents, studies suggest a modest reduction in effectiveness may occur (Klorman, et al., 1987; Varley, 1983; Klorman, et al., 1988; Varley, 1986; Wender, 1985; Brown & Sexton, 1988).

Chapter 15

Clinical Diversity of ADHD

Clinical Diversity of ADHD

Children with attention deficit disorder come in all kinds of sizes and shapes. Their behavior and cognition vary in patterns that we imprecisely refer to as "with hyperactivity," "without hyperactivity," and "undifferentiated ADHD." The subtypes of ADHD are suggested by the diversity of clinical patterns linked to the pharmacologically different medications that benefit these children. This diversity implies that there is no singular neurobiological pattern to the ADD-spectrum disorders. Our current neurochemical and brain imaging data suggests that there are several neurobiological substrates relating to the different clinical subgroups of the attention disorders. There is a need for a model that relates clinical, developmental, and treatment response characteristics to neurobiological subtypes of ADD.

This model suggests that some children have symptoms of ADHD secondary to neurobiological overarousal that may reflect increased basal brain norepinephrine activity and be responsive to medications such as clonidine. Others with ADD may have a primary cognitive (information processing) deficit that reflects diminished dopamine activity in midbrain mesocortical regulatory mechanisms and input systems into the prefrontal cortex. These patients respond optimally to the psychostimulants. Others who meet the general criteria for ADD have a primary deficit in functioning of the behavioral system localized in the prefrontal cortex. This deficit may be mediated by a decrease in efferent serotonergic output systems that diminish impulse and drive intensity. Optimal response may require modest doses of both. This group responds to psychostimulants and possibly to serotonergic antidepressants. Another subgroup may have a primary dysfunction in attachment and reward processes that ultimately underlie self-directed attention. Although speculative, neuropeptides and endorphins appear to mediate this process.

These differences may assist in defining more clinically and biologically homogenous subgroups that are differentiable by means of neurobiological tests and respond optimally to different individual or collective medications. This is an empirically testable model that is subject to modification from ongoing research.

Clinical Patterns of ADHD

ADHD is one of the most frequent disorders of childhood. Epidemiological surveys suggest an incidence of about 3.5% in elementary-school-aged children; it persists with decreasing frequency through adulthood (Trites, et al., 1983; Hechtman, 1985). ADHD is more frequent in boys than girls (about 6 to 1) and has a peak incidence at, or near, age eight—a time when high levels of energy intersect with more demanding educational tasks. Children with the earliest onset often have the highest degree of overactivity and appear frenetically overaroused (Hunt, et al., 1987; 1987; 1991). The differentiation of two syndromes of ADD is supported by cluster and factor analytic studies that indicate two dimensions of maladjustment: (1) inattention and disorganization, and (2) motor hyperactivity and impulsive responding that correspond to the DSM-III subtypes (Lahey & Carlson, 1991; Barkley, et al., 1990). ADHD is often associated with aggression, oppositional defiant disorder (ODD), and learning difficulties (Biederman, et al., 1991). ADHD often persists into adulthood and may predispose to subsequent antisocial, delinquent behavior (Hunt, 1988; Hunt, et al., 1987; Cantwell & Baker, 1988; Pelham & Murphy, 1986).

Patients with ADD-spectrum disorders vary in several important parameters: severity of symptoms, onset and course of illness, associated problems, and response to medications. Differences in these aspects may reflect a variety of neurobiological substrates that underlie related, but distinguishable, clinical patterns.

The differences in the severity of the symptoms across patients provide a window into understanding the varied neurobiological substrates of the spectrum of ADD disorders. Efforts to understand ADHD subtypes have been reflected in the evolution of the nosology of this disorder. The term "Minimal Brain Dysfunction" implied that this spectrum of impaired thinking, excessive activity, and decreased motor control, often associated with minor physical anomalies was expressed in disruption of brain function. The predominance of the heightened activity prompted the term "hyperactivity" or "hyperkinesis" in DSM-III. In DSM-III the emphasis on attention, rather than activity, prompted the term attention deficit disorder with or without hyperactivity. In DSM-III R, the classification of specific behaviors attributed to overactivity, inattention, and impulsiveness, yielded to an ordinal menu of symptoms that collectively constituted criteria for the diagnosis. DSM-IV returned to the hierarchical emphasis of specific symptoms that reflects the principal triad of inattention, impulsivity, and overactivity. Historically, the symptoms of activity, inattention, and impulsiveness have been considered the unifying expression of an underlying disturbance in brain function. The question has always been, how are these symptoms related and what do they signify about brain dysfunction and treatment?

Behavioral Dimensions of ADHD

Inattention: Inattention can be a primary or secondary deficit. It is primary when the major difficulties consist of deficits in filtering, gating, and linking components of cognition. It is secondary when the inattention is a derivative of altered arousal, diminished inhibition, or failure of attachment and reward. The cognitive system that transmits information in the brain is affected by three basic neurobiological modulating systems: the arousal system, the behavioral inhibition system, and the reward or attachment system. This model addresses the relationship among these clinical symptoms and these neurobiological systems in ADD.

Those who are most inattentive experience a complicated set of disruptions that affects not only filtering, but self-cueing and reasoning. They have failure in sequencing, not because they are stupid, but because they cannot appropriately connect how one event is linked to another.

Imagine a typical ADHD child, Steven, dragged into the principal's office after he has just fought with David.

Steven immediately launches his excuse: "I didn't start it. It's all David's fault." Having somehow heard all this before, the principal asks Steven, "How did it start?" Steven: "He hit me." When the full story is told, Steven was calling David "a twerp" for the first half hour before David finally hauled off and hit him. Steven has no appreciation of the fact that his being so provocative precipitated his getting hit. The inability to link together these cognitive and social events also affects reading, self-cueing, and completion of homework. It is not just filtering that is impaired in ADD—it is linking.

The core concept of "attention" is that of continuity of cognitive processing. Attention is the thread that weaves together the complex tapestry of thought. It is the chain that binds together the stages and locations of information processing. Disruption in this chain may occur with equal frequency in girls or boys, and may persist into adulthood in spite of compensatory strategies such as making lists and using a computer. Attention is fragile and easily disrupted.

Hyperactivity: Some inattentive individuals experience extremely high levels of hyperactivity, while others are hypoactive. The preschool children whom we treat around age three may be characterized as "tornado toddlers." These children differ from those with diminished fine motor difficulties that may reflect decreased inhibition, integration, and attention—the ADD without "hyperactivity."

Children with high levels of arousal may be the most motorically overactive. This hyperactivity may affect both gross and fine motor control. The severe hyperactivity problem frequently leads to accidents due to excessive energy unchallenged by impulse judgment. Consequently, ADHD children often have to explain their way out of trouble.

ADHD children who are overly aroused experience not only too much activity, but too much reactivity. They are affected cognitively as well as emotionally and physically by high levels of arousal and low frustration tolerance. With too much internal energy intersecting with too many external stressors, their cognitive environment becomes flooded. Their accelerator is stuck to the floorboard. When frustrated or excessively challenged, these children with this subtype become frustrated and overwhelmed; they cannot pay attention or stay on a task. When trying to do their homework, these ADHD children not only have trouble staying seated, they glance at a page of math assignments and immediately panic. But this panic is expressed physically, not affectively. They quarrel, complain, fight, and whine to avoid the task that has flooded their consciousness. This "hyperactive-hyperreactive" mechanism of inattention is distinguishable from processes of cognitive distractibility and filtering. Their distractibility and dysfunction is not due to a failure of the "zoom lens" of inattention, always shifting from one narrow close-up to another. Rather, they are distracted and derailed by the excitability of low frustration tolerance secondary to high arousal that floods their otherwise intact cognitive system. When overexcited and overstimulated, they can no longer process information correctly.

Their "cognitive computer" becomes overloaded by a power surge of excessive voltage. Their high level of energy overwhelms their capacity for behavioral inhibition. They are like a VW Beetle with a Maserati engine. There is an imbalance between the power of their engine and the strength of their brakes that overwhelms their ability to steer and direct themselves. These individuals have high levels of energy evident by sustained vigor and endurance, even if the objects of their energy change repeatedly.

Impulsiveness: A primary deficit in impulsiveness is evident by excessive touching, talking, even heightened emotional dependency. Impulsive behavior may be secondary to extreme increases in energy in the hyperactive children. Due to excessive energy, a hyperactive child may be "driven to distraction." He may also be driven to talk all the time, to touch too much, to say too much. Some individuals with ADD-spectrum difficulties are not particularly "driven." They just talk, touch, flounder or flop around, but they are not excessively hyperactive. In that group we may be witnessing a primary prefrontal cortical deficit—not an excess of activity secondary to excessive arousal.

This failure to inhibit is often overlooked or misinterpreted in young children. Many children with ADHD cannot effectively self-inhibit. They need external controls to limit their showing off and to promote using secondary ways of gratifying their narcissism. Part of the narcissism, which eventually becomes internalized psychologically, reflects the impact of ADHD on the character structure and personality. A child may begin to believe that he cannot pay attention, he cannot handle stress, he cannot inhibit himself. A failure to appreciate the obvious signs of danger may extend into adulthood.

For these children, a failure of the behavioral inhibition system, most evident in terms of impulsiveness, may produce the symptoms of ADHD. Children who have diminished prefrontal cortical inhibition, the predominant mechanism associated with this disorder, cannot stop themselves. They have trouble with the brakes. This trouble affects cognition, behavior, and attention.

The impact of failure of inhibition depends on what one needs to inhibit. What comes out depends on what is behind or beneath. To understand disinhibition, consider what type of experiences individuals need to inhibit: drive states, distractions, feelings of profound dependency, excessive anger or overwhelming anxiety. We also must inhibit recurring thoughts and exaggerated appetites. Obsessive-compulsive disorders ("binges of thought"), bulimia ("binges of eating"), and some forms of violence ("binges of anger") are disorders of disinhibition. This subgroup consists of ADD children who are not particularly hyperactive, but who are always touching everything, talking, or acting "immature." They simply cannot inhibit or shut out response to internal drive states or external stimuli.

Attachment and Reward Insensitivity: Some children with ADHD have symptoms reminiscent of autism. Their interpersonal relationships are impaired by an apparent failure of attachment. Their eye contact is poor. They are so oversensitive to touch that they may resist being held. They seem impervious to pain and to consequences. Behavior modification fails because rewards and punishment lack meaning. Praise and punishment are not internalized or generalized to shape patterns of self-directed behavior.

Since most meaningful attention is internally guided—not simply externally prompted—these children also have profound difficulties with attention. As adults, we pay attention to internal thoughts and stimuli when we compose a paper, write a song, develop a business plan, or even write a shopping or "to do" list. Attention to these activities is not the same process as listening to a lecture or monitoring signals on a screen. It is internally directed and goal-driven. The capacity for this form of problem-solving, this self-directed attention, requires the experience of meaning, the ability to shape goals. Ultimately, this ability derives from a fundamental capacity for attachment and for reward. This ability relates to, but is distinct from, experiences of pleasure and pain. Attention to long-term goals is directed by meaning and values, not by the immediacy of pleasure and pain. A failure in the neurobiological processes that facilitate attachment and reward can produce secondary deficits in volitional, goal-directed attention.

Chapter 16

Neurobiological Systems for Cognition and Attention

Neurobiological Systems for Cognition and Attention

Visual System
Attentional Filtering and Gating
Alerting and Warning
Recognition and Association
Memory Encoding and Retrieval

How might systems of difficulties that complicate the lives of ADHD individuals provide a window into the secrets of the brain? The brain is not a homogenous pool of neuronal goulash, but instead consists of regionally specialized areas of specific architecture and distinct functions. These diverse areas are functionally interlinked by a neuronal information highway that connects signals in one area to information and modification in another.

Attention links the processing of this information across all of these sites. Any disturbance in attention can easily disrupt this process. Each brain area is affected by the activity of other brain centers. There is also a close connection between the feeling or affective functions and the cognitive and sensory systems. Information is selectively amplified or diminished—even at the level of the sensory organ. It is then transmitted to other brain areas for pattern recognition, identification, interpretation, prioritization, analysis, and response selection. Many of these processes occur preconsciously, without interrupting conscious, on-going thought. All of these areas in the brain are interlinked by attention.

Information Processing Systems

The Visual System: To appreciate the circuitry of brain areas in cognition, consider this simplified model of

---

Neurobiological Systems in ADHD

A. *Information processing system*
B. *Arousal system*
C. *Behavioral inhibition system*
D. *Limbic system*

Brain Regional Systems—Neuroanatomy of ADHD

1. **Arousal and alerting—** *Reticular activating system and locus coeruleus*
2. **Perception and localization—** *Sensory organs; parietal and occipital cortex*
3. **Association and recognition—** *Temporal lobe and associative cortices*
4. **Recognition of change—** *Hippocampus*
5. **Relay and interruption—** *Nucleus accumbens and striatum, mesocortex*
6. **Affective, emotional significance—** *Limbic system*
7. **Delay, analysis, and judgment—** *Prefrontal cortex*

Visual Information

Attention is the process that links visual information—including pattern recognition, symbolization, and cognitive-emotional interpretation.

Information Processing—Attention

Attention is involved in visual-motor coordination of eye movement and in memory storage and retrieval processes.

Recognition

Recognition of change and of significance alerts us to danger or opportunity.

visual attention. When reading, the retina anticipates where the eye will be moving next and heightens the responsiveness of the rods and cones in the retina that are preparing for activation. A light stimulus then activates the retina bilaterally, and travels down the optic tracts across the optic chiasm where the images from the two eyes intersect. At the lateral geniculate bodies, connections are made between what you see and what you hear. It is this link that prompts us to look in the direction of a strange sound, or to listen for sounds accompanying a movement sighted in the woods. The visual information is then transmitted back along tracts to the occipital cortex where complex decoding and integration occurs.

The visual receptor cells in the occipital cortex organize information in a hierarchy of triadic overlapping layers that enable pattern detection. Each point on the retinal screen is projected back to the occipital cortex, and then deciphered into recognizable patterns. A similar process also occurs with other kinds of sensory information such as sound and smell.

Closely linked to these tracts, the hippocampus recognizes whether anything has changed. If someone raises his or her hand, the visual field appears different than it did a moment ago. The hippocampus energizes and passes messages to other areas of the brain, activating further analysis. The hippocampus identifies change by continuously recycling a 300-millisecond loop that monitors whether something is new or changed. This filtering process is highly noradrenergic and is primarily mediated by norepinephrine.

The nucleus accumbens is the key gatekeeper that regulates whether this new stimulus merits significance to interrupt ongoing conscious processing. As the preconscious characterization of a new stimulus event proceeds in immediate memory, a judgment is made regarding significance to the importance of the current thought or focus. The nucleus accumbens filters: "This is new, but is it important?" A new stimulus may partially or completely interrupt overt processing of a prior idea, or may be minimally assessed and discarded. Much of the early formulation of this "shift/stay" judgment occurs in the nucleus accumbens that receives efferent stimuli from the prefrontal cortex and inputs from the preoptical areas and the amygdala (Margulies, 1985).

The amygdala is the alerting or "emergency early warning system" in the brain that continuously asks the survival question: "Is it danger—or opportunity? Is this going to eat me or am I going to eat it?"

In the midbrain, the thalamus monitors and integrates internal drive states. The striatum is a relay station between what's going on inside the body and outside in the world. We continuously monitor which of these actions are given attention. "Am I too thirsty to go to this meeting without first getting a drink of water? Am I curious or interested in what I am hearing?" (We ask that question all the time.)

> **Monitoring**
>
> *Monitoring of our internal physical and emotional states involves attention.*

Initiation of motor movement begins in the cortex, is transmitted through the striatum, coordinated in the cerebellum and conveyed to the peripheral nerves that control muscles. The frontal (motor) cortex houses memories of learned response routines involving speech and movement. Well-rehearsed behaviors, stories or talks can be accessed with minimal effort. New learning, or execution of a motor response in the face of peripheral muscle or orthopedic injury, requires greater cognitive effort and volitional attention.

Concurrently, the stimulus is being identified back in the occipital cortex where it is recognized as a pattern: "Oh, that's a face. It's Sally." Quickly, the pattern is analyzed in memory in the temporal lobe leading to recognition and identification. "We went to college together. I wonder what happened between Bill and her." Memory retrieval begins as a complex process of approximations that include pattern recognition and associations encoded by concept, event, sequence, and affect. In associative cortical areas, the visual, auditory, tactile, and olfactory components of the stimulus are interlinked in order to coordinate multisensory construction of an event.

> **Attention**
>
> *Attention is required to sequence and implement complex motor responses.*

The signal is simultaneously processed by the limbic system where feelings are evoked. The limbic lobes become engaged in attribution of affective components to the experience. This may occur partially by the addition of "emotion color" to long-term memory in the sensory register. "I really like Sally. We had some great talks together."

The prefrontal cortex assesses the appropriateness of rule-governed behavior in situations: "Is it OK to hug Sally,

> **Cognitive and Emotional Information**
>
> *Linking of cognitive and emotional information to social context requires judgment and attention.*

or should I just say 'hi' first? How will she feel about seeing me after all this time?" These processes are transmitted anteriorly and upwards to the frontal cortex to the "speech generation system" and then connected back and down through the midbrain to the cerebellum. You reach out your hand and say, "Hi, Sally." It takes a lot of coordinated brain power just to greet Sally.

PET scans show the activation of these brain regions as the brain perceives language in the auditory cortex (towards the back), and initiates speech more toward the front and top (the prefrontal and frontal cortexes). These are the areas involved in hearing, in seeing words, in spelling words, and in generating words.

> **Attention in ADD**
>
> *Attention in ADD is impaired at many levels: sensory perception and discrimination, recognition and interpretation, appreciation of sequence and context, and selection of response.*

Relevance to ADHD: Errors in information processing can occur any place along this cognitive sequence. Attention is the thread of continuity that entrains the diverse activities of these centers required for information processing of perception, recognition, association, memory, response selection, and identification. Some cognitively-impaired ADHD children have such breadth of attention that they cannot ignore any intense incoming stimuli.

Deficits in filtering may burden attention by increasing the processing load. Capacity to sustain attention may be impaired at the level of the hippocampus (familiar things are inaccurately considered novel), or at the level of the nucleus accumbens that inadequately buffers against interruption of ongoing thought.

More diffuse connections within the cortex are essential for contemplation and abstraction. Such complex processes require additional accessing of long-term memory and creative or novel restructuring essential for problem solving (Oades, 1987). This process of conscious direction of thinking and cognitive effort occurs on several levels of brain functioning.

> **Sustain Attention**
>
> *Ability to sustain attention requires emotional regulation of boredom and frustrations.*

Memory and Attention in ADHD: Cognitive psychology is the science of information processing. Information that enters the cognitive system is identified based on a signal-to-noise discrimination and early (preconscious) analysis of significance. Stimuli that are considered potentially significant are processed in immediate memory. Information that requires active, conscious manipulation or consideration is held in active, short-term memory.

By analogy, the sensory input system in the brain is similar to the keyboard of the computer. The input quickly passes through a BIOS (brain input/output system) that regulates input and output and routes information to and from its appropriate locations. Short-term or "working memory" in the brain is similar to RAM (random access memory) in the computer where information can be temporarily stored, altered, and compared to other information available in long-term memory (similar to information stored and indexed on the hard disk). For example, to remember a phone number or a complex name, you have to create other reinforcements or links.

Information that is important and needs further processing must be shifted into active or working memory. Short-term memory, meaning anything from immediate to several minutes, has an automatic decrement since short-term memory has limited resources. However, increased concentration and motivation can temporarily expand the capacity of short-term memory. This is the area of active memory where associations are constructed.

A shift of information to long-term memory is encoded in several ways. This encoding occurs partly in sequence (what happened first, second, and so on). "I first met Sally in 1984, when I was in medical school, before graduation." Remote memories are also encoded by content or concept—what the information is about. "This article about ADHD reminds me about patterns of behavior I saw in my child when he was ten years old." Memories are also filed by their emotional meaning (affective significance). "I was very disappointed when Sally and Bill split up. It reminded me of my losing Carol." These associative links are partially generated during sleep and dreaming. Part of the dream process is protein synthesis, enabling information to be encoded and consolidated into long-term memory.

The linking of all of those processes is what is endangered in children with attention deficit disorder. But it is particularly impaired in those children where the attention deficit is primarily a filtering and processing deficit. They often seem to store information relatively randomly—and often have difficulty retrieving it when needed.

Functional Attention

Functional attention occurs in short-term working memory, and must be linked to immediate and long-term memory.

Long-Term Memory

Story in long-term memory depends on emotional and cognitive significant and requires protein synthesis.

Effective Retrieval

Effective retrieval requires attention to labeling and search strategies.

Chapter 17

Measures of Attention and Learning

Measures of Attention and Learning

Continuous Performance Task (CPT)
Matching Familiar Figures Task (MFFT)
Paired Associate Learning Task (PAL)
Inhibition Tasks

Cognitive Measures in ADHD: The primary method of measuring attention in ADHD consists of using a battery of stimulus-dependent tasks that recruit increasingly complex cognitive processes. Several tasks have been widely applied in studies of ADHD. Most tasks can be scored to reflect a combination of speed and accuracy that can be integrated to measure caution, oppositionality, or impulsivity. The use of tasks in ADHD have been reviewed by Barkley (1988) and Swanson (1985). These tasks include:

Attention

- *Filtering*
- *Gating*
- *Linking*

Continuous Performance Task (CPT)

The Continuous Performance Task provides a measure of reaction time (latency), impulsivity (errors of commission) and sustained attention (Sykes, et al., 1971; 1973; Nuechterlein, 1983; Klorman, et al., 1988). We have previously studied ten ADHD children using the CPT and found them to be easily frustrated, very oppositional, impulsive and apt to make more errors of commission than nonaggressive ADD patients ($p<0.01$).

To measure sustained attention, clinicians administer tests like the CPT which samples the ability to tolerate boredom and to inhibit response (the B & A task). Tracking latency and errors of omission and commission, the basic CPT measures: "How long can you sit there and be bored by a stimulus flashing in front of you? How impulsive are your responses?" Although relevant to ADHD, the CPT is a stimulus-based task. More sophisticated versions of the CPT (Conners and Swanson versions) tap more complex domains of inhibition by introducing variable intervals between stimuli. However, the CPT does not probe more complex processes of reasoning and problem-solving—the ability to contemplate things that are important. Furthermore, results of this vigilance task do not correlate highly with classroom learning or overall behavior.

Matching Familiar Figures Test (MFFT)

The Matching Familiar Figures Test is a type of "matching to sample" task. The MFFT assesses selective attention, distractibility and impulsivity (Sargent, et al., 1979; Kagan, 1966). ADHD patients make rapid, impulsive, and inaccurate selections due to low frustration tolerance. ADD subjects may demonstrate greater cognitive effort (increased latency), but have difficulty with perceptual discrimination resulting in an increased error rate.

Paired Associate Learning Task (PAL)

The PAL measures the rate and accuracy of learning an arbitrarily assigned match of unrelated stimuli, and assesses "effortful" learning and memory (Douglas, et al., 1988; Swanson, et al., 1983). ADHD patients are expected to quickly become impatient, oppositional, and make errors of commission, while having greater variability in their latency.

The measuring of attention is fundamental to research about brain functioning and medication effects in ADHD. Given our interest in new drug development, we are developing new measures that address the connection between attention, problem-solving, frustration tolerance and motivation. We are currently creating an integrated computer system for analysis of clinical, pharmacological, and cognitive data with links to educational systems to pilot and normalize new behavior and cognitive ratings.

Inhibition Tasks

The intolerance of boredom is not pathognomonic or diagnostic of all the problems for ADHD. Also of concern in ADHD is the allocation of attention to areas of interest, the capacity to pay attention to various internal or external experiences. The attention of ADHD individuals appears excessively stimulus-bound—these children are stimulus-captive. Whatever is bright and moving grabs their attention. But events that are quiet, sad, or reflective do not sustain their interest. Usually, when adults pay attention to something complex, it involves solving a problem, thinking about a relationship, or considering ideas; initiation is fundamentally internal. Our capacity to objectively measure that dimension of internal attention and problem-solving is very limited.

There are a number of tasks to assess these processes of selective attention including the Matching-to-Sample Task, the Dichotic Listening Task (which helps separate or identify our ability to distinguish stimuli), the Stroop Color Naming Task (an interesting task where the subject sees the written word "red" displayed in the color blue and must respond to the color, not the word). Other inhibitory tasks measure the ability to stop doing one thing and shift our attention to something new. Other tasks assess the ability to respond to stimuli in different locations and to disconnect from an activity prior to shifting attention. These tasks can distinguish motor from cognitive aspects of response.

Chapter 18

Neurobiological Systems That Modulate Cognition and Attention

Neurobiological Systems That Modulate Cognition and Attention

Arousal System
Behavioral Inhibition System
Affect Regulation (Limbic) System
Attachment/Reward System

These cognitive functions that interpret, store and link information among brain regions are affected by at least three general modulating systems—the arousal system (basal brain), the inhibition system (prefrontal cortex), and the affective system (limbic system.) These modulating systems affect the amplitude of signals, their intensity, clarity, and significance. They regulate the importance attributed to a cognitive task—the ability to attribute meaning and motivation and to regulate frustration associated with a task.

The Arousal System

The basal areas of the brain contain the energy and drive systems essential to survival. The reticular activating system and the locus coeruleus, where norepinephrine cell bodies are concentrated, regulate alertness, sleep-wake, startle response, and reaction to immediate danger.

The arousal system has much of its origin in the basal part of the brain. The locus coeruleus is the area in the brain where norepinephrine has its core cell bodies. Norepinephrine is the neurotransmitter most involved in arousal processes associated with energy level and responsivity. Arousal pathways connect to the cortex and to many areas of the brain, including the hippocampus. Norepinephrine does not function as a specific neurotransmitter; rather, it is a more general neuromodulator. Norepinephrine does not convey specific information; it regulates the intensity of information being analyzed.

> **The Arousal System**
>
> *The arousal system enables alerting and active information processing. It includes many brain systems and neurotransmitters—especially norepinephrine.*

Inadequate Arousal

Inadequate arousal slows information processing.

Excessive Arousal

Excessive arousal may lead to cognitive flooding.

Increased Arousal

Increased arousal enables alert scanning of the environment.

Physiology of Arousal: Firing of the locus coeruleus produces a state of alert arousal. Locus coeruleus firing occurs in response to novel stimuli and activates secondary analytic processes to facilitate identification, to determine threat or opportunity, and to initiate analysis of significance and response.

At the level of the cortex, variations in arousal have significant effects on attention and activity. Diminished arousal during fatigue or depression slows cognitive rate, and diminishes effort and perceptual and analytic acuity. Moderate increases in arousal in the mature brain can enhance attention by increasing alertness and focus. Moderate stress, or heightened reward or interest, may enhance receptive and analytic capacity, and improve processing efficiency of effortful cognition.

Excessive arousal, especially in an immature cortex, can disturb attentional focusing by diminishing the effectiveness of the primary perceptual filters. Familiar or intense stimuli are considered novel and fail to be rejected. This results in flooding the analytic processes with irrelevant stimuli and shifting conscious focus. Background "noise" becomes indistinguishable from significant external signals or internal ongoing cognition, compromising prioritization of selective and sustained attention. Attentional focus becomes shallow and scattered. Also, increased basal brain arousal may increase the experience of anxiety and diminish frustration tolerance. Also, excessive arousal increases motor output which results in restlessness, fidgeting, and overactivity including rapid rate of speech.

Animal Models of Arousal: As evident from work by Foote and colleagues (Foote, et al., 1980), locus coeruleus stimulation in unanesthetized monkeys produces a state of alert activation and visual scanning. Norepinephrine stimulation affecting the hippocampus labels stimuli as being "new" or "changed," thereby necessitating further cognitive analysis by cortical processing systems (Gray, et al., 1982; Quay, 1984). Thus, excessive norepinephrine release seems to burden and ultimately overload intact information processing systems.

In the mature animal, norepinephrine stimulation also activates compensatory (cortical) behavioral inhibition systems, producing a state of controlled, prepared vigilance. However, in developing children, this excessive basal brain activation, unbalanced by sufficient prefrontal cortical inhibition, may produce a state of hyperactive behavior in which many stimuli are deemed significant and require further processing, or generate excessive response. Thus, the high level of basal arousal may impair cortical processing and intensify behavioral activity.

For an ADHD child experiencing such a hyperaroused state, trivial stimuli become distractions to more pertinent ones and attention is repeatedly shifted from stimulus to stimulus. Frustration that accompanies trying to process too much unselected information may lead to secondary oppositionality, as a child attempts to ward off the task demands (such as homework) that have become cognitively overwhelming and emotionally demoralizing. In such a state, an ADHD child would rather fight than work. The fight refocuses attention, redefines identity and purpose, and eventually produces a release of energy that diminishes hyperarousal. After a two-hour fight, the ADHD child frequently completes his or her assignment in 15 minutes.

> **Excessive Arousal in ADHD**
>
> *In ADHD, excessive arousal may be uninhibited, producing increase, unselected action and activity.*

Behavioral Inhibition System

Another major neurofunctional system that affects multiple aspects of behavior is the behavioral inhibition system (Gray, 1982). If arousal is the neurophysiological equivalent of acceleration and activation, inhibition is analogous to the neural brake.

The prefrontal cortex is where delay, evaluation, and judgment occur. This is the area that oversees and monitors other activities of the brain. The prefrontal cortex is the executive area of the brain—responsible for arbitrating disputes between immediate impulses and long-range goals. The prefrontal cortex provides the brakes needed to delay action long enough to insert reflection. It is the librarian that cross-references new information with old. The prefrontal cortex searches memory for relevant new and old information. Here facts are integrated into meaning and context. It is the censor that stops inappropriate behavior; the policeman who enforces the rules. It is the minister who

> **Behavioral Inhibition System**
>
> *The behavioral inhibition system provides delay, judgement, and selection of response.*

> **Behavioral Inhibition System**
>
> *The behavioral inhibition system is the respository of values and priorities.*

> **Managing Stress**
>
> *Strategies for managing stress and completing projects and goals require conscious inhibition and organization.*

integrates values, identity, and continuity into behavior. The prefrontal cortex is the CEO who judges and determines the course of action, establishes priorities, executes values, imposes needed delays. It is the inhibitory brake and analytical computer that governs behavior. It provides the fingerprint for personality and identity; it is the fountain of civilization, culture, and law; it tames the tyranny of impulses.

As events are integrated that require further conscious processing (in short-term memory), the prefrontal cortex becomes engaged in judgments about meaning, prioritization, and response preparation. The prefrontal cortex performs much of the functions commonly attributed to executive ego functioning. It is engaged in determining what additional information might be needed in order to enhance analysis or clarify opportunity or risk. Similarly, the prefrontal cortex is essential to the determination of judgment about the execution of response. For example, in the face of danger, the prefrontal cortex may determine that negotiation is a better strategy than running or fighting. Issues of competing values and commitments, empathy and social learning may all be employed in making such a judgment.

The prefrontal cortex executes volitional processing essential to self-directed or goal-directed behavior. This center is vital to decision-making, value acquisition, and strategy formation. Lesions or damage to the prefrontal cortex are frequently associated with the inability to plan and direct willful, goal-oriented behavior and utilize appropriate social judgment.

The prefrontal cortex of the brain is in charge of executive functioning, the ego functions of personality. Other areas pass information along to the prefrontal cortex, where decisions must be made as to whether it is worth interrupting ongoing information to shift to new stimuli. Is this information really worth thinking about? Does it remind me of something else that I already know? "I remember the time Sally…. Boy, if I said this, she would be so embarrassed and I'll bet she would really laugh. No, she wouldn't laugh. She'd just be embarrassed. I won't talk about it." Hyperactive children do not make these contextual connections. They blurt out before they process the information.

Physiology of Inhibition: On a cellular level, many neurotransmitters inhibit cellular activity firing on a behavioral level. Throughout much of the cardiovascular system, norepinephrine activates vasoconstriction while serotonin facilitates vasodilation. Similarly, on the gross behavioral level, emission of many forms of behavior are delayed or aborted by the behavioral inhibition system. Behavioral inhibition is essential to the expression and direction of sexual activity, appetite, and motor activity and aggression. In addition, inhibitory processes affect persistence of thought and complex behavior as evidenced by excessive inhibition in obsessive-compulsive disorder. The site of the altered inhibitory process in obsessive-compulsive disorder (OCD) and ADHD may differ.

> **Inhibition**
>
> *Inhibition involves control of impulses and the guidance by purpose and goals.*

The cingulate gyrus functions as an internal "motivation detector" (prioritizer) for innate impulses; the striatum functions as an external stimulus transmitter (prioritizer) for external cortical signal content. Both structures have input to the globus pallidus that has inhibitory effects to the thalamus. In OCD, excessive firing of the cingulate gyrus decreases the inhibitory action of the globus pallidus, thereby liberating the thalamic transmission of basal brain impulses (grooming and territorial protection) to the cortex. Activation of the globus pallidus via serotonin diminishes obsessionality; diminished globus pallidus output could increase obsessionality. Serotonergic medications (SSRI's) ultimately reduce serotonergic receptors in the globus pallidus thereby facilitating (reducing inhibitory control) globus pallidus inhibition of thalamic impulses that can repetitively dominate thought. Similar behavioral inhibition processes in ADHD may occur at the level of the striatum and involve prefrontal cortical systems. (Flament, et al., 1987; Rapoport, 1988).

> **Serotonin and Inhibition**
>
> *Serotonin enables inhibition of drives and impulses.*

Input to the prefrontal cortex in man is substantially dopaminergic. A major clinical effect of the psychostimulants is to enhance transmission into the prefrontal cortex in order to facilitate judgment. The output systems from this are two major tracts. One neurotransmitter, the serotonin tract, contributes to the active inhibition from the prefrontal cortex. The second tract was recently described from work in monkeys at Yale by Goldman-Rakic and Arnsten (1985).

> **Norepinephrine**
>
> *Norepinephrine in the cortex decreases distraction from other sensory inputs.*

> **Attention Shift**
>
> *The ability to shift attention requires active inhibition and release.*

> **Inhibition**
>
> *ADHD individuals have difficulty inhibiting drives and selecting and prioritizing behavior.*

They found important output tracts of norepinephrine in the third layer of the prefrontal cortex that inhibit brain activity in the striatum and other areas. These inhibitory tracts are activated by norepinephrine and are enhanced by drugs like Clonidine and Tenex that act very specifically on norepinephrine receptors in those areas (Arnesein & Hunt, 1993).

Attention also requires inhibition to appropriately delay activity to allow reflection and consideration of response options. An active, albeit inhibitory, process is also involved in letting go of a thought or cognitive focus in order to shift attention to a new subject (Posner, 1986).

This component of the behavioral inhibition system may occur at several levels of brain function. Caudate-based inhibitory processes act to control movements. The major site of cortical inhibition is the prefrontal cortex that is involved in judgment, information searching, prioritization, and inhibiting behavior pending adequate consideration.

Relevance to ADHD: Many children with symptoms of ADHD, especially those characterized by impulsivity without high levels of arousal, may have a deficit in response inhibition. They act and speak without thinking. Frequently, their fists or words hit their opponent before their thoughts can reach their hands. They are almost surprised at their reflexive, aggressive actions. They cannot override the expression of their needs, affects, or drives. Sometimes this is expressed as excessive emotional need for support and attention—frequently labeled as "immaturity." Other times the lack of inhibition is behaviorally evident as an inability to stop behaviors such as talking, playing with a pencil, or eating. In the face of inadequate inhibition, their needs or impulses are tyrannical. They blurt out inappropriate thoughts, tease and "unintentionally" insult peers, and require the vigilance of teachers. They require continual external monitoring to maintain focus and avoid danger. Their uninhibited behavior is evident in their lack of direction of activity. While they do not exhibit the excessive energy of the highly aroused ADHD patients, and do not have a primary cognitive deficit in information processing, they qualify as ADHD by their impulsivity, fidgetiness, and inattention.

Neurochemistry of Inhibition: Cortical inhibitory

processes reflect a synchrony of affect, or input signals, that may be primarily dopaminergic, and output tracts that are primarily serotonergic. The effective power of these inhibitory processes must be considered in relation to the strength of the underlying drive states and the degree of overall arousal. If norepinephrine is the principal behavioral activating neurotransmitter, serotonin is the predominant central behavioral inhibiting neurotransmitter.

The neurochemical tracts into the human prefrontal cortex are highly dopaminergic. This differs even from monkeys, which have little dopamine in the cortex. In the last two years, anatomical scanning of the human brain at the prefrontal cortex, along with labeling using PET and SPECT scans, has demonstrated a high concentration of dopaminergic innervation in the prefrontal cortex. Much of the behavioral inhibition system appears to be serotonergically mediated.

While an increase in serotonin may be associated with obsessional thinking, a decrease in serotonin is associated with impulsive action, aggression and perhaps fragmented or inadequately persistent thought. A primary deficit in serotonergically mediated inhibition systems may constitute an alternative route to ADHD. Other neurotransmitters also have profound effects on behavioral inhibition, including GABA (Gamma Amino Butyric Acid) systems, which appear to be functionally related to the experience of anxiety.

Affect Regulation System

The limbic system is a complex series of connections that include emotional experiences essential to attachment, anger, fear, sadness, pleasure, and dreaming. There are many interconnected areas because so many diverse feelings must be connected to memory and to response selection and execution. Much of this affective system involves the autonomic, or peripheral nervous system. These systems are also linked to other cognitive pathways so that thoughts and feelings can be integrated. A primary disturbance within either the cognitive or affective system will burden the other.

Norepinephrine

Norepinephrine facilitates arousal.

Dopamine

Dopamine is essential to getting information into the prefrontal cortex for analysis.

Serotonin

Serotonin is involved in stopping or inhibiting emotions, thoughts, and behavior.

Limbic System

The limbic system processes emotional information.

Reward System

Reward and meaning are important components of attention and information processing (Haenlein & Caul, 1988). This system is involved in attribution of emotional significance relevant to motivation and short-and long-term goals. These rewards may be external (such as praise, smiles, nickels or ice cream) or internal, as defined by one's sense of identity or values. While initially connected to a sense of pleasure and gratification, values that direct subjective attention ultimately comprise a sense of personal identity and long-term ambition. Reinforcement initially reflects emotional processes of attachment that during development shift from preoccupation with parental approval to investment in curiosity, intimacy, and task performance. The ability to willfully direct attention requires a sense of identity, goals, and rewards that constitutes a framework for prioritization of effort. This competence requires input from limbic as well as cognitive systems.

An inability to experience reward occurs at two different levels. Cognitive impairment may reduce the ability to integrate values and social awareness into thought processes. Thus, it may be difficult to assign meaning to rewards, resulting in no sense of fulfillment or pleasure. In some children, however, the reward system itself may be intact, with meaning assigned to specific events and emotions attached to specific behavioral responses, yet the child remains unable to access the system.

Relevance to ADHD: Severe deficits in reward processing occur in pervasive psychiatric disorders, such as autism, and in atypical personality development. Some ADHD children demonstrate deficits in processes of consequence or of significance. Even when unstressed and relaxed, they are relatively unresponsive to consequences of praise or punishment. They seem indifferent to the emotional significance of their actions. Unless they are threatened with immediate punishment or pain, their actions have little meaningful direction. They may become obsessively preoccupied with a redundant task, such as a puzzle, and protest violently if interrupted. Their thoughts and behavior appear disorganized due to a lack of emotional, rather than cognitive, integration.

Neurochemistry of Brain Systems in ADHD

1. *Dopamine—attention*
2. *Norepinephrine—arousal*
3. *Serotonin—inhibition*
4. *Endorphins—attachment and reward*

Reward

There is an important difference between immediate pleasure and long-term reward.

Long-Range Goals

Many ADHD individuals struggle to define and implement long-range goals and plans.

The neurochemistry of each of these three systems is probably different. Hyperarousal and hyperactivity may reflect excessive norepinephrine activity. Primary difficulties with filtering may be linked to deficits in dopamine systems. Deficits in impulsive control may be associated with diminished functioning in serotonin systems, the major output tracts from the prefrontal cortex involved in stopping and inhibiting. Attachment and reward may be mediated by endorphins.

Brain Systems In Attention and ADHD

1. **The cognitive system: selective attention**
    a. *Breadth of attention: analysis, association, response*
    b. *Dopamine effects on attention: the zoom lens.*
        - *Specific tracts and receptors—mesolimbic, cortical*
        - *Evidence for dopamine effects on attention: psychostimulants*

2. **The arousal system: fatigue and mania, hyperactivity and attention**
    a. *Locus coeruleus and reticular activating system*
    b. *Noradrenergic projections to the hypothalamus and cortex*
    c. *Arousal-dependent ADHD*

3. **The behavioral inhibition system: controlled response**
    a. *Ability to select and inhibit response*
    b. *Serotonin in inhibition of aggression, impulsivity, thought*
    c. *Serotonergic receptors and medications*

4. **The reward system: motivation, attention, reward and meeting**
    a. *Ability to direct attention towards a meaningful goal*
    b. *Limbic system and attachment processes*
    c. *Possible role of endorphins*

Chapter 19

Potential Role of Neurobiological Systems in ADHD/ADD

Chapter 19 Born To Be Wild

Potential Role of Neurobiological Systems in ADHD

Cognitive Failure in ADHD/ADD

The spectrum of ADHD behavior suggests that these diverse problems reflect dysfunction in specific components of brain functioning in children. Attention may fail due to difficulties at several levels of cognition: perception, recognition, integration, memory, expression, or initiation of sustained activity.

At the level of sensory perception and integration, peripheral mechanisms of attention may fail to activate sense organs in preparation for processing important information. Alerting may be inadequate or excessive—leading to ignoring or exploding when a threat is perceived. Visual-motor coordination essential to reading may fail at the level of visual movement. ADHD patients may need to allocate so much attentional capacity to the regulation of eye movements that they forget what they have just read. When they return to thinking about what they have read, they lose eye control, experience visual regressions or loss of convergence. The content of what they read may prompt loose associations of thoughts, further fragmenting the tracking information from the text. Attentional failure may also occur at the level of linking information among brain locations and modalities. Some people learn much better through visual stimuli (what they see), others by auditory processing (what they hear). Difficulties encoding or decoding from storage reservoirs (as evident in learning disabilities) may also place an added burden on attentional processes.

Since much of the linking between sensory information and cognitive processing must be transmitted through the striatum, Lou and colleagues (1990) postulated the "striatal theory" of disregulation. Using xenon inhalation to trace blood flow, he demonstrated that cerebral blood flow in the striatum is decreased in some ADHD patients in comparison

---

Neurobiological Systems in ADHD/ADD

A **Cognitive—**
- *primary effects seen on information processing; secondary effects on activity and impulsivity*

B **Arousal—**
- *primary effects seen on frustration; secondary effects on cognition and inhibition*

C **Inhibition—**
- *primary effects seen on impulsiveness; secondary effects on activity and cognition*

D **Attachment/Reward—**
- *primary effects on self-directed behavior; secondary effects on attention and activity*

to those with other syndromes. Psychostimulant treatment increases flow to the striatum and the periventricular region. This diminished flow through the brain relay station may reflect part of the mechanism of attention fragmentation in ADHD.

Overarousal in ADHD

Excessive arousal may overload intact information processing systems. This is analogous to the amplifier in a stereo system. The arousal amplifier does not change the channels, as attention does; it does not process information, it is the volume control. Too much volume in the system can produce static, feedback and overwhelm the speakers and distort the sound. Speakers and amplifiers are rated to reflect their tolerance of distortion as a function of the amplitude of the signal being processed, or their ability to buffer or modulate various intensities of stimuli. The distortion increases when the signal gets too strong. Similarly in the brain, when stimuli become too intense, the brain processes become overwhelmed. Many hyperactive children are virtually unable to modulate their response to intense stimuli—the excitement of a birthday party, or the stress of a test. High levels of norepinephrine intensify baseline activity and stimulus response. Altered arousal may secondarily ablate information-processing in hyperactive and hypoactive behavior in ADHD children.

Inhibition in ADHD

Deficits in the behavioral inhibition system have been suggested by several behavioral observations, as well as by pharmacological response and neurobiological indices such as brain imaging. Some children and adults with ADHD appear to have symptoms of disinhibition that reflect a neurobiological deficit in the prefrontal cortex. Behaviorally, many ADHD children fail to access that area which makes judgments, inhibits them from offending people, improperly touching and fighting. The prefrontal cortex is involved in processes of integration, evaluation, judgment, and initiation—processes impaired in children and adults with

ADHD. PET scan studies of adults with residual ADHD suggest diminished brain metabolism in the prefrontal cortex (Zametkin, et al., 1991).

Reward Insensitivity in ADHD

A failure of the attachment/reward system in the limbic cortex may lead to inappropriate affect regulation. Failures in emotional attachment may ultimately lead to diminished capacity for meaningful judgments and definition of goals that guide volitional attention. You cannot self-direct attention if you are unable to experience and establish purposeful direction.

> **Arousal and Attention**
>
> - *Attention depends on the level of arousal*
> - *Excess arousal can overwhelm cognition*
> - *Excessive arousal can produce frustration and anxiety*

Neurotransmitter Systems That Modulate Attention and Behavior

Neurotransmitters

Neurotransmitters

Brain pathways to ADHD symptoms.

This model of brain function suggests that there may be multiple pathways though which children come to exhibit similar behavioral symptoms of overactivity, inattention, and impulsivity. It also suggests that these varied sites of brain dysfunction may respond optimally to different medications. Medications directed toward decreasing noradrenergic activation (clonidine) may normalize arousal; medications that increase dopaminergic functioning appear to enhance cognition (methylphenidate or amphetamine). Perhaps medications that increase serotonergic functioning, such as the serotonergic antidepressants, will both stabilize mood and diminish impulsiveness. Other medications may eventually be found to enhance the experience of reward.

How do these medications act on the spectrum of symptoms of ADD as described within this model? The varied response patterns of ADD children to a variety of medications with different mechanisms of action suggest possible differences in underlying neuropathology. The effects of medications that alter functioning of systems ultimately occur at the level of the synapse—the communicative bridge between neurons. Behavior and the effects of medication are further modulated by genetically controlled processes that regulate receptor response and the transfer of information beyond the receptor. By analogy, the radio signal coming into a stereo is detected and decoded before it is amplified and transmitted to the speakers. Yet differences in the sensitivity and processing of the signal by the speakers greatly alters the final sound produced.

Synapses

Synapses provide the chemical connection between brain cells.

An appreciation of brain function and attention requires consideration of events at the level of the synapse. There neurotransmitters and neuropeptides bridge the information between nerve cells essential to perception, cognitive processing, arousal, inhibition, and reward. In the axons (the endings of neurons), neurotransmitters such as norepinephrine and dopamine are synthesized and stored. There are very specific sites in the brain where serotonin, norepinephrine, dopamine, and other neurotransmitters are concentrated. Alterations in specific neurotransmitter levels in the synaptic cleft can affect attention and the modulation intensity of thoughts, feelings and activities. Disturbances in these brain regions or in brain functional systems may also impair attentional competence.

Synaptic Regulation and Effects of Medications

Multiple levels of regulation affect the activity of a neuron or a synapse. Neuronal activity can be regulated by alteration in neurotransmitter synthesis, release, reuptake, metabolism, or by alteration in receptor sensitivity. Synthesis, or production of neurotransmitters, usually begins in the cell body and involves a chain of chemical reactions and transformations that produce a particular neurotransmitter from its precursor. The rate of production is partially controlled by enzymes that catalyze these reactions. Most neurotransmitters are stored presynaptically in vesicles near the synapse where they await release and possible final transformation. The process is analogous to the supply line that allows an army to amass units in strategic locations before being called into action.

Synaptic Effects: Most signals within the brain must be rapidly transmitted and deactivated. The tone, or level of response of a neuronal system, must remain relatively constant—but be able to respond quickly to danger and emergency. But the content of the specific information being transmitted changes instantaneously. The concentration of neurotransmitters that provide is this chemical communication must be tightly regulated—not only by controlling the neurotransimitters' production and release—but their fate, once they enter the synaptic cleft. A rapid removal and deactivation of neurotransmitters is necessary to generate

Synaptic Regulation in the Brain

- *Neurotransmitters cross brain synapses to convey information.*
- *Neuronal activity can be regulated by alteration in production, release, reuptake or by changes in receptor responses.*
- *Presynaptic receptors regulate production and release of neurotransmitters.*
- *Dopamine regulates attentional focusing and gaiting of information and activity.*

Neurotransmitter Effects on Behavior

- *Norepinephrine regulates arousal and responsivity to reinforcement.*
- *Serotonin regulates inhibition of impulses and drives.*

Deactivation of Chemical Signals

The deactivation of chemical signals primarily occurs by active reuptake of released neurotransmitter.

Brain Receptors

Brain receptors are self monitoring. They can vary greatly in their response to a neurochemical signal.

brief pulses and changes of information and prevent perseveration, "sticking," or fixation on a prior signal. The most immediate regulation of neurotransmitters occurs through a process of reuptake into the releasing neuron, resulting in rapid removal of the neurotransmitter from the synapse. This occurs through a "pump," an active chemical process that removes the transmitter from the synapse. Once the neurotransmitter is taken back into the presynaptic neuron, it is deactivated and recycled. Neurotransmitters are broken down and metabolized within the axons and the synapse by enzymes that "deactivate" their effect through a chemical. There are very specific sites in the brain where serotonin, norepinephrine, dopamine and other neurotransmitters are concentrated. Attentions in release, reuptake, or in post-synaptic receptors sensitivity can change functioning of specific receptor response. Enzymatic processes within the cell may inactivate the neurotransmitter by removing a carbon group (decarboxylation), or a nitrogen group (deamination), or an oxygen/hydroxyl group (oxidation/dehydroxylation). The core material comprising the neurotransmitter is then recycled by reactivating the process of synthesis and storage.

Receptor Effects: Once released, neurotransmitters bind to and activate receptors. The sensitivity of the receptors themselves may be altered by the concentration of neurotransmitter they have been exposed to recently, or by medications that stimulate or block the receptor. If a receptor has been chronically exposed to a high concentration of a neurotransmitter, its sensitivity is likely to become reduced. If it has been chronically blocked, the receptor is likely to become super-sensitive to stimuli.

The presynaptic receptors are generally much more sensitive than the postsynaptic receptors. The presynaptic receptors are regulating production and monitoring what the neuron is releasing. These autoreceptors regulate how much is being released by tracking how much is in the pipeline. This process is similar to regulating output of cars at the end of an automobile assembly line. "How many cars did we make today?" This is a means of controlling the activity close to the site of production.

The postsynaptic receptor, located on the axon, responds to what the "downstream" neuron is receiving. To maintain stability, the highest priority is to regulate what the presynaptic neuron is releasing, rather than what the downstream neuron is receiving.

Much regulation of neuronal response occurs postsynaptically—and is as important a site for regulation as the presynaptic neuron. The sensitivity of postsynaptic receptors is regulated by enzymatic activity and genetically-controlled protein synthesis. Reactions occur here that involve adenylate cyclase, adenosine triphosphatase, and cyclic adenosine monophosphate that are secondary messengers. These chemical reactions regulate the release of energy and transmission of information deep within the neuron. The sensitivity of the system can be changed not only by regulating release, reuptake, and production, but many events that happen postsynaptically. The sensitivity of this postsynaptic cascade can change the response to a stimulus a thousand fold.

In children who have modulatory difficulties, affecting attentional and disruptive behavior, the site of "chemical imbalance" may be postsynaptic as well as presynaptic. The behavior ultimately reflects changes in receptor response and secondary messengers, not just the levels of neurotransmitters. One area of research that may develop in the next decade is the creation of medications that act at postsynaptic second messenger sites.

In order to maintain balance, or homeostasis, the sensitivity of the receptor changes in response to the strength of the signal detected. If receptors are chronically deprived of a neurotransmitter (either due to a reduction of neurotransmitter release or a blockage of the receptor), the system may increase (up-regulate) its response to a rare signal. Conversely, if the receptor is chronically bombarded by excessive neurotransmitter signals, it may decrease (down-regulate) its response.

Postsynaptic Response

Postsynaptic response is highly dependent on receptor sensitivity.

Medication Effect Receptor Response

The effect of a medication depends on receptor response in addition to dose and blood level.

Epilogue

Will Beyer and Robert Hunt

Epilogue

With so many books now available to parents, educators, and clinicians, the authors of *Born to Be Wild* did not wish to simply replicate available information on ADHD. It is the hope that this book has created new insights into the management of this disorder. It is the authors' opinion that ADHD has been ignored and neglected in the treatment of alcoholism and addictive illness. We are hopeful that this book will establish this connection.

We are indeed thankful for the scientists and clinicians who have contributed enormously to our knowledge of this and similar disorders through their dedicated research. We are also thankful to Judy Wood, Scott Wood, Eddie Wood, and their staff who believed in the value of this book and have provided their professional expertise in publishing.

We are indebted to our clients and patients for teaching us through sharing their lives with us at our clinics. We thank you for your trust in our care. And finally, we thank our families, friends, and staff who have been patient, understanding, and encouraging to us daily in our work.

Will Beyer, M.Ed. and Robert Hunt, M.D.

For further assistance with ADHD, consultation, training, and so forth, you may contact the authors at the following addresses:

Will Beyer, LPE
The ADHD/LD Clinic of Tennessee
49 Murray Guard Drive
Jackson, Tennessee 38305
(901) 661-9860

Robert Hunt, M.D.
The Center for Attention and Hyperactivity Disorders
2129 Belcourt Ave
Nashville, Tennessee 37212
(615) 383-1222

References

References

American Psychiatric Association. (1995). *Diagnostic and Statistical Manual*. 4th ed. Washington, DC: Author.

Barkley, R.A. (1990). *Attention Deficit Hyperactivity Disorder: A Handbook for Diagnosis and Treatment*.

Barkley, R.A., et al. (1990). "The Adolescent Outcome of Hyperactive Children Diagnosed by Research Criteria: I. An 8-Year Prospective Follow-Up Study." *Journal of the American Academy of Child and Adolescent Psychiatry*.

Barkley, R.A., et al. (1990). "Comprehensive Evaluation of Attention Deficit Disorder with and without Hyperactivity as Defined by Research Criteria." *Journal of Consulting and Clinical Psychology*, pp. 775-789.

Begleiter, H., et al. (1987). "Auditory Recovery Function and P3 in Boys at High Risk for Alcoholism." *Alcohol*, 4, pp. 315-321.

Begleiter, H., and B. Porjesz. (1988). "Potential Biological Markers in Individuals at High Risk for Developing Alcoholism." *Alcoholism*, 12, pp. 488-493.

Biederman, J., et al. (1989). "A Double-Blind Placebo Controlled Study of Desipramine in the Treatment of ADD." *Journal of the American Academy of Child Adolescent Psychiatry*, 28(5), pp. 777-784.

Beiderman, J., (1998). "Attention Deficit Hyperactivity Disorder: A Life-Span Perspective." *Journal of Clinical Psychiatry*, Suppl. 59(7), pp. 4-16.

Biederman, J., et al. (1986). "Desipramine in the Treatment of Children with Attention Deficit Disorder." *Journal of Clinical Psychopharmacology*, 6, pp. 359-363.

Biederman, J., et al. (1988). "Desipramine and Cutaneous Reactions in Pediatric Outpatients." *Journal of Clinical Psychiatry*, 49, pp. 178-183.

Blau, A. (1936). "Mental Changes Following Head Trauma in Children." *Archives of Neurology and Psychiatry*, 35, pp. 772-769.

Blouin, A., R. Bornstein, and R. Trites. (1978). "Teenage Alcohol Use Among Hyperactive Children: A 5-Year Follow-Up Study." *Journal of Pediatric Society*, 3, pp. 188-194.

Blum, K. and J. Payne. (1991). *Alcohol and the Addictive Brain.* New York, NY: The Free Press, pp. 174-175.

Blum, K., et al. (1990). "Allelic Association of Human Dopamine D2 Receptor Gene in Alcoholism." *Journal of American Medical Association*, 263(15), pp. 2055-2060.

Bradley, W. (1937). "The Behavior of Children Receiving Benzedrine." *American Journal of Psychiatry*, 94, pp. 577-585.

Bunney, B.S., and S.A. DeRiemer. (1982). "Effects of Clonidine on Nigral Dopamine Cell Activity: Possible Mediation by Noradrenergic Regulation of Serotonergic Raphe System." In: Friedhoff, A.J., and T.N. Chase, eds., *Gilles de la Tourette Syndrome.* New York: Raven.

Burton, R. (1906). *The Anatomy of Melancholy.* William Tegg: London.

Campbell, M., L.T. Anderson, and W.H. Green. (1983). "Behavior-Disordered and Aggressive Children: New Advances in Pharmacotherapy." *Developmental and Behavioral Pediatrics,* 4(4), pp. 265-271.

Cantwell, D.P. (1972). "Psychiatric Illness in the Families of Hyperactive Children." *Archives of General Psychiatry*, 27, pp. 414-427.

Carroll, K.M. & B.J. Rounsaville. (1993). "History and Significance of Childhood Attention Deficit Disorder in Treatment-Seeking Cocaine Abusers." *Comprehensive Psychiatry*, 64(2), pp. 75-82.

Casat, C.D., et al. (1989). "Bupropion in Children with Attention Deficit Disorder." *Psychopharmacology Bulletin,* 125(2), pp. 198-201.

Chen, S.W., and D.G. Vidt. (1989). "Patient Acceptance of Transdermal Clonidine." A retrospective review of 25 patients. *Cleveland Clinical Journal of Medicine*, 56(1), pp. 21-26.

Cloninger, C.R., M. Bohman, and S. Sigvardsson. (1981). "Inheritance of Alcohol Abuse." *Archives of General Psychiatry,* 38, pp. 861-868.

Cloninger, R. (1987). "Neurogenetic Adaptive Mechanisms in Alcoholism." *Science,* pp. 236-410.

Cohen, D.J., R.D. Bruun, and J.F. Leckman, eds. (1988). *Tourette's Syndrome and Tic Disorders: Clinical Understanding and Treatment.* New York: John Wiley & Sons.

Cohen, D.J., et al. (1980). "Clonidine Ameliorates Gilles de la Tourette Syndrome." *Archives of General Psychiatry,* 37, pp. 1350-1357.

Comings, D., et al. (1991). "The Dopamine D2 Receptor Locus as a Modifying Gene in Neuropsychiatric Disorders." *Journal of American Medical Association,* 266, pp. 1793-1798.

Comings, D.E., et al. (1993). "Serotonin and the Biochemical Genetics of Alcoholism: Lessons from Studies of Attention Deficit Hyperactivity Disorder (ADHD) and Tourette Syndrome." *Alcohol & Alcoholism,* 2, pp. 237-241.

Conners, C.K., et al. (1996). "Nicotine and Attention in Adult Attention Deficit Hyperactivity Disorder." *Psychopharmacology Bulletin,* 32(1), pp. 67-73.

Conners, C.K., et al. (1976). "Food Additives and Hyperkinesis: A Controlled Double-Blind Experiment." *Pediatrics,* 58(2), pp. 154-166.

Crook, W.G. (1978). "Adverse Reactions to Food Can Cause Hyperkinesis." Letter. *American Journal of Diseases in Children, 132,* pp. 819.

Cynn, V. "Persistence and Problem-Solving Skills in Young Male Alcoholics." *Journal of Studies on Alcohol,* 53(1), pp. 57-62.

Dawson, P.M., et al. (1989). "Cardiac Dysrhythmia with the Use of Clonidine in Explosive Disorder." *DICP,* 23(6), pp. 465-466.

DeObaldia, R., O. Parson, and R. Yohman. (1983). "Minimal Brain Dysfunction Symptoms Claimed by Primary and Secondary Alcoholics: Relation to Cognitive Functioning." *International Journal of Neuroscience,* 20, pp. 173-182.

Donnelly, M., et al. (1986). "Treatment of Childhood Hyperactivity with Desipramine: Plasma Drug Concentration, Cardiovascular Effects, Plasma and Urinary Catecholamine Levels, and Clinical Response." *Clinical Pharmacology and Therapeutics,* 39, pp. 72-81.

Douglas, V. I. (1983). "Attention and Cognitive Problems." In: Rutter, M., ed., *Developmental Neuropsychiatry,* New York: Guilford Press, pp. 280-329.

Ebaugh, C.S. (1923). "Neuropsychiatric Sequelae of Acute Encephalitis in Children." *American Journal of Diseases in Children,* 25, pp. 89-97.

Egger, J., et al. (1985). "Controlled Trial of Oligoantigenic Treatment in the Hyperkinetic Syndrome." *The Lancet,* pp. 540-545.

Erickson, W.D., et al. (1984). "The Effects of Neuroleptics on Attention in Adolescent Schizophrenics." *Biological Psychiatry,* 19(5), pp. 745-752.

Feingold, B. (1975). *Why Your Child Is Hyperactive?* New York: Random House.

Filipeck & Colleagues. (1998). "Volumetic MRI Analysis Comparing Subjects Having Attention-Deficit Hyperactivity Disorder with Normal Controls." Department of Pediatrics, University of California College of Medicine, Irvine. 92868-3298, USA.

Gabel, S., and R. Shindeldecker. (1992). "Behavior Problems in Sons and Daughters of Substance Abusing Parents." *Child Psychiatry and Human Development,* 23(2), pp. 99-115.

Garfinkel, B.D., P.H. Wender, and L. Sloman. (1983). "Tricyclic Antidepressants and Methylphenidate Treatment of Attention Deficit Disorder in Children." *Journal of the American Academy Child Psychiatry,* 2, pp. 343-348.

Gastfriend, D.R., J. Biederman, and M.S. Jellinek. (1984). "Desipramine in the Treatment of Adolescents with Attention Deficit Disorder." *American Journal of Psychiatry,* 141, pp. 906-908.

Gillberg, C., et al. (1997). "LonTerm Stimulant Treatment of Children with Attention Deficit Hyperactivity Disorder Symptoms. A Randomized, Double-Blind, Placebo Controlled Trial." *Archives of General Psychiatry*, September, 54(9), pp. 957-864.

Gittelman-Klein, R. (1974). "Pilot Clinical Trial of Imipramine in Hyperkinetic Children." In: Conners, C.K., ed., *Clinical Uses of Stimulant Drugs in Children*, The Hague, Netherlands: Excerpta Medica Foundation, pp. 192-201.

Gittelman-Klein, R., et al. (1976). "Comparative Effects of Methylphenidate and Thioridazine in Hyperkinetic Children." *Archives of General Psychiatry*, 33, pp. 1217-1231.

Goetz, C.G., et al. (1987). "Clonidine and Gilles de la Tourette Syndrome: Double-Blind Study Using Objective Rating Methods." *Annals of Neurology*, 21, pp. 307-310.

Goldman, D., R.G. Lister, and J.C. Crabbe. (1987). "Mapping of a Putative Genetic Locus Determining Ethanol Intake in the Mouse." *Brain Research*, 420, pp. 220-226.

Goodman, R. (1989). "Genetic Factors in Hyperactivity." *British Medical Journal*, 298(6685), pp. 1081-1086.

Goodwin, D. (1971). Review and critique of "Is Alcoholism Hereditary?" *Archives of General Psychiatry*, 25, pp. 545-549.

Goodwin, D.W., et al. (1973). "Alcohol Problems in Adoptees Raised Apart from Alcoholic Biological Parents." *Archives of General Psychiatry*, 28, pp. 238-243.

Goodwin, D.W. (1985). "Alcoholism and Genetics: The Sins of the Fathers." *Archives of General Psychiatry*, 6, pp. 171-174.

Goodwin, D.W., et al. (1975). "Alcoholism and the Hyperactive Child Syndrome." *The Journal of Nervous and Mental Disorders*, 160, pp. 349-353.

Gorelick, D.A. (1986). "Effect of Fluoxetine on Alcohol Consumption." *Alcoholism: Clinical and Experimental Research*, 10, p. 113.

Greenberg, L., et al. (1975). "Clinical Effects of Imipramine and Methylphenidate in Hyperactive Children." *International Journal of Mental Health,* 4, pp. 144-156.

Gross, M.D. (1973). "Imipramine in the Treatment of Minimal Brain Dysfunction in Children." *Psychosomatics,* 14, pp. 283-285.

Gross, M.D., et al. (1987). "The Effects of Diets Rich in and Free from Additives on the Behavior of Children with Hyperkinetic and Learning Disorders." *Journal of the American Academy of Child Adolescent Psychiatry,* 26(1), pp. 53-55.

Gualtieri, C.T., and R.E. Hicks. (1985). Letter: "Stimulants and Neuroleptics in Hyperactive Children." *Journal of the American Academy of Child Adolescent Psychiatry,* 24(3), pp. 363-364.

Hallahan, D.P., et al. (1979). "Self-Monitoring of Attention as a Treatment for a Learning Disabled Boy's Off-Task Behavior." *Learning Disability Quarterly,* 2, pp. 24-32.

Halliday, R., E. Callaway, and R. Lannon. (1989). "The Effects of Clonidine and Yohimbine on Human Information Processing." *Psychopharmacology Berlin,* 99(4), pp. 563-566.

Harley, J.P., et al. (1978). "Hyperkinesis and Food Additives: Testing the Feingold Hypothesis." *Pediatrics,* 61(6), pp. 818-828.

Hartsough, C.S., and N.M. Lambert. (1985). "Medical Factors in Hyperactive and Normal Children: Prenatal, Developmental, and Health History Findings." *American Journal of Orthopsychiatry,* 55, pp. 190-210.

Heiligenstein, E., H.F. Johnston, and J.K. Nielsen, (1996). "Pemoline Therapy in College Students with Attention Deficit Hyperactivity Disorder: A Retrospective Study (Comment)." *Journal of the American College of Health,* July, 45(1), pp. 35-39.

Hesselbrock, V.M., J.R. Stabenau, and M.N. Hesselbrock. (1985). "Minimal Brain Dysfunction and Neuropsychological Test Performance in Offspring of Alcoholics." In: Galanter, M., ed., *Recent Developments in Alcoholism,* New York: Plenum Press.

Huessy, H.R., and A.L. Wright. (1970). "The Use of Imipramine in Children's Behavior Disorders." *Acta Paedopsychiatrie,* 37, pp. 194-199.

Hunt, R.D. (1987). "Treatment Effects of Oral and Transdermal Clonidine in Relation to Methylphenidate—an Open Pilot Study in ADHD." *Psychopharmacology Bulletin,* 23(1), pp. 111-114.

Hunt, R.D. (1988). "Treatment of ADHD with Clonidine: Guidelines for Physicians." *Psychiatric Times,* September, 1988.

Hunt, R.D., L. Clapper, and M.H. Ebert. (1989). "Clonidine and Methylphenidate: Combined Use in Treatment of Selected ADHD Children." Presentation: American Academy of Child and Adolescent Psychiatry.

Hunt, R.D., et al. (1988). "Noradrenergic Mechanisms in ADHD." In Bloomingdale, L.M., ed., *Attention Deficit Disorder: New Research in Attention, Treatment, and Psychopharmacology,* New York: Pergamon Press.

Hunt, R.D., L. Capper, and P. O'Connell. (1990). "Clonidine in Child and Adolescent Psychiatry." *Journal of Child and Adolescent Psychopharmacology,* 1(1), pp. 87-102.

Hunt, R.D., et al. (1984). "Possible Change in Noradrenergic Receptor Sensitivity with Attention Deficit Disorder and Hyperactivity: Response to Chronic Methylphenidate Treatment." *Life Sciences,* 35, pp. 885-897.

Hunt, R.D., R.B. Minderaa, and D.J. Cohen. (1985). "Clonidine Benefits Children with Attention Deficit Disorder and Hyperactivity: Report of a Double-Blind Placebo-Controlled Crossover Study." *Journal of the American Academy of Child Psychiatry,* 24(5), pp. 617-629.

Hunt, R.D., D.J. Cohen, and D.J. Cohen. (1985). "Clonidine Benefits Children with Attention Deficit Disorder and Hyperactivity: Report of a Double-Blind Placebo Cross-Over Therapeutic Trial." *Journal of the American Academy of Child and Adolescent Psychiatry*, 24, pp. 617-629.

Hunt, R.D., R.B. Minderaa, and D.J. Cohen. (1986). "The Therapeutic Effect of Clonidine in Attention Deficit Disorder with Hyperactivity: A Comparison with Placebo." *Psychopharmacology Bulletin,* 22(1), pp. 229-236.

Israel, Kim. (1998). "Treat Them Kind."

Jouvent, R., et al. (1988). Letter: "Clonidine and Neuroleptic-Resistant Mania." *British Journal of Psychiatry,* 152, pp. 293-294.

Kaplan, B.J., et al. (1989). "Dietary Replacement in Preschool-Aged Hyperactive Boys." *Pediatrics,* 83(1), pp. 7-17.

Kaplan, B.J., et al. (1987). "Sleep Disturbance in Preschool-Aged Hyperactive and Non-Hyperactive Children." *Pediatrics,* 80, pp. 839-844.

Kaij, L. (1960). "Studies on the Etiology and Sequels of Abuse of Alcohol." Sweden: University of Lund, Dept. of Psychiatry.

Lang A.R., et al. (1989). "Levels of Adult Alcohol Consumption Induced by Interactions with Child Confederates Exhibiting Normal Versus Externalizing Behaviors." *Journal of Abnormal Psychology,* 98(3), pp. 294-299.

Laufer, M., and E. Denhoff. (1957). "Hyperkinetic Behavior in Children." *Journal of Pediatrics,* 50, pp. 463-474.

Leckman, J.F., J.T. Walkup, and D.J. Cohen. (1988). "Clonidine Treatment of Tourette's Syndrome." In: Cohen, D.J., R.D. Bruun, and J.F. Leckman, eds., *Tourette's Syndrome and Tic Disorders: Clinical Understanding and Treatment,* New York: John Wiley & Sons.

Levin, F.R., et al. (1998). "Methylphenidate Treatment for Cocaine Abusers with Adult Attention Deficit Hyperactivity Disorder: A Pilot Study." *Journal of Clinical Psychiatry,* 59(6) pp. 300-305.

Levine, P.M., (1998). "Methylphenidate Treatment for Cocaine Abusers with Adult Attention Deficit Hyperactivity Disorder: A Pilot Study." *Journal of Clinical Pyschiatry,* June, 59(6), pp. 300-305.

Levine, P.M., (1938). "Restlessness in Children." *Archives of Neurology and Psychiatry,* 39, pp. 764-770.

Levy, F. and G. Hobbes. (1988). "The Action of Stimulant Medication in Attention Deficit Disorder with Hyperactivity: Dopaminergic, Noradrenergic, or Both?" *Journal of the American Academy of Child Psychiatry,* 27, pp. 802-805.

Liskow, B.I., and D.W.Goodwin. (1987). "Pharmacological Treatment of Alcohol Intoxication, Withdrawal and Dependence: A Critical Review." *Journal of Studies on Alcohol,* 48, pp. 356-370.

Lou, H.C., L. Henriksen, and P. Bruhn. (1984). "Focal Cerebral Hypoperfusion in Children with Dysphasia and/or Attention Deficit Disorder." *Archives of Neurology,* 41, pp. 48-52.

Lou, H. C., et al. (1989). "Striatal Dysfunction in Attention Deficit and Hyperkinetic Disorder." *Archives of Neurology,* 46, pp. 48-52.

Lowenthal, D.T., K.M. Matzek, and T.R. MacGregor. (1988). "Clinical Pharmacokinetics of Clonidine." *Clinical Pharmacokinetics,* 14(5), pp. 287-310.

Mannuzza, S., et al. (1989). "Hyperactive Boys Almost Grown Up: V.I. Criminality and Its Relationship to Psychiatric Status." *Archives of General Psychiatry,* 46, pp. 1073-1079.

Mannuzza, S., et al. (1993). "Adult Outcome of Hyperactive Boys, Educational Achievement, Occupational Rank, and Psychiatric Status." *Archives of General Psychiatry,* 50, pp. 565-576.

Martin, P.R., et al. (1984). "Effects of Clonidine on Central and Peripheral Catecholamine Metabolism." *Clinical Pharmacology & Therapeutics,* 35(3), pp. 322-327.

Milberger, S., et al. (1997). "ADHD Is Associated with Early Initiation of Cigarette Smoking in Children and Adolescents." *Journal of the American Academy of Child and Adolescent Psychiatry,* 36(1), pp. 37-44.

Milberger, S., et al. (1997). "Further Evidence of an Association Between Attention Deficit Hyperactivity Disorder and Cigarette Smoking. Findings from a High Risk Sample of Siblings." *American Journal of Addictions,* 6(3), pp 205-217.

Milberger, S., et al. (1997), "Associations Between ADHD and Psychoactive Substance Use Disorders. Findings from a Longitudinal Study of High-Risk Siblings of ADHD Children." *American Journal of Addictions*, 6(4), pp. 318-329.

Milin, R., et al. (1991). "Psychopathology Among Substance Abusing Juvenile Offenders." *Journal of the American Academy of Child and Adolescent Psychiatry*, 30(4), pp. 569-574.

Mitchell, E.A., et al. "Clinical Characteristics and Serum Essential Fatty Acid Levels in Hyperactive Children." *Clinical Pediatrics*, 26, pp. 406-411.

Morrison, J., and M.A. Stewart. (1973). "Evidence for Polygenetic Inheritance in the Hyperactive Child Syndrome." *American Journal of Psychiatry*, 130, pp. 791-792.

Murphy, J.M., et al. (1987). "Contents of Monoamines in Forebrain Regions of Alcohol-Preferring (P) and Nonpreferring (NP) Lines of Rats." *Pharmacology, Biochemistry and Behavior*, 26(2), pp. 389-392.

Murphy, J.M., et al. (1988). Abstract. *Alcoholism*, 12, p. 306.

Nemzer, E.D., et al. (1986). "Amino Acid Supplementation as Therapy for Attention Deficit Disorder." *Journal of the American Academy of Child and Adolescent Psychiatry*, 25(4), pp. 509-513.

O'Connor, S., et al. (1987). "P3 Amplitudes in Two Distinct Tasks Are Decreased in Young Men with a History of Paternal Alcoholism." *Alcoholism*, 4, pp. 323-330.

Peterson, J., and P. Finn. (1990). "Inherited Predisposition to Alcoholism: Characteristics of Sons of Male Alcoholics." *Journal of Abnormal Psychology*, 99(3), pp. 291-301.

Pfeffer, A.O., and H.H. Samson. (1986). "Effects of Pimozide on Home Case Ethanol Drinking in the Rat: Dependence on Drinking Session Length." *Drug Alcohol Dependence*, 17, pp. 47-55.

Phelan, T. (1987). "1-2-3 Magic."

Physicians Desk Reference. (1999).

Pliszka, S.R., (1998). "The Use of Psychostimulants in the Pediatric Patient." *Pediatric Clinic of North America*, Oct. 45(5), pp. 1085-1098.

Pliszka, R. (1987). "Tricyclic Antidepressants in the Treatment of Children with Attention Deficit Disorder." *Journal of the American Academy of Child Psychiatry,* 26, pp. 127-132.

Pogge, D.L., J. Stokes, and P.D. Harvey. (1992). "Psychometric vs. Attentional Correlates of Early Onset Alcohol and Substance Abuse." *Journal of Abnormal Child Psychology*, April 20, pp. 151-162.

Quinn, P.O., and J.L. Rapoport. (1975). "One-Year Follow Up of Hyperactive Boys Treated with Imipramine or Methylphenidate." *American Journal of Psychiatry,* 10, pp. 387-390.

Rapoport, J.L. (1986). "Antidepressants in Childhood Attention Deficit Disorder and Obsessive-Compulsive Disorder." *Psychosomatics,* 27(11), pp. 30-36.

Rapport, M.D., H.A. Murphy, and J.S. Bailey. (1982). "Ritalin vs. Response Cost in Control of Hyperactive Children: A Within-Subject Comparison." *Journal of Applied Behavior Analysis,* 15, pp. 205-216.

Rapoport, J.L., et al. (1974). "Imipramine and Methylphenidate Treatment of Hyperactive Boys: A Double-Blind Comparison." *Archives of General Psychiatry,* 30, pp. 789-793.

Riddle, M.A., et al. (1988). "Desipramine Treatment of Boys with Attention Deficit Hyperactivity Disorder and Tics: Preliminary Clinical Experience." *Journal of the American Academy of Child Adolescent Psychiatry,* 27(6), pp. 811-814.

Rogeness, G.A., and C.A. Macedo. (1983). "Therapeutic Response of a Schizophrenic Boy to a Methylphenidate-Chlorpromazine Combination." *American Journal of Psychiatry,* 140(7), pp. 932-933.

Rugle. (1993). "Neuropsychological Assessment of Attention Problems in Pathological Gamblers." *Journal of Nervous and Mental Disorders,* 181(2), pp. 107-112.

Rounsaville, B. J., et al. (1991). "Psychiatric Diagnosis of Treatment-Seeking Cocaine Abusers." *Archives of General Psychiatry,* 48, pp. 43-51.

Safer, D.J., and J.M. Krager. (1983). "Trends in Medication Treatment of Hyperactive School Children." *Clinical Pediatrics,* 22, pp. 500-504.

Safer, D.J., and J.M. Krager. (1988). "A Survey of Medication Treatment for Hyperactive/Inattentive Students." *Journal of American Medical Association,* 260, pp. 2256-2258.

Saul, R.C. (1985). Letter: "Nortriptyline in Attention Deficit Disorder." *Clinical Neuropharmacology,* 8(4), pp. 382-383.

Shekim, W.O., et al. (1990). "A Clinical and Demographic Profile of a Sample of Adults with Attention Deficit Hyperactivity Disorder, Residual State." *Comprehensive Psychiatry,* 31, pp. 416-425.

Shirley, M. (1939). "A Behavior Syndrome Characterizing Prematurely Born Children." *Child Development,* 10, pp. 115-128.

Simeon, J.G., H.B. Ferguson, and J. Van Wyck Fleet. (1986)."Bupropion Effects in Attention Deficit and Conduct Disorders." *Canadian Journal of Psychiatry,* 31, pp. 581-585.

Smith, B.H., et al. (1998). "Dosage Effects of Methylphenidate on the Social Behavior of Adolescents Diagnosed with Attention Deficit Hyperactivity Disorder." *Experimental Clinical Psychopharmacology,* May, 6(2), pp. 187-204.

Smith, B.H., et al. (1998). "Equivalent Effects of Stimulant Treatment for Attention Deficit Hyperactivity Disorder During Childhood and Adolescence." *Journal of the American Acadamy of Child and Adolescent Psychiatry,* March, 37(3), pp. 314-321.

Spencer, T., et al. (1998). "Adults with Attention Deficit Hyperactivity Disorder: A Controversial Diagnosis." *Journal of Clinical Psychiatry.*

Sprague, R., and E. Sleator. (1977). "Methylphenidate in Hyperkinetic Children: Differences in Dose Effects on Learning and Social Behavior." *Science*, 198, pp. 1274-1276.

Still, G.F. (1902). "Some Abnormal Psychical Conditions in Children." *Journal of Abnormal Psychology*, 9, pp. 407-418.

Swanson, J.M. (1985). "Measures of Cognitive Functioning Appropriate for Use in Pediatric Psychopharmacology Research Studies." *Psychopharmacology Bulletin*, 21, pp. 887-890.

Swanson, J.M., et al. (1998). "Analog Classroom Assessment of Adderall in Children with ADHD." *Journal of the American Acadamy of Child and Adolescent Psychiatry*, May, 37(5), pp. 519-526.

Swanson, J., et al. (1998). "Objective and Subjective Measures of the Pharmacodynamic Effects of Adderall in the Treatment of Children with ADHD in a Controlled Laboratory Classroom Setting." *Psychopharmacology Bulletin*, 34(1), pp. 55-60.

Tabakoff, B., and P.L. Hoffman. (1988). "Genetics and Biologic Markers of Risk for Alcoholism." *Public Health Report*, 103(6), pp. 690-698.

Tarter, R.E., A.I. Alterman, and K.L. Edwards. (1985). "Vulnerability to Alcoholism in Men: A Behavior-Genetic Perspective." *Journal of Studies on Alcohol*, 46, pp. 329-356.

Tarter, R. (1981). "Minimal Brain Dysfunction as an Etiological Predisposition in Alcoholism." In: Meyer, R., J. Glueck, T. Babor, J. Jaffe, and J. Stabenau, eds., Evaluation of the Alcoholic: Implications for Research, Theory, and Practice, research monograph. U.S. Department of Health and Human Services, 1981, chapter 12.

Tarter, R.E. (1988). "Are There Inherited Behavioral Traits That Predispose to Substance Abuse?" *Journal of Consulting Clinical Psychology*, 56(2), pp. 189-196.

Trommer, B.L., et al. (1988). "Sleep Disturbances in Children with Attention Deficit Disorder." *Annals of Neurology*, 24, p. 325.

von Knorring, A.L., et al. (1985). "Platelet MAO Activity as a Biological Marker in Subgroups of Alcoholism." *Acta Psychiatrica Scandanevica,* 72, pp. 52-58.

von Knorring, L., L. Oreland, and A.L. von Knorring. (1987). "Personality Traits and Platelet MAO Activity in Alcohol and Drug Abusing Teenage Boys." *Acta Psychiatrica Scandanevica,* 75, pp. 307-314.

Waizer, J., et al. (1974). "Outpatient Treatment of Hyperactive School Children with Imipramine." *American Journal of Psychiatry,* 131, pp. 587-591.

Webster's Collegiate Dictionary. (1996).

Weinberg, W.A., and R.A. Brumback. (1990). "Primary Disorder of Vigilance: A Novel Explanation of Inattentiveness, Day-Dreaming, Boredom, Restlessness, and Sleepiness." *Journal of Pediatrics,* 116(5), pp. 720-725.

Weiss, G., et al. (1985). "Psychiatric Status of Hyperactives as Adults: A Controlled Prospective 15-Year Follow Up of 63 Hyperactive Children." *Journal of the American Academy of Child Psychiatry,* 23, pp. 211-223.

Wender, E.H. (1986). "The Food Additive-Free Diet in the Treatment of Behavior Disorders: A Review." *Developmental and Behavioral Pediatrics,* 7(1), pp. 35-42.

Werner, E.E. (1986). "Resilient Offspring of Alcoholics: A Longitudinal Study from Birth to Age 18." *Journal of Studies on Alcohol,* 47(1), pp. 34-40.

Werry, J., and M. Aman. (1975). "Methylphenidate and Haloperidol in Children: Effects on Memory and Activity." *Archives of General Psychiatry,* 32, pp. 790-795.

Werry, J. (1980). "Imipramine and Methylphenidate in Hyperactive Children." *Journal of Child Psychology and Psychiatry and Allied Disciplines,* 21, pp. 27-35.

Williams, J.I., et al. (1978). "Relative Effects of Drugs and Diet on Hyperactive Behaviors: An Experimental Study." *Pediatrics,* 61(6), pp. 811-817.

Wilens. (1999). Personal Communications.

Wong, D.T., et al. (1988). "Serotonergic and Adrenergic Receptors in Alcohol-Preferring and Non-Preferring Rats." *Journal of Neural Transmission.* 71, pp. 207-218.

Wood, D.R., F.W. Reimherr, and P.H. Wender. (1985). "Treatment of Attention Deficit Disorder with dl-Phenylalanine." *Psychiatry Research,* 16, pp. 21-26.

Yepes, L.E., et al. (1977). "Amitriptyline and Methylphenidate Treatment of Behaviorally Disordered Children." *Journal of Child Psychology and Psychiatry and Allied Disciplines,* 18, pp. 39-52.

Zametkin, A., and J.L. Rapoport. (1983). "Tricyclic Antidepressants and Children." In: Burrows, G.D., T.R. Norman, and B. Davis, eds., *Drugs in Psychiatry, Vol I. Antidepressants,* Amsterdam; Elsevier, pp. 129-147.

Zametkin, A., et al. (1985). "Treatment of Hyperactive Children with Monoamine Oxidase Inhibitors." *Archives of General Psychiatry,* 42, pp. 962-966.

Zametkin, A.J., and B.G. Borcherding. (1989). "The Neuropharmacology of Attention Deficit Hyperactivity Disorder." *Annual Review of Medicine,* 40, pp. 447-451.

Zametkin, A.J., and J.L. Rapoport. (1986). "The Pathophysiology of Attention Deficit Disorder with Hyperactivity: A Review." In Lahey, B. and A. Kazdin, eds., *Advances in Clinical Child Psychology,* 9, pp. 177-216.

Zentall, S.S. (1986). "Effects of Color Stimulation on Performance and Activity of Hyperactive and Non-Hyperactive Children." *Journal of Educational Psychology,* 78, pp. 159-165.

Zucker, R.A., and E.S.L. Gomberg. (1986). "Etiology of Alcoholism Reconsidered: The Case for a Biopsychosocial Process." *American Psychologist,* 41, pp. 783-793.

Zuckerman, M. (1990). "The Psychophysiology of Sensation Seeking." *Journal of Personality,* 58(1), pp. 313-345.

Index

Index

A

Activity *111*
ADD
   adult *148*
   behavioral disability of *15*
   comorbid problems
      associated with *18*
   comorbidity of *17, 19*
   differences between ADHD *55*
   emergence of *5*
   genetic substrate for *21*
   interventions for *14*
   pathways to *9*
Adderall *142*
   clinical significance of longer
      duration of action *143*
   compared to Ritalin *143,
      146, 147*
   daily dose *147*
   difference between Dexedrine
      and *142, 147*
   IND study of *144*
   patients' preferences to *144, 145*
   recommendations for use *147*
Addictive behaviors *17*
Addictive outcome of ADHD in
   children *40*
ADHD
   addiction & cognition *39*
   adults in *8, 196, 232*
   age of diagnosis *54*
   amphetamine use in *149*
   are males more likely to have
      ADHD than females? *49*
   attention and learning in
      alcoholism and *40*
   clinical diversity *249*
   clinical patterns of *239, 250*
   clinical symptoms *7*
   COA *25*
   cocaine and *38*
   cognitive failure *285*
   comorbidity of *19, 33*
   consequences of *71*
   developmental aspects of *244*
      in high school *244*
      in middle school *244*
      onset *244*
      outcome *245*
   diagnostic process in *243*
   differences between ADD
      and *55*
   distinguishing from COA *24*
   early onset alcoholism, and *37*
   education services for students *83*
   environmental influences *12*
   environmental-social *23*
   etiology *124*
   genetic-biological *23, 124*
   historical influences &
      perspectives *10*
   history & etiology *10*
   how diagnosed *56*
   how does ADHD negatively
      impact the family? *49*
   how may individuals have *52*
   inhibition in *286*
   medications used in treatment
      53, 222
   nicotine and *37*
   overarousal in *286*
   recognition of *76*
   reward insensitivity in *287*
   scapegoat *20, 22*
   shared characteristics *22*
   situational versus pervasive *242*
   substance abuse, and *37*
   ten keys to managing ADHD in
      adulthood *232*
   what are the causes of *47*
   with & without
      hyperactivity *10*
ADHD and alcoholism—behavioral
   similarities *34*
ADHD—CD/ODD *240*
ADHD Spectrum/Pharmacological
   Diversity *149*
Adjuster *27*
Affective & regulatory disorders *18*
Affective system (limbic system) *273*
Alcohol craving *11, 42*
Alcoholics
   adopted sons of *36*
   Alcoholics Anonymous *17, 230*
   behavior of SOMAs *37*
   behavioral & cognitive
      deficits in at-risk *35*
   children of *20, 23*
   predisposing factors in *24*
   primary versus secondary *36*
Alcoholism
   ADHD and *34*
   ADHD and early onset *37*
   age of onset *33*
   attention and learning *40*
   comorbidity *33*
   drinking in rats *41*
   evoked potential in SOMAs *35*
   follow up studies *37*
   neurochemical components and
      ADHD *40*
   overlying symptoms *34*
   pharmacologic treatment of *125*
   predictors of *33*
   predisposing factors in *24*
   problem solving, and *39*
   psychiatric problems *37*
   twin studies for *33*
   type l and type ll *35*
   sons of male alcoholics (SOMAs)
      33
   SOMAs and cognition *39*
   symptom overlap *37*
   vigilance, and *39*
Amygdala *261*
Anafranil *127, 167*
Anger *50*
Animal models of arousal *274*
Antabuse
   pharmacologic treatments for
      alcohol and drug abuse *125*
Anticipate ahead of the child *88*
Anticonvulsants
   listing of *121*
   medications *203*
Antidepressants *119*
   advantages over stimulants *155*
   clinical effects *153*
   comments on use of *175*
   listing of *121*
   neurochemical effects *153*
   summary of *167*
Antisocial Personality
   Disorder *55*
Arousal
   alerting *259, 273*
   modulating *9*
   modulating medications *179*
   stimulus seeking and *8*
   system (basal brain) *273*
Arousal Modulating Medications
   listing of *121, 179*
Assist with organization *88*
Associated tics *175*
Association & Recognition *259*
Attachment & Reward
   Insensitivity *254*
Attachment/Reward Process
   Dysfuntion *249*
Attention

bias *11*
learning in alcoholism and ADHD and *40*
training system *91*
Attention deficit disorder *11*

B

Barkley, Ph.D., Russell *29, 58*
Begleiter *35*
Behavior
addictive *18*
characteristics of children of alcoholics *23*
disruptive *18*
emotional causes of addictive *20*
impact of children's on parents *26*
of SOMAs *37*
symptoms of ADHD versus ADD *34*
Behavioral dimensions of ADHD *251*
attachment and reward insensitivity *254*
hyperactivity *252*
impulsiveness *253*
inattention *251*
Behavioral Inhibition System *9, 275*
neurochemistry of inhibition *278*
physiology of inhibition *277*
relevance to ADHD *278*
Biofeedback *52*
Borderline Personality Disorder *114*
Bradley, Charles *123*
Brain
imaging *13, 109*
lesions *9*
measure of functioning *109*
Brain Regional Systems—Neuroanatomy of ADHD *259*
Brain Systems in Attention and ADHD *281*
Brooks, Ph.D., Robert *90*
Bupropion (Wellbutrin) *126, 169*
bupropion study *169*
in alcoholism *126*
study on preadolescent males *170*
summary of *172*

C

Carbatrol (Tegretol) *203*
Career guidance *102*
Case managers *96*
Catecholamines *136*
Change how you see your child *68*

Change your environment *70*
Children of Alcoholics (COA) *20, 23*
Chunking *87*
Cingulate gyrus *277*
Classroom rules *98*
Clinical Diversity of ADHD *249*
Clinical Patterns of ADHD *239, 250*
Clinical patterns of comorbid symptoms *34*
Clomipramine hydrochloride (Anafranil) *127, 167*
Clonicel *190*
Clonidine (Catapres) *179*
adult ADHD *196*
cardiovascular effects *197*
clinical indications *180*
clinical guidelines for using in ADHD *192*
clinical management in ADHD *196*
combined clonidine and methylphenidate side effects of *186*
differential effects of clonidine and methylphenidate *185*
drug interaction *198*
duration of treatment *196*
in ADHD *179*
long-term effects of *196*
medical work-up and follow-up *198*
monitoring response to *193*
neurobehavioral mechanisms of action *188*
neurochemical mechanisms of action *189, 195*
overdose *197*
pharmacokinetics of *190*
physiological mechanism of action *195*
plus Ritalin—side effects *187*
side effects *181, 193*
side effects and toxicity *196-197*
starting of *192*
summary of *198*
tolerance *197*
transdermal clonidine *183, 193*
versus methylphenidate *182*
versus placebo *180*
Clonidine Skin Patch (Transdermal) *183, 193*
COA *23*

Cocaine & ADHD *38*
Cognition versus activity *239*
Cognitive disorders *18*
Cognitive dysfunction *9, 107*
Cognitive processing deficit *35, 109, 110*
Comorbidity *7*
ADHD & addictive behaviors *17, 33*
ADHD/ADD of *19, 240*
clinical patterns of symptoms *34*
of ADHD and addictions *33*
Competency development *89*
Complex diagnosis *58*
Computer instruction *85*
Conduct disorder *8, 36, 240*
Confront your anger *68*
Confusion *50*
Conners' Questionnaire *157, 169, 170, 171, 216*
Continuous Performance Task (CPT) *58, 267*
Contracts and reward systems *101*
Cooperation versus competition *86*
Crack babies *62*
Crook, M.D., William *12*
Cylert (magnesium pemoline) *141*

D

Defense of mothers, in *29*
Defiance *73*
Deficient reward systems *115*
Depakote (Valproic Acid) *204*
Delaying gratification *15*
Denial *51*
Depression *166, 168, 172, 175*
Desipramine Hydrochloride (Norpramine) *154, 161*
compared to placebo *162*
in ADHD boys *163*
in ADHD with associated tics *165*
summary of *166*
Desoxyn *140*
Developmental aspects of ADHD *244*
onset *244*
outcome *245*
Dexedrine (dextroamphetamine) *140*
Adderall to *142*
comparison of Adderall *147*
differences between Adderall and *142*
Diagnosis
an increasing *62*

Index

Diagnostic criteria *7*
Diagnostic tests *58*
Dichotic Listening Task *269*
Dietary intervention *61, 215*
   amino acid supplementation *219*
   conclusion *220*
   Feingold diet studies *215*
      and stimulants *217*
      Feingold diet versus placebo *218*
Discipline *98*
Discrepancy formulas *84*
Disinhibition *15*
Disorder
   affective & regulatory *18*
   cognitive *18*
Disruptive behaviors *18*
Distinguish between distractibility and defiance *73*
Distracter *21*
Distractibility *56, 73*
Dopamine *12, 48*
   levels *41*
   receptors *41*
Douglas, Virginia *11*
DRD2 gene *17, 40*
Drinking in rats *41*
DSM-IV *83, 251*
   diagnostic criteria *7-8*
Dysfunction *27*

E

Earplugs *96*
Educational interventions *53, 84*
EEG *58, 84, 109*
Effexor *172, 173*
Elavil (amitriptyline) *121, 154*
Elementary school
   developmental aspects of ADHD in *244*
Emergence of ADHD *5*
Emotional case of addictive behavior *20*
Emotionally disturbed (ED) *83*
Encephalitis *10*
Endorphins *98*
Environmental
   agents *12*
   influences *12*
Environmental causes of ADHD *49*
Exercise *98*
Exhaustion *50*
Expressive language impairment *62*

F

Failure of inhibition *19, 107*
Family genetic relationships *18*
Family patterns of repetition *31*
Fear *50*
Feingold *215*
Feingold diet studies *215*
   and stimulants *217*
   Feingold diet versus placebo *218*
   food allergies *218*
Fetal alcohol affected children *62*
Filtering
   attention *259, 262*
   the visual system *259*
Find the right teacher *76*
Fluoxetine hydrochloride (prozac) *41, 174*
Food allergies *218*
Fragile X *58, 64*
Free Appropriate Public Education (FAPE) *77*
Free inquiry, encourage *99*
Freedom from distractibility formulas *58, 60*
Frontal lobe *11*
Frontal (motor) cortex *261*
Frustration *49*

G

GABA *12, 279*
Gamblers & attention *38*
Gating
   attention *259*
Gender differences *40, 244*
Gene (TDO2) *17*
Genetic
   age of onset *33*
   aspects of addictive illness *40*
   behavioral symptoms of ADHD versus ADD *34*
   comorbidity *34*
   determinism *15*
   familial *33*
   family relationships *18*
   genetic connection, the *32*
   overlapping and symptomatic characteristics *32*
   overlying symptoms *34*
   predictors of alcoholism *33*
   similarity *17*
   sons of male alcoholics *33*
   studies *14*
   substrate for ADHD *21*
   twin studies *15*
   twin studies for alcoholism *33*
Gibran, Kahlil *67*
Glasser, William *75*
Globus pallidus *277*
Grandma's rule *89*
Guanfacine *199*
Guilt *50*

H

Haloperidol (Haldol) *209*
Head injuries *11*
"hero" child *21*
Hippocampus *260*
Hippocampus dysfunction *56*
Historical influences and perspectives *10*
Holt, John *83*
Humor, use of *99*
Hyperactive child syndrome *10, 11*
Hyperactive-impulsive disorder *55*
Hyperactivity *7, 9, 11, 36, 216, 252*
Hyperkinetic impulse disorder *10*

I

Imipramine hydrochloride (Tofranil) *48, 156*
   compared to methylphenidate and placebo *157*
   effectiveness for classroom *159*
   in Ritalin non-responders *160*
   summary of *160*
Immediate memory *262*
Impact of children's behavior on parents *26*
Impaired behavioral inhibition system *113*
Implications for attributions and treatment *25*
Impulsiveness *253*
Impulsivity *7, 9, 111-113, 115*
Inattention *7, 239, 241, 251*
Individuals with Disabilities Education Act—IDEA *53, 77*
Information processing—attention *260*
Inhibition *253*
Inhibition system *254, 275*
Inhibition Tasks *269*
Instruction
   core subjects in the morning *98*
   supervision of socialization, and *97*
   word processing, about *97*

Intermittent explosive disorder *114*
Island of competence *90*
Isolation *51*

J

Join a support group *73*
Juvenile offenders *36*

K

Keymakers *57*
King, Jr., Martin Luther *227*

L

Learning disabled (LD) *84*
Learning Styles, recognition *100*
Legal advocacy *83*
Lethargy *56*
Limbic lobes *225, 261*
Limbic system *259, 261, 279*
Linking *263*
  attention *259*
Lithium *204*
Local Education Agency (LEA) *77*
Locke, John *15*
Locus coeruleus *273-274*
Lovable, make yourself *69, 102*

M

M-Teams *100*
Magnesium pemoline (Cylert) *141*
Magnetic Resonance Imaging (MRI) *13, 49*
Magnetoencephalography (MEG) *49*
Mannuzza, Salvatore *54*
Mascot *21*
Matching Familiar Figures Test (MFFT) *268*
Measures of Attention and Learning *267*
  Continuous Performance Task (CPT) *267*
  Inhibition Task *269*
  Matching Familiar Figures Test (MFFT) *268*
  Paired Associate Learning Task (PAL) *268*
Medications for bipolar disorder (Lithium) *204*
Medications in ADHD
  summary of *222*
Mellaril *211*
Mental Activity Network Scanner (MANSCAN) *49*

Methamphetamine hydrochloride (Desoxyn) *140*
Methylphenidate (MPH) *137*
  addictiveness *138*
  effect of MPH on catecholamines in ADHD *136*
  for substance abusers *139*
  mechanism of action *135*
  neurochemical effects of *135, 195*
  physiological mechanism of action *195*
  plus clonidine *186*
Midbrain *261*
Minimal Brain Dysfunction *10, 11, 250*
Monitoring *261*
Monoamine Oxidase Inhibitors, 168
  Nardil & Parnate *121*
  platelet in type II alcoholics *35*
  summary of *169*
Moral deficit *16*
Motivational model of alcohol craving *42*
Motor movement *261*
Multi-modal/multi-disciplinary treatment *31*
Multi-modal treatment *25*
Multisensory learning *86*
Music *94*

N

Nature versus nurture *15, 22*
Neurobiological
  subtypes of ADHD *107*
  validation of clinical model *109*
Neurobiological Systems for Cognition and Attention *259*
  memory and attention in ADHD *262*
  relevance to ADHD *262*
  visual system *259*
    information processing—attention *260*
    monitoring *261*
    recognition *260*
Neurobiological Systems that Modulate Cognition and Attention *273*
  affect regulation system *279*
  arousal system *273*
    physiology of arousal *274*
    animal models of arousal *274*
  behavioral inhibition system *275*
    neurochemistry of inhibition *278*

  physiology of inhibition *277*
  relevance to ADHD *278*
  reward system *280*
    relevance to ADHD *280*
Neurochemical components of alcoholism and ADHD *40*
Neurochemistry of Inhibition *278*
Neuroleptics 209
  clinical efficacy *209*
  listing of *121*
  summary of *212*
Neurotransmitters *12*
Neurotransmitter Systems that Modulate Attention and Behavior *288*
  neurotransmitters *288*
  synaptic regulation and effects of medications *289*
    receptor effects *290*
    synaptic effects *289*
Normalcy
  grieve your loss *67*
  grieving the loss of *51*
Norpramine (desipramine) *118, 161*
Nortriptyline (Pamelor/Aventyl) *166*
Nucleus accumbens *260*
Nurturance *22*

O

Obsessive-compulsive disorder *167, 277*
Obtain a tutor *74*
Occipital cortex *260, 261*
Office of Civil Rights *83*
Oral Clonidine *190*
Other health impaired category *53, 83. See also* Legal Advocacy

P

P300 wave *35*
Paired Associate Learning Task (PAL) *268*
Paxil (paroxetine) *48, 172, 173, 175*
Peacekeeper *27*
Persistence of disorganization *30*
Phelan, Dr. Thomas *73*
Physical contact *94*
Physical coordination *100*
Physiology of arousal *274*
Physiology of inhibition *277*
Placebo or appropriate treatment *61*
Plutarch *18*
Positive addictions *227, 233*

Index

Positive incentive programs 88
Positron Emission Tomography (PET) Scans 13, 49
Postencephalitic behavior disorder 10
Potential Role of Neurobiological Systems in ADHD 285
    cognitive failure in ADHD 285
    inhibition in ADHD 286
    overarousal in ADHD 286
    reward insensitivity in ADHD 287
Prefrontal cortex 261, 273, 275, 276
Preparation, provide ample time 75
Pre/Perinatal Influences 61
Premack principle 89
Primary alcoholic 31
Primary modulatory difficulties 107
Processing speed 56
Prompts 87
Proposed relationship between symptoms, neurochemistry, and treatment in ADHD 194
Prozac 48, 172, 174
Psychostimulants 121
    behavioral effects of 131, 132
    cognitive effects of 133
    comparative effects of 134
    mechanism of action 131
Purkey, William 10

Q
Quality over quantity 84

R
Rapport, M.D. 91
Reality Therapy 75
Recognition 260
Research into clinical typology 239
    ADD-H 241
    ADHD-CD/ODD 240
    cognition versus activity 239
    comorbidity of ADHD and ADD 240
    situational versus pervasive ADHD 242
Receptive language impairment 62
Recognition of change 259, 260
Regulating mood and temperament 15
Regulatory Disorders 18
Rehabilitation Act of 1973 77, 83
Relay & interruption 259
Repeated relapses 31
Resilient children 27

Reward 72
    and meaning 9
    deficient 108
    insensitive 108
Reward system 280
    relevance to ADHD 280
Ritlan (methylphenidate) 137
Ross, Elizabeth Kubler 51

S
Sadness 51
Salicylates 12
Scapegoat 20
Scatter 23
Secret signal 96
Section 504 of the Rehabilitation Act of 1973 53, 77, 83
Selective filtering 131
Selective seating 85
Selective serotonin reuptake inhibitors (SSRIs) 121, 172
Self-monitoring 90
Self-motivate 15
Sensation Seeking Scale (SSS) 8
Sense of shame 27
Sensitivity 34
Serotonin 12
Shaming 28
    child to parent 28
    parent to child 28
Short-term memory 262
Signal-to-noise 262
Silkworth, M.D., William 17
Single-Photon Emission Computed Tomography (SPECT) 49
Situational versus pervasive ADHD 242
Sleep 94
Slow neural processing 62
Snorting Ritalin 138
Sociobiological view of addictive illness 41
SOMAs (Sons of Male Alcoholics) 33, 34
Somnambulence 56
Sons of alcoholic fathers 39
Special education, know your rights 77
SPECT analysis 13
Still, Dr. George 5
Stimulus
    enrichment 92
    reduction 92

Stimulus seeking 15, 19, 227
    positive addictions 227
    treatment or punishment 228
Stress-dopamine-genotype hypothesis of craving 18
Striatal region 13
Striatum 13, 261, 277
Stroop Color Naming Task 269
Substance abusers
    methylphenidate for 139
    use of stimulants 139
Summer tutoring 95
Support group 73
Sustained attention 131
Synaptic regulation and effects of medications 289
    receptor effects 290
    synaptic effects 289

T
Tabula rasa 15
TDO2 17
Teacher prompts 87
Teach with activity 94
Teasdale, Sara 67
Tegretol (Carbatrol) 203
Temperament 15
Temporal lobe 259, 261
Tenex (guanfacine) 199
Textbooks on tape 91
Thalamus 261, 277
The visual system 259
Therapeutic alternatives 31
Thorazine 210
Tofranil (imipramine) 156
Tourette's Syndrome 17, 64, 165
Transdermal clonidine 183, 193
Traumatic brain injury 61
Treat Them Kind 69
Treatment implications 25
Treatment or punishment 228
Tricyclics
    antidepressant medications for ADHD 121, 154
Tryptophan levels 17
Tutor 74
Twin studies 15
Typology 239

V
Valproic Acid (Depakote) 204
Values training 101

Visual system *259*
   information processing—attention
      260
   monitoring *261*
   recognition *260*

W
Wellbutrin (bupropion) *169*
Wechsler Intelligence Scale for
   Children-Version III *58*
White noise *74*

Y
Yohimbine *109*

Z
Zoloft *48, 172*
Zuckerman, Marvin *8*